SOUTH PLATTE

ROCKCLIMBING

SOUTH PLATTE

ROCK CLIMBING

AND

THE GARDEN OF THE GODS

PETER HUBBEL • MARK ROLOFSON

CHOCKSTONE PRESS

Denver, Colorado

1988

Published by
Chockstone Press, Inc.
526 Franklin Street
Denver, Colorado 80218

ISBN 0-934641-10-2

Cover photos:
(front) The Bishop and The Dome; photo by Dan Hare
(back) Mississippi Half Step; photo by Ken Trout

PREFACE

This book describes rocks and routes across a broad area of Colorado. There is probably more rock covered here than in all the remaining guides to the state combined. Despite this, the areas described in this book – with the exception of The Garden of the Gods – have not historically seen much documentation; this was not for lack of routes. Rather, the task of this book, the first comprehensive look at the *other* Front Range climbing areas, awaited individuals up to the daunting task.

This book was produced by two people, Mark Rolofson and Peter Hubbel. While they reviewed the other's work, each of the authors was responsible for compiling the information to specific areas, and in that respect, the end result is really two books under one cover. Despite the overall presentation of the book, the reader/user of this guide will undoubtedly be aware of slightly different presentations of route information, reflecting the authors' personal imprint.

Mark Rolofson provided the information for the Garden of the Gods section, as well as that for Big Rock and the Turkey Rocks Area of The Platte. Peter Hubbel compiled the remaining information for The Platte section of this book, in addition to drawing all the topos and taking all of the cliff photos (except where credited). Peter got this book off the ground, and adopted the role of general overseer of the project from start to finish.

Inaccuracies will be found, however, and the authors hope that new route information, changes, and more detailed route corrections can be sent to them for use in subsequent editions of this book in care of the publisher, Chockstone Press, 526 Franklin Street, Denver, Colorado 80218.

CONTENTS

Olaf Mitchell and Peter Prandoni, Mississippi Half Step, Poe Buttress

Dan Hare

INTRODUCTION

This book describes over 1,200 routes that lie amid the foothills of the Colorado Front Range. These cliffs and formations, located in an area roughly between U.S. Highways 285 and 24, provide the closest climbing to residents of Denver and Colorado Springs, Colorado's largest metropolitan areas. The rocks and routes of this broad region also provide some of the best rock climbing in the greater Rocky Mountains area.

The rock climbing areas are presented as two major geographical groups. Within the city limits of Colorado Springs is the well-known Garden of the Gods, a concise area – mostly face climbing – on sandstone towers and spires. From a point west of the Springs and running north 60 miles to Highway 285, west of Denver, is an extensive area of rolling hills, forested with pines and interspersed with rushing creeks and boulder- strewn rivers. The two forks of the South Platte River drain this foothill area, and provide a name for the scattered but extensive climbing to be found here. Unlike the concentrated presence of rock one feels in areas outside Boulder, the domes and cliffs of The Platte are dotted along hidden valleys, on ridges and hilltops throughout a broad region of over 500 square miles.

The climbing described in this book is, with the notable exception of The Garden of the Gods, on various types of granite. The rock formations range in height from 40 feet to 1,300 feet, and offer a wide variety of face and crack climbs. The rock quality varies as well, from the soft sandstone of The Garden, to exquisite, Tuolumne-like rock in the upper reaches of The Platte.

Some climbing areas that might fall geographically within the scope of this guide were intentionally omitted due to a lack of space, access problems, lack of information, or because of requests from climbers developing the area. These areas include Eagle Cliffs, outside of Aspen Park, Ocelot Cliffs, at Turkey Creek Road and Highway 74, the granite of Pike's Peak, The Crags, and the Four Mile Dome Area.

WARNING
This is only a guide book. It is not intended to teach anyone to climb. This book is simply a compilation of hearsay descriptions of the routes up various rocks and in no way should be construed to be correct. No responsibility is assumed by either the authors or the publisher for any misfortunes resulting from use of this guide. As much a part of the sport of rock climbing as the rock, personal judgment is the basis for your safety. If something seems wrong, it probably is; your judgment should always override this guide in making decisions. When you are on the rock, you are on your own.

HOW TO USE THIS BOOK

The cliffs of this book are, in general, listed in a north to south fashion. There are two sections to this guide, each with its own introduction. The Platte is the largest section, describing a large area south of U.S. Highway 285. Next follows the Garden of the Gods, a small and concise sandstone area in Colorado Springs. The maps on the next few pages are reproduced from the US Forest Service Pike National Forest Map, and outline the major areas in this guide.

The topos that are found throughout the book are formatted as follows:

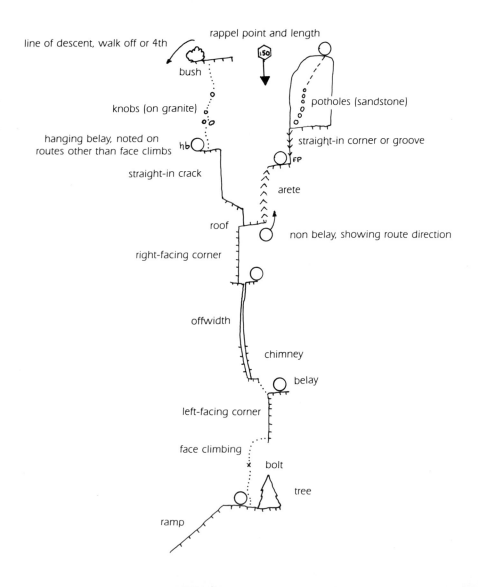

RECOMMENDED ROUTES

The following list was compiled by Noel Childs and Ken Trout and is intended to provide an overview of the best climbing to be found in The Platte. The routes are listed in no particular order.

Wunsch's Dihedral   (Cynical Pinnacle) This route is considerd to be **the** most classic Platte route. Steep, sustained, good pro, and history make this route a gem. Best crack climbing in the Front Range.

Center Route   (Cynical Pinnacle) This is the best 5.9 crack climb anywhere (maybe). Classic hands; link it up with **Class Act** for a great 5.11.

Standard Route   (Sunshine Wall) Great variety in four pitches of 5.10.

El Supremo   (Wigwam Dome) For the face climber.

Mississippi Half Step   (Poe Buttress) Thin cracks, incredible exposure, and two desperate 5.11 + cruxes; this route, and all the hard routes on Poe Buttress are great. The hard man's playground.

Bishop Finger Crack   (The Bishop) This is the best one- pitch route in the Platte, best finger crack in the Front Range.

Classic Dihedral   (Bucksnort Slabs) The classic 5.7.

Drumstick Direct   (Turkey Tail) Great wide hands, fist, nice roof.

Whimsical Dreams   (Turkey Tail) Thin hands; a good pump for the 5.11 − climber.

Journey to Ixtlan   (Turkey Tail) Variety; classic 5.12 −

Heart of Darkness   (Sunshine Dome) Best route on the rock, or in the whole inner Platte, for that matter.

Shining Path   (Sunshine Dome) Some think it is as good as Tuolumne

Turkey Shoot   (Turkey Rocks) 5.8 Yee-Haw!

Straw Turkey   (Turkey Rocks) 5.10.

Beam Me up Scotty   Helen's Dome Best 5.9 + /5.10 face climbing.

Four Eyes   (Acid Rock) One of the best of the easier (5.9) routes.

Bishop's Jaggers   (The Dome) Nice, friendly friction.

Childhood's End   (Big Rock) The best route on the biggest rock.

Topographic Oceans (The Dome) Super-protected friction. A harder start uses **Sea of Holes.**

Turkey Foot Crack   (Sunshine Wall) Nice crack in a clean wall.

Great White Crime   (Turkey Rocks)

Ramblin' Rose   (Wigwam Dome)

Vanishing Point   (Turkey Rocks)

Throne Room   (The Castle) Every route here is worth the $3.

Acid Crack   (Sheep Rock) The best 5.5

TURKEY PERCH   This is the best place for moderate 5.7-5.9 routes.

Halogen Angels to **Better Lock Next Time**   (The Sun)

Buffalo Tears   (Helen's Dome) 5.10a face

Brothers in Arms   (Poe Buttress) 5.12 cracks

Bad Ju Ju   (Bad Ju Ju Formation) Biggest roof in the Platte.

Not many easy routes, but The Platte, even more than Yosemite, is not a good place for climbs easier than 5.9.

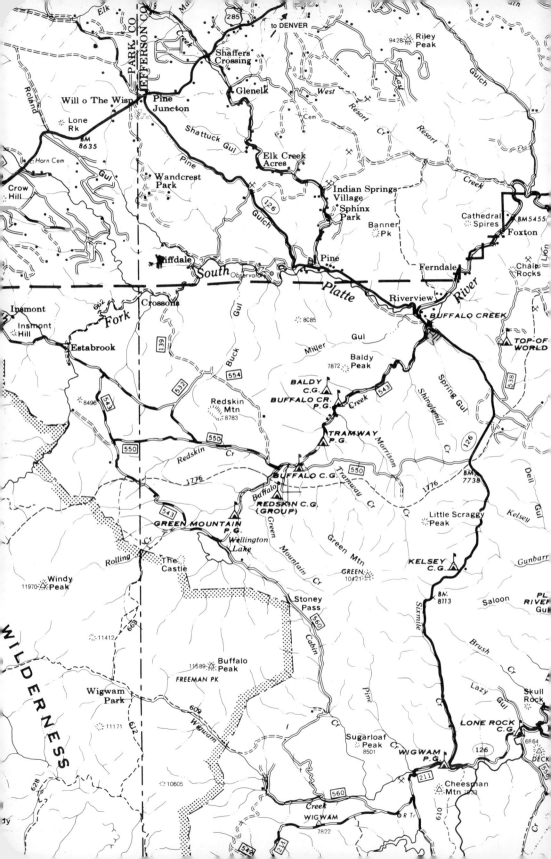

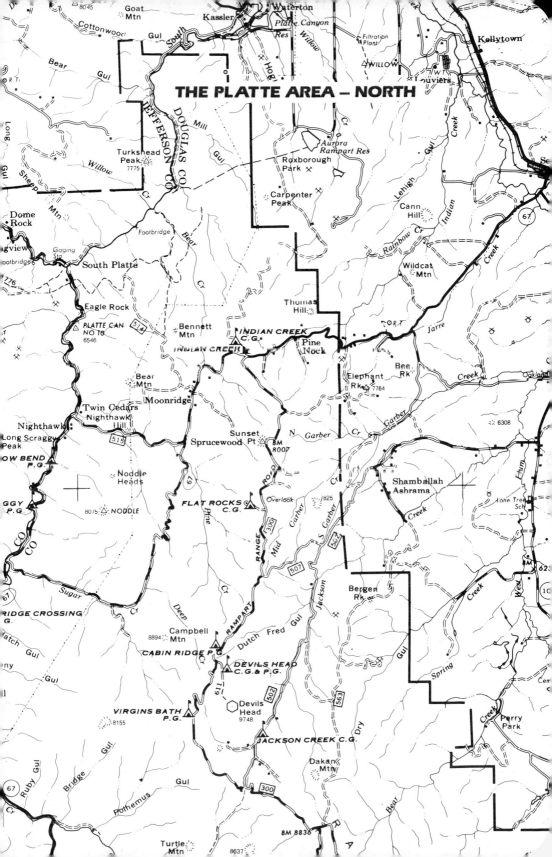

THE PLATTE AREA – NORTH

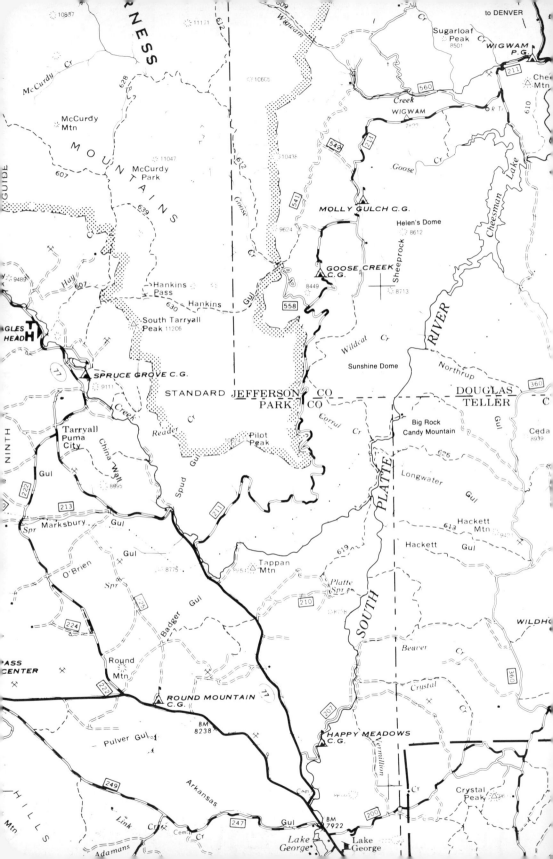

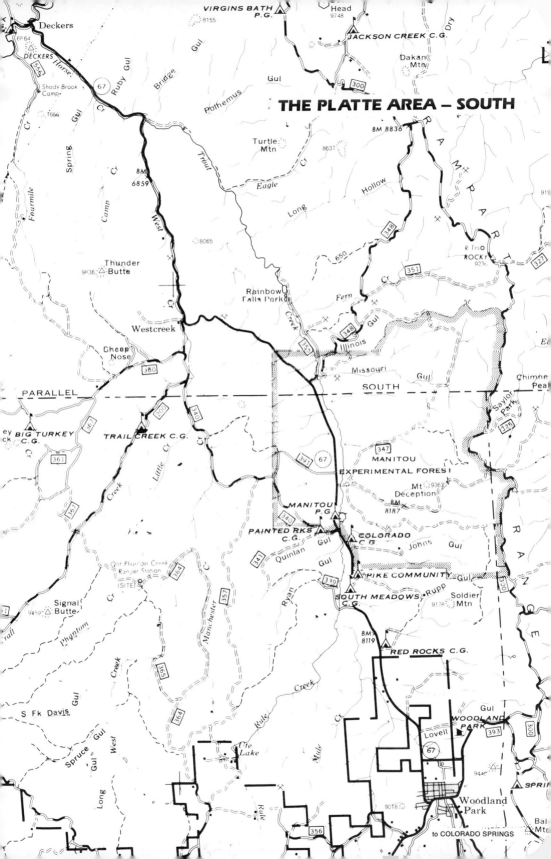

THE PLATTE

The climbing found alongside the upper reaches of Colorado's Platte River consists of granite bluffs, crags and domes. The rock quality varies widely, from granular, almost rotten granite, to fine, hard, and flawless faces that provide excellent routes. Unfortunately for those with an addiction to short approaches, the best rock seems to require at least a good half-hour walk. Fortunately for those who savor good climbing away from the madding crowd, there is a lot of rock in The Platte.

The climbing season for this region is primarily spring and fall, though mild winter and moderate summer days assure a comfortable outing. With few exceptions, most of the rocks in the area have southern, southeastern, or southwest faces, receiving a large amount of sun all year round. In winter, access to some climbs is restricted by unplowed roads. The elevation of many of the rock outcrops that dot the ridges and hilltops of The Platte range between 6,500 to almost 9,000 feet, providing a somewhat cooler retreat from flatland heat. During the Colorado thunderstorm season of late spring and summer, storms will often build over the upper reaches of The Platte before moving out over Denver and the plains. Although these showers are usually of short duration, they are often accompanied by hail. It is wise to carry rain gear.

WEATHER SUMMARY

Months	Temperatures	Precipitation
Nov-Mar	10-40s	medium
Apr-May	30-60s	med/high
Jun-Aug	50-80s	medium
Sep-Oct	30-60s	low

Due to its proximity to the great populations of Denver and Colorado Springs, The Platte, almost entirely under the auspices of Pike National Forest, provides an outdoor recreational environment for a great number of people besides climbers. Access to most climbs is by dirt roads, which, though providing shorter walks for climbers, also allows backcountry access to people with few or nonexistant wilderness ethics. As a result, some areas are polluted with the noise of dirt bikes, others with the trash-and-hack ethics of city-bred campers. Most cliffs and climbs are remote from such problems, however, and climbing in The Platte is characterized by feelings of adventure, exploration, and wilderness not found in the Boulder areas.

As some of the rocks are on or close to private land, more than standard care should be taken to minimize the climbers' impact. Please take the additional time to pick up stray trash. This will serve two purposes: It will provide climbers with a nicer area in which to climb, and will alleviate potential access problems that could result as a result of climber traffic. It is beyond the scope of this guide to establish what is or isn't on private land. Obey all no trespassing signs. If a rock is close to a house and you are in doubt, ask first before crossing someone's land.

Drinking water is scarce in The Platte. Springs may be noted on the map, but it is wise to carry an ample supply of water at all times.

NOTE: Cynical Pinnacle, the prominent tower of the Cathedral Spires Area, is off limits to climbing from May through August due to peregrine falcon nesting.

RATINGS

The so-called Yosemite Decimal System is the rating of choice for American climbers, and that is the system in use in this book. The style by which routes have been established is not generally available and thus is not included in this book. First ascent data simply reflects the first known recorded ascent based on the available information at the time of publication. Although good Euro-style and traditional routes have been put up in the Platte, both types of routes have also been chopped. Even without a clear standard for putting up new routes it could be said that if you wish to see your route remain in existence, it would be better to establish it in traditional style, that is, from the ground up.

In addition to the difficulty rating, there occasionally will be found an R or X suffix that indicates the seriousness of the climb, though not necessarily on the crux pitch. All the climbs in this guide are rated based on the assumption that a competent climber has placed the best protection available. An R means a long or damaging fall potential. An X indicates the potential of serious injury or death as the result of a fall. The lack of such a rating in no way indicates that a particular pitch is easily protected, but merely that the author was not aware of information to indicate otherwise. Indeed, when in doubt as to the seriousness of a face climb, count the number of bolts between the belays. Though this number may not be strictly accurate, it will give an indication of the protection of the pitch. Many face routes in The Platte would warrant an R rating, although the falls are not usually serious. As a result, this rating has been omitted from all but the most serious climbs.

A quality rating – by means of up to three stars – is given some climbs. Due to the variety of granite found in The Platte and the fact that the rocks are fairly spread out, the star ratings are based on the best climbs at specific locations. Thus a 2-star route at one cliff may not rate a star at all at another cliff. A separate listing is found on page 3 that details routes that would stand out anywhere.

BOLTS AND EQUIPMENT

Due to the variety of climbs covered in this guide, a standard rack is hard to define. A rack consisting of a set of RPs, a set of Stoppers through #8, some Tri-cams through 1½, Hexentrics or Friends through 4", four or five standard slings, and seven or eight quickdraws (QDs) and extra mid to hand-size pieces will usually suffice. A lot of the newer climbs have been done using TCUs, Rollers, Quickies, Aliens, and the like. Some bolted face routes require nothing more than quickdraws and runners. It is advisable to have some keyhole hangers or some unepoxied small wire stoppers handy for use on bolts without hangers. Most routes require two ropes for the descent and 165-foot ropes are common if not always necessary.

Most of the bolts in The Platte are Rawl Drives. The older climbs usually have ¼" by 1¼" bolts between belays and ¼" by 1½" protecting the cruxes and belays. Most of the newer climbs have been established with 5⁄16" or 3⁄8" by 2" bolts. Hopefully this trend to stronger bolts will continue. Regardless of size, however, it must be remembered that the very nature of bolts is such that on the surface they tend to look alike – and very comforting – but that their quality depends on the unknown factors of how well they were placed and on their unseen structural integrity.

HOW TO USE THIS SECTION

Due to the spread-out nature of The Platte, the rocks are presented in a north to south order, grouped according to prominent geographical landmarks. Written descriptions of approaches to the cliffs are found either at the beginning of each section or accompanying the topos of the cliffs themselves.

Notes about a route's particular protection needs may appear along with the route name and rating.

Unless otherwise specified, all mileage readings are taken from the junction of U.S. Highway 285 and the Soda Lakes Road, at the base of the foothills west of the Denver metropolitan area. For the sake of organization, the rocks are arranged in this section of the book as part of a geographical group around major landmarks (such as town, junctions of roads, etcetera). Each grouping of rocks is preceded by mileage distance and approach directions. Routes are listed from left to right as you face the rock. Approach times are approximations based on the amount of time it takes a reasonably fit party to reach the base of the rock.

ACKNOWLEDGEMENTS

The authors would like to thank all those who took the time and energy to help make this a better guide. Among those who contributed information were Marty Alfred, Phil Ayers, Diana Baily, Andy Beal, Phil Berggren, "Bo" Bohannon, Brett Bristol, Steve Brodhead, Ed Brown, Emily Busch, Elaine Chandler, Noel Childs, Tripp Collins, Kevin Cooney, Greg DeWitt, Rick Dulin, John Durr, Marion Durr, Lynn Fletcher, Dave Gottenburg, Larry Griffin, Mike Griffin, Jon Hall, Stephen Hart, Leon Henkleman, Bruce Hildebrand, Paul Hyliger, Ron Kirk, David Kozak, Keith Liggert, Lee Marsh, Mac McKiel, Dave McCanless, Dan McGee, Olaf Mitchell, Alan Mossiman, Sharon Murra, Brian Parsons, Brian Perkins, Carl Perkins, Deaun Schovaysa, Paul Sibley, Kevin Smythe, Ed Tobler, Claude Traufield, Ken Trout, Steve Turner, George Watson, Doug Werme, and Jay Wilson.

Thanks also to the following people for reviewing the text:
Phil Ayers, Dave Bell, Brett Bristol, Noel Childs, John Durr, Marion Durr, Dan Hare, Ron Kirk, Lee Marsh, Dave McCanliss, Mac McKeel, Paul Midkiff, Claude Traufield, Ken Trout, and Dave Twinam.

Thanks to Scott Mohr, Gordon Hubbel, and Mimi Hubbel for proofreading.

Very special thanks to the following people:

Phil Berggren for the many hours of flying to get aerial photos.

Dave Gottenburg for the massive amount of computer time keying in all this information.

Brenda Langenberg and Gordon Hubbel for the use of their cars to verify mileages since my odometer wasn't working.

HIGHWAY 285 AREA

LOVERS LEAP

This 450-foot high rock has both a northeast and a northwest face. Most of the climbs lie on the northwest face and the climbing is characterized by steep, downward-sloping holds. Most of the climbs follow crack systems, with the harder climbs following discontinuous cracks that are somewhat shallow and hard to protect.
Approach: Take Hwy. 285 3.1 miles from the junction with the Soda Lakes Road; Lovers Leap is the rock on the south side of the road. Drive to the first possible turnaround, and go back east to the turnoff directly under the rock. Cross Turkey Creek to the obvious break where a subsidiary stream meets Turkey Creek. Follow a trail on the east side, then bear left at the junction with a faint trail that puts you on a scree field directly below the northwest face (15 minutes).
Descent: For routes on the northeast face, climb down easy rock and ledges to the east. For routes on the northwest face, descend easy rock and scree to the south.

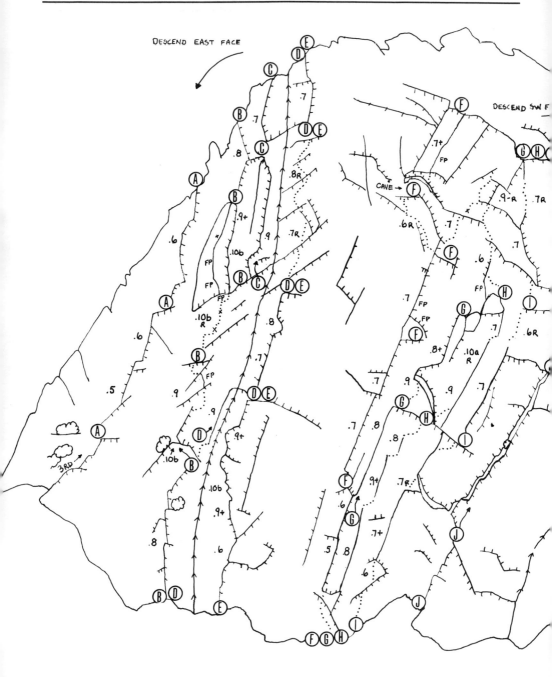

LOVER'S LEAP

A Original Route 5.6
B Ye Olde Hysterical Route 5.10b ★
C Yohr Variation 5.9
D Hubbel/Drier Route 5.9 R
E Where Tunas Flop 5.10b ★
F Lovers' Leap 5.7+ ★★★ pro: to 5"
(This is an excellent mixed route in winter; it ices up top to bottom in some years.)
G No Holds Barred 5.9 ★
H Something For Nothing 5.10a
R pro: TCUs, Quickies, HBs
I Procrastination 5.7 R
J Winter Route rating depends on conditions; ice on the 2nd and 3rd pitches.
K Winter Route II rating depends on conditions; ice on 1st and 3rd pitches.

LICORICE REUNION BUTTRESS

L Scare Tactics 5.10a ★★
M Shadow Dancer 5.10c ★★

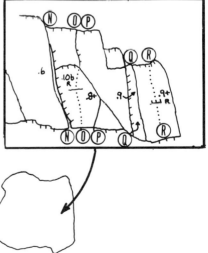

WIMPY'S BURGER STAND

This is hidden in trees 150 feet northwest of the bottom of the rock.
N Love Me Do 5.6
O Where's The Beef 5.10b R
P The Cutting Board 5.8+
Q Mind Games 5.9
R Leon's Way 5.9+ R on the west wall

NORTH TURKEY CREEK

North Turkey Creek Canyon offers a vast number of climbs and boulder problems ranging from 15 feet to 160 feet high. Most of these are in the 5.5 to 5.10 range, which makes this a very appealing area for beginning and intermediate climbers. Only the most popular routes have been shown and top-rope problems are noted with a (tr) following the rating. 90 percent of the routes can be top-roped easily; bring some very long runners for this.

At present, this property is for sale by the landowners, who have not objected to climbers. This could change any time, so please respect any no trespassing signs should they appear.

Approach: Three miles past Lovers Leap (6.1 miles on Hwy. 285 from the Soda Lakes Road) turn west on the North Turkey Creek Road and drive 0.7 miles to a turnoff on the left. The climbing is on the north side of the road.

SOUTHWEST SIDE

A   **Dotage**   5.10a (tr) ★
B   **Shadow Foxing**   5.8
C   **A Bit of the Old One-Two**   5.10b (tr)
D   **Win One for the Zipper**   5.9
E   **Captain's Corner**   5.7+
F   **Tonic**   5.8+ R ★
G   **Beginner's Route**   5.6 ★★
H   **Pot Boiler**   5.9− R

I   **Chalk Talk**   5.9
J   **Young Lizards**   5.9+ ★
K   **Warts 'n' All**   5.8
L   **Bound for Glory**   5.9
M   **Glory Hunters**   5.10a (tr)
N   **Aid Route**   A2/A3   pins, hooks
O   **Bell Route**   5.9   ★

SOUTHEAST SIDE

A **Roof Route** 5.7+ ★
B **Queen of Hearts** 5.6 or 5.9 ★★★
C **5.12 Crack** 5.11c/d (tr) ★★ bolts on top
D **5.10 Face** (tr)
E **5.9 Crack** (tr) ★★ bolts on top
F **5.8 Crack** (tr) ★-bolts on top
G **Marginal Error** 5.9+ ★
H **Warhead** 5.6
I **King of the Jungle** 5.10b (tr)
J **Young Lizards** 5.9+ ★
K **Chimney** 5.7
L **Valley Rescue** 5.8
M **Glory Hunters** 5.10a (tr)

N **Aid Route** A2/A3 pins, hooks
O **Bell Route** 5.9 ★
P **Bell Route Variation** 5.8+
Q **Sucker** 5.8+ ★
R **Green Slab** 5.7 ★★★
S **Green Slab Indirect** 5.9+ ★★★
T **Wuthering Corner** 5.8 ★★
U **5.8 Crack** (tr) ★★★ pin on top
V **Finger Crack** 5.10b (tr) ★ pin on top
W **5.7 Corner**
X **Left Crack** 5.9+ (tr) ★★ bolt on top
Y **Right Crack** 5.7+ (tr) bolt on top

PINE AREA

There are many rocks loosely grouped around the small town of Pine, located 7 miles southeast of U.S. 285 and Pine Junction on State Highway 126. Almost all of these rocks are within a short hike from the road, with the exception of Banner Peak. The climbs are mostly in the 100 to 200-foot range and cover a full spectrum of climbing difficulty and techniques. Etive Slabs are about a mile west of town on the north side of the road and offer some nice, although somewhat runout, bolt-protected slab climbs of moderate difficulty. Sphinx Rock is due north of Pine and has one of the hardest crack climbs found in the United States. Climbs on Sphinx Rock vary from crack to face climbs, as do the climbs on Squat Rock (about a quarter mile farther north) and Bucksnort Slabs (1¾ mile farther). The Ding Domes offer slab climbs of up to 300 feet and are approached by a 20-minute hike.

Access and Approach

For Little Etive Slabs, drive 5.6 miles south of U.S. 285 on Highway 126 to a turnout located on the left (north) side of the road. Little Etive Slabs are found above and north of the turnout. Take a trail up a valley that heads towards the slabs. Just before the top of the first ridge, Lower Etive Slabs are found to the right, about a 15-minute hike. Just past this first ridge and across a small valley are the Upper Etive Slabs, an additional 5 minute hike.

Sphinx Rock is located 0.4 miles east of the Pine Grocery Store on State Road 83. Park at any of the turnouts by the road and boulder-hop across the river. About 10 minutes.

Squat Rock is located 1.1 miles north of the Pine Grocery Store on State Road 83, hidden in a tight valley on the east side of the river. Park in turnouts by the road (as far off the road as possible) and cross the river via a makeshift bridge. 5 minutes.

The Ding Domes are about 2 miles past the Pine Grocery Store on State Road 83. Park at a small dirt road/turnout and hike straight up the valley to the west. About 15 minutes brings you to Ding Domes. This is all private property and is used extensively on the weekends for paint pellet war games; it also provides good intermediate climbing.

Bucksnort Slabs are located 2.1 miles up State Road 83 from the Pine Grocery Store. Park on either side of the road slightly north of the slabs. Please use as little space as possible as there is limited parking and lots of traffic. 0.1 miles past the slabs are the Bucksnort Boulders, located on the north side of the road; 0.1 miles past this are the practice slabs, just east of the turn. 0.1 past the practice slabs and on the west side of the road is Psych Dike, just above the river. 0.3 miles past this (2.7 miles from Pine) is the Bucksnort Saloon, where they serve beer, burgers, and Mexican food.

The Wave and The Beach are approached as follows: Just in front of the Bucksnort Saloon (2.7 miles from Pine on State Road 83) is a road that heads due east. Take this to where there is a dead end sign and a sharp right turn. Take this right turn and park at the first major left switchback. The Wave is to the right, a 5 minute approach. The next (right turning) switchback in the road past The Wave parking is directly under The Beach.

To approach Banner Peak take the road to The Wave and The Beach but continue past these rocks to the top of the ridge. From here take a sharp left turn downhill, passing a house. Continue up this road, bearing mostly northeast, until you can go no farther. Banner Peak **should** be just 20 minutes east of where you park. There is a maze of roads here. Take your best guess and mark your trail in! The approach is somewhat tedious and involves either crossing some private land or hiking 45 minutes from the backside of The Dome.

ETIVE SLABS – South Face

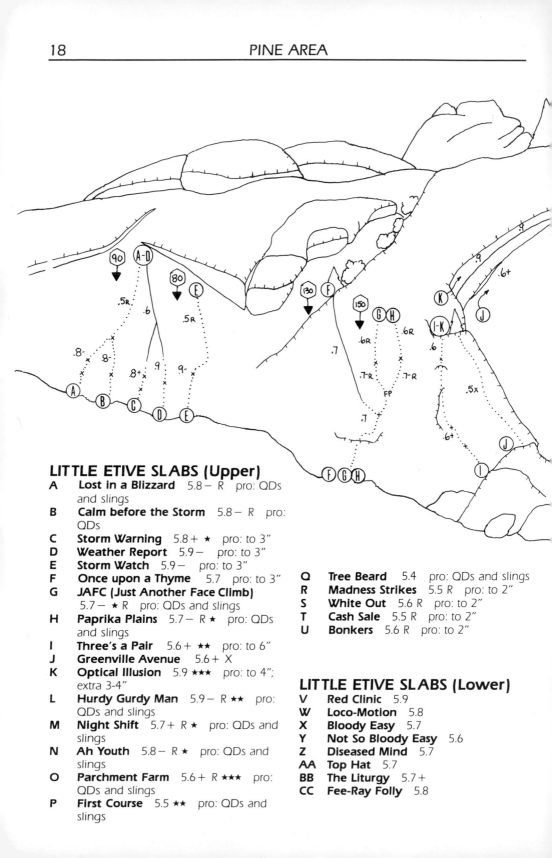

LITTLE ETIVE SLABS (Upper)

A   **Lost in a Blizzard**   5.8 − R   pro: QDs and slings

B   **Calm before the Storm**   5.8 − R   pro: QDs

C   **Storm Warning**   5.8 + ★   pro: to 3"

D   **Weather Report**   5.9 −   pro: to 3"

E   **Storm Watch**   5.9 −   pro: to 3"

F   **Once upon a Thyme**   5.7   pro: to 3"

G   **JAFC (Just Another Face Climb)**   5.7 − ★ R   pro: QDs and slings

H   **Paprika Plains**   5.7 − R ★   pro: QDs and slings

I   **Three's a Pair**   5.6 + ★★   pro: to 6"

J   **Greenville Avenue**   5.6 + X

K   **Optical Illusion**   5.9 ★★★   pro: to 4"; extra 3-4"

L   **Hurdy Gurdy Man**   5.9 − R ★★   pro: QDs and slings

M   **Night Shift**   5.7 + R ★   pro: QDs and slings

N   **Ah Youth**   5.8 − R ★   pro: QDs and slings

O   **Parchment Farm**   5.6 + R ★★★   pro: QDs and slings

P   **First Course**   5.5 ★★   pro: QDs and slings

Q   **Tree Beard**   5.4   pro: QDs and slings

R   **Madness Strikes**   5.5 R   pro: to 2"

S   **White Out**   5.6 R   pro: to 2"

T   **Cash Sale**   5.5 R   pro: to 2"

U   **Bonkers**   5.6 R   pro: to 2"

LITTLE ETIVE SLABS (Lower)

V   **Red Clinic**   5.9

W   **Loco-Motion**   5.8

X   **Bloody Easy**   5.7

Y   **Not So Bloody Easy**   5.6

Z   **Diseased Mind**   5.7

AA   **Top Hat**   5.7

BB   **The Liturgy**   5.7 +

CC   **Fee-Ray Folly**   5.8

HIDDEN IN TREES JUST RIGHT
OF THE TRAIL BEFORE RIDGE.

All the routes are without protection.

LOWER ETIVE SLABS

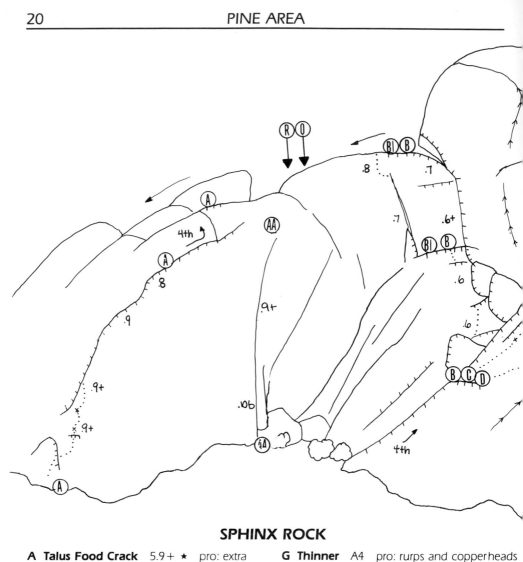

SPHINX ROCK

A Talus Food Crack 5.9+ ★ pro: extra 3-4"

AA Black Crack 5.10

B Exit Stage Right 5.7 ★★

B1 Variation 5.8

C Plinth 5.7+ R ★★ pro: to 2", incl. TCUs, Quickies

D Lickety Split 5.7 R ★★★ pro: QDs; #2-3 Friend for belay

E Locksmith (Dihedral Route) 5.9+ ★★ pro: extra 2-3"

F Choeps 5.10c ★★★ pro: Friends, QDs, slings

G Thinner A4 pro: rurps and copperheads

H Crossing The River Styx 5.10a R pro: to 3"

I Sphinx Crack (Fate Crack) 5.13b ★★★ pro: extra ¾-3"

J The Crunch 5.9+ (tr)

K Joint Venture 5.10a R pro: 3" for belay

L Laundry Shoot 5.9 R pro: 3" for belay

M The Turner Route 5.7+ R pro: to 3"

N Uh-Oh 5.6 R pro: 3" for belay

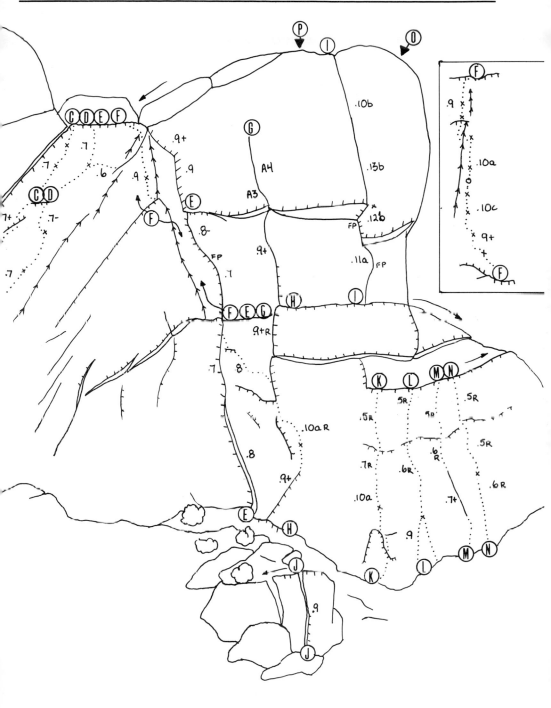

SPHINX ROCK – East Face

O Return to Forever (Southeast Corner) 5.11a ★★ pro: to 3", incl. extra 1-2"

P Bottom Line 5.7 A4 pro: pins

Q The Slug 5.8 pro: to 6"

R Ptooeey Factor 5.10a ★ pro: to 6"

SIDE SHOW SLAB

S Mind over Matter 5.12a ★ pro: #2-3
Friend for belay

T Weekend Warrior 5.11b ★ pro: #2-3
Friend for belay

HONED ROCK

U Mary's First Time 5.3 R pro: #1-3
Friends

V So Honed yet so Stoned 5.10c
★ pro: to 2"

W Snowbody's Business 5.8 pro: to 4"

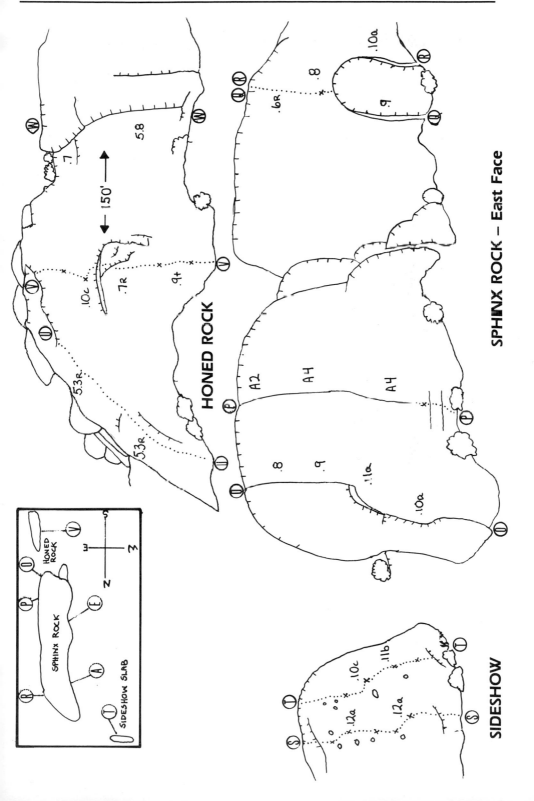

HONED ROCK

SPHINX ROCK – East Face

SIDESHOW

SQUAT ROCK

A Serenade 5.3 R/X
B Miss Conception 5.9+   pro: to 3", incl. #2 Slider or similar
C Sex Favors 5.8+ ★★   pro: QDs and slings
D Jelly Omelet 5.10c R ★   pro: QDs and slings
E Elusive Wapiti 5.9+ ★★★   pro: RPs; keyhole hangers
F Elusive Wapiti Direct 5.10b R   pro: RPs, QDs
G Higher Education 5.10b ★★★   pro: TCUs, keyhole hangers
H Dead Gumbies Can't Dance 5.10d (tr)
I Ghost Images 5.12a (tr)
J Slimy Slit 5.7+ ★   pro: extra 3- 4"
K Sticky Fingers 5.9 R ★★
L Peter's Out 5.9+ R
M Hob Goblin 5.10c (tr)
N Gob Knobbler 5.9 (tr)
O Casual Corner 5.8

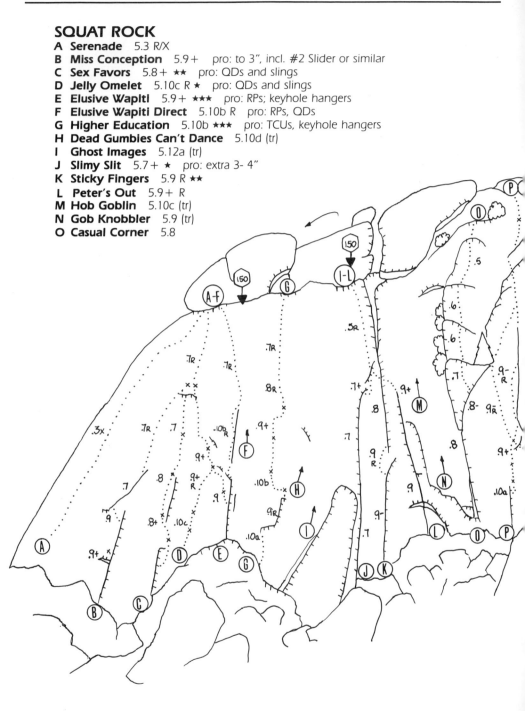

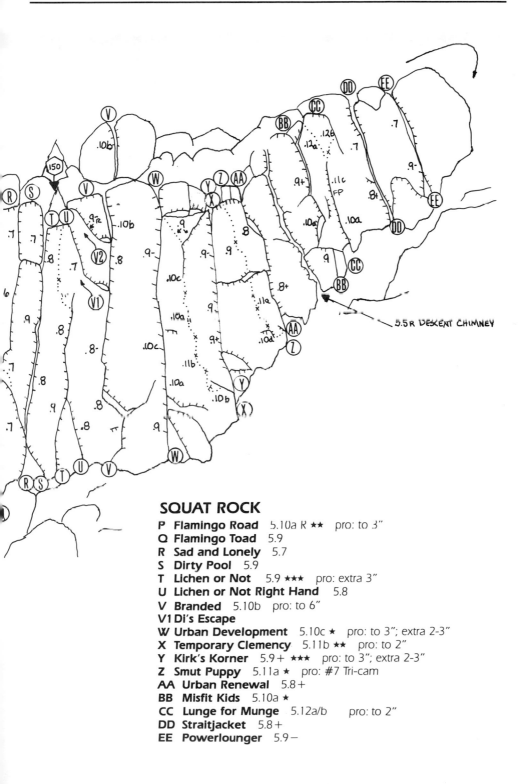

5.5R DESCENT CHIMNEY

SQUAT ROCK

P Flamingo Road 5.10a R ★★   pro: to 3"
Q Flamingo Toad 5.9
R Sad and Lonely 5.7
S Dirty Pool 5.9
T Lichen or Not   5.9 ★★★   pro: extra 3"
U Lichen or Not Right Hand   5.8
V Branded 5.10b   pro: to 6"
V1 Di's Escape
W Urban Development 5.10c ★   pro: to 3"; extra 2-3"
X Temporary Clemency 5.11b ★★   pro: to 2"
Y Kirk's Korner 5.9+ ★★★   pro: to 3"; extra 2-3"
Z Smut Puppy 5.11a ★   pro: #7 Tri-cam
AA Urban Renewal 5.8+
BB Misfit Kids 5.10a ★
CC Lunge for Munge 5.12a/b   pro: to 2"
DD Straitjacket 5.8+
EE Powerlounger 5.9−

Ghost Image, Squat Rock

DING DOMES

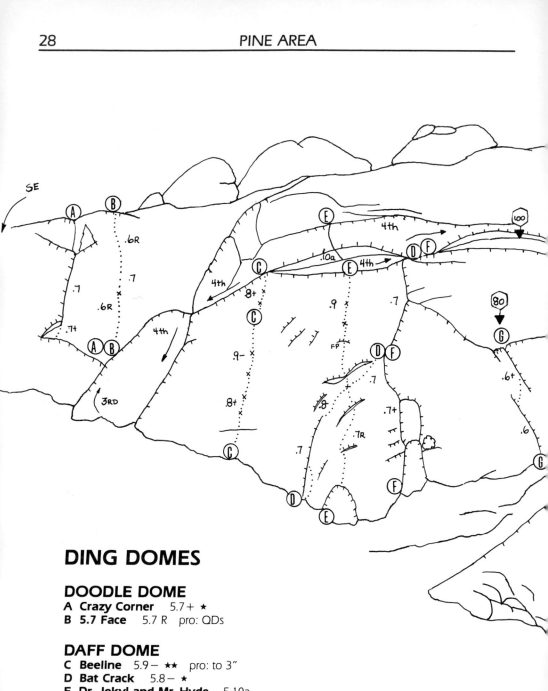

DING DOMES

DOODLE DOME
A Crazy Corner   5.7+ ★
B 5.7 Face   5.7 R   pro: QDs

DAFF DOME
C Beeline   5.9− ★★   pro: to 3"
D Bat Crack   5.8− ★
E Dr. Jekyl and Mr. Hyde   5.10a
     ★★★   pro: extra 3-4"
F Daffy Duck   5.7+ ★   pro: extra 3- 4"
G Rye Crisp   5.6+

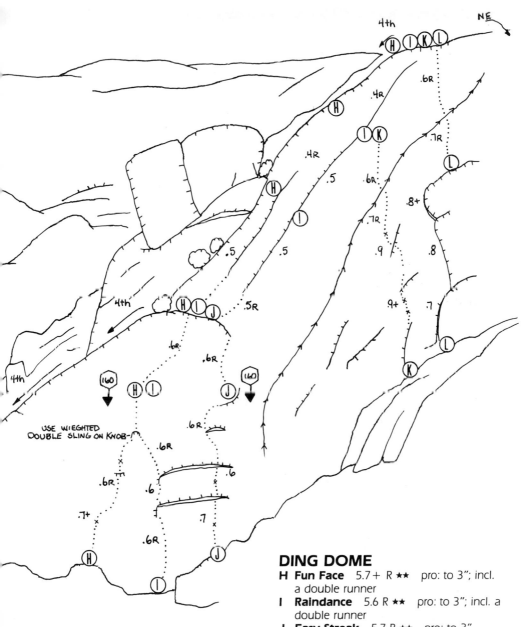

DING DOME
H Fun Face 5.7+ R ★★ pro: to 3"; incl. a double runner

I Raindance 5.6 R ★★ pro: to 3"; incl. a double runner

J Easy Streak 5.7 R ★★ pro: to 3"

NOTE: Routes H, I, and J are usually done as one pitch, then rappelled from the anchors.

K Ding Dang Doodle 5.9+ R pro: to 3"

L Captain Crunch 5.8+ pro: to 4"; extra 3-4"

Robby Baker, Gumbi Groove, Bucksnort Slab   Dan Hare

BUCKSNORT SLABS

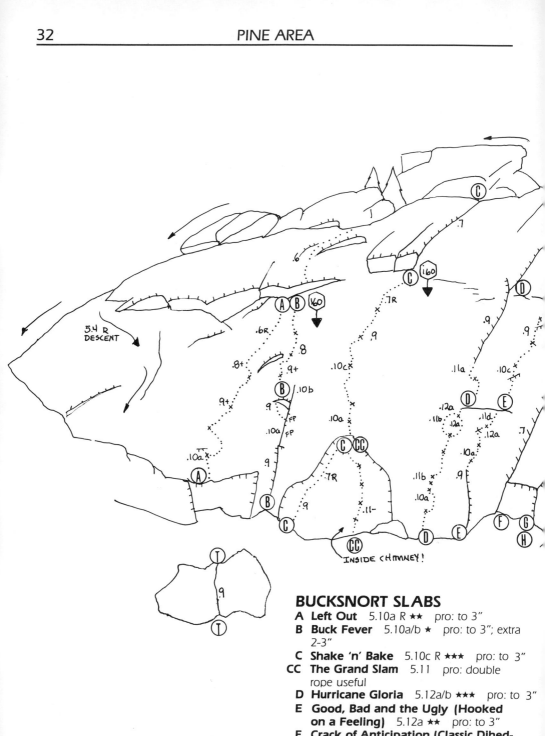

BUCKSNORT SLABS

A Left Out   5.10a R ★★   pro: to 3"
B Buck Fever   5.10a/b ★   pro: to 3"; extra 2-3"
C Shake 'n' Bake   5.10c R ★★★   pro: to 3"
CC The Grand Slam   5.11   pro: double rope useful
D Hurricane Gloria   5.12a/b ★★★   pro: to 3"
E Good, Bad and the Ugly (Hooked on a Feeling)   5.12a ★★   pro: to 3"
F Crack of Anticipation (Classic Dihedral)   5.7+ ★★★
G Slippery when Wet   5.11b ★★★   pro: to 3"
H Slippery when Dry   5.11d/5.12a ★   pro: to 3"

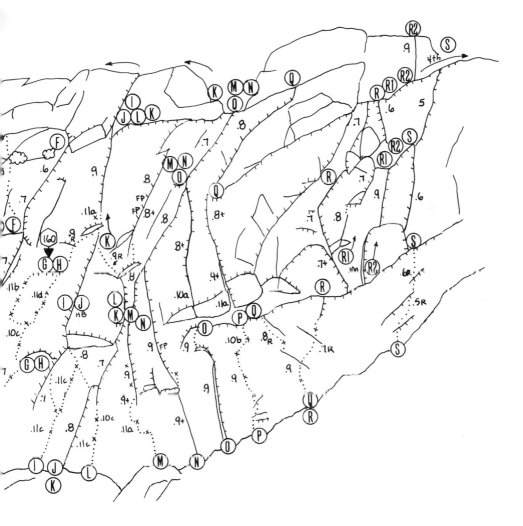

BUCKSNORT SLABS

I   **Nuclear Burn/China Syndrome**   5.11c ★   pro: to 3"
J   **Bushes of Beelzebub**   5.8 ★★   pro: extra 3"
K   **Out and About**   5.11a ★
L   **Core Dump**   5.11c   pro: to 3"
M   **Crazy Face**   5.11a ★   pro: to 3"
N   **Motor Mouth**   5.9+ ★   pro: to 3"
O   **Bats in the Belfry**   5.10a ★
P   **Gumbi Groove**   5.10b ★   pro: QDs and slings
Q   **The Boys are Back**   5.11a   pro: to 5"
R   **Over and Out**   5.9 R
S   **Easy Out**   5.6 R
T   **One for the Road**   5.9 (tr) or pro: to 2"

MOTHERLODE DOME
A No Glory for You 5.10a R pro: to 3"

THE EGGSHELL
B The Terminator 5.9– R pro: to 3"

Access and Approach:
These two rocks are visible from the Bucksnort Saloon by looking north and west. Access appears to be somewhat restricted due to the summer houses in the area. Use your best judgment.

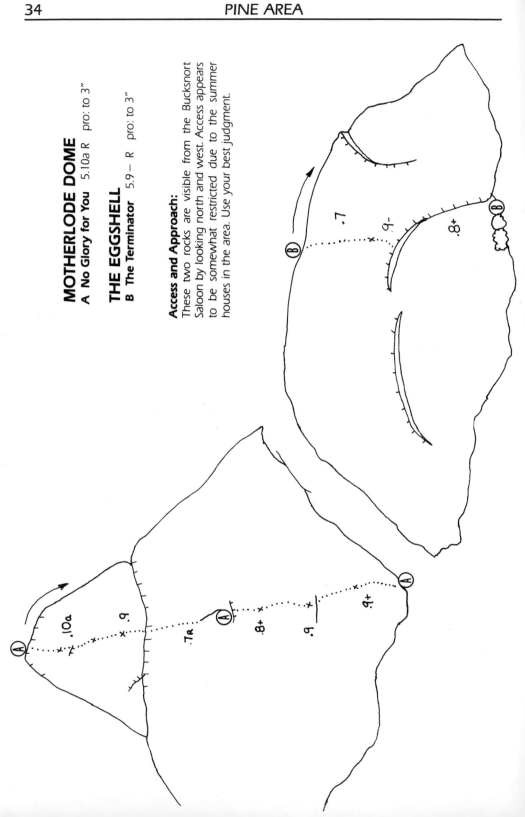

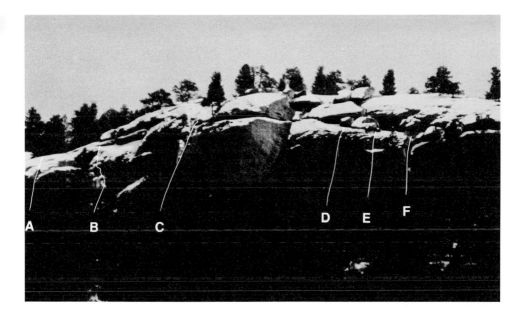

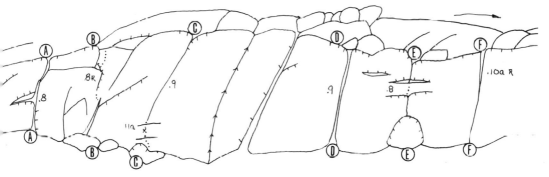

THE BEACH

A Pirate's Cove 5.8 pro: to 5"
B Sunburn 5.8 R
C Riptide 5.11a
D Blonde Bomb 5.9 pro: to 5"
E Cardiac Police 5.8
F Clamdigger 5.10a R pro: to 5"

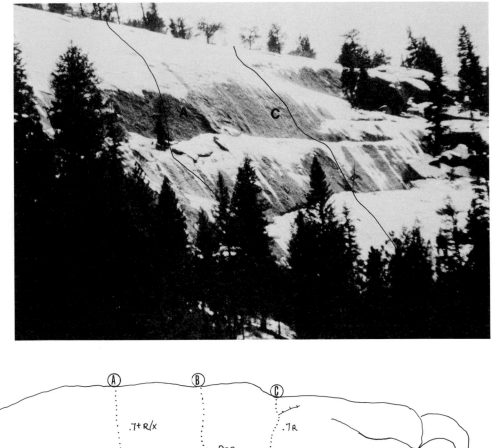

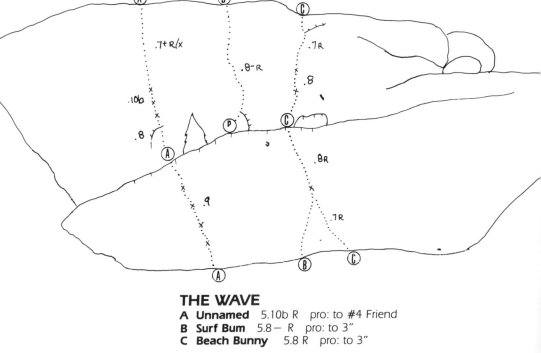

THE WAVE
A Unnamed 5.10b R   pro: to #4 Friend
B Surf Bum 5.8 − R   pro: to 3"
C Beach Bunny 5.8 R   pro: to 3"

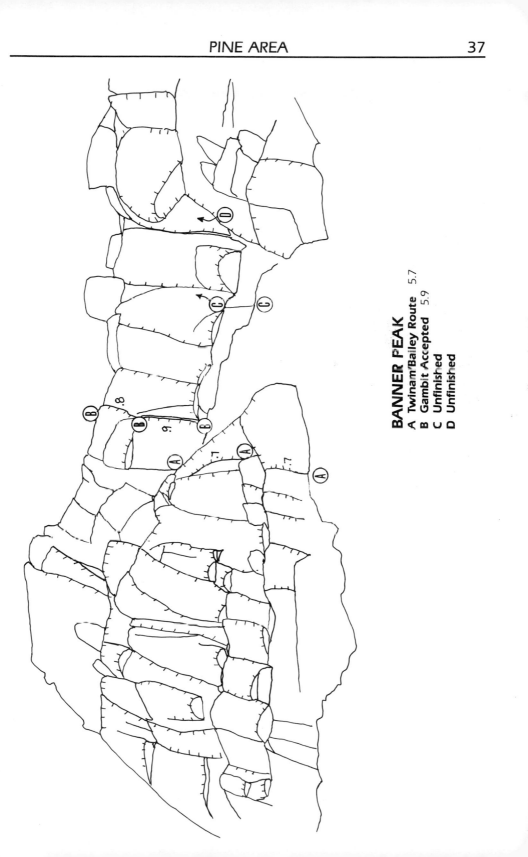

BANNER PEAK
A Twinam/Bailey Route 5.7
B Gambit Accepted 5.9
C Unfinished
D Unfinished

THE DOME AREA

This group of rocks faces the Cynical Pinnacle Area. Most of the climbs are on The Dome massif; the balance are on the two other formations, Little Dome and The Bishop. The climbs vary in height from 150 to 450 feet and are mostly bolt-protected friction climbs. Some short crack climbs of moderate difficulty are found on Little Dome and the south side of The Dome, while crack climbs of considerable difficulty can be found on the steep to slightly overhanging rock on The Bishop.

Access and Approaches:

Driving west on U.S. Highway 285 from the town of Conifer, Jefferson County Road 97 (the Foxton/Reynolds Park Road) appears to the south in 0.6 miles. Follow this 8.3 miles to the junction with Jeffco 96 at the South Platte River. Turn right and drive 3.8 miles to a large parking area on the west side of the road next to an old mining road that winds steeply up the hillside. Park here for climbs on Angle Iron Slabs, The Dome, Little Dome, The Bishop, Sunshine Wall, and Sunshine Face.

Angle Iron Slabs are located immediately off the road north of the parking area on the west side. For all other rocks, start up the old mining road.

Sunshine Wall and Sunshine Face: After about 15 minutes of hiking up the old mining road, and past where the road levels out, the road turns to the left. To get to Sunshine Wall bear right and follow a ridge up to the lowest southwest section of Sunshine Wall, about 45 minutes from the parking area.

For climbs on the Dome, Little Dome, and The Bishop, continue up the road past the point where it turns to the left. After less than five minutes, there is a sharp switchback to the west. Either turn off the road here and follow a trail on the ridge or follow the road to the next switchback and follow a gully that leads up off the road, eventually joining the trail that goes up the ridge just south of The Dome. For climbs on Little Dome, traverse right across a boulder field slightly below Little Dome. To get to the climbs on the southeast face of The Dome, continue up the ridge about another 300 feet, then traverse right across boulders. To get to climbs on the south side of The Dome near **Stars of Mars,** walk up a little higher, then go right. For climbs still farther up, hike over the saddle to the west of The Dome, and, staying high, traverse right. For all these approaches, stay on the ridge south of The Dome, Little Dome, and off of the valley floor.

For climbs on The Bishop and Round the Corner Rock, continue on the old mining road past trails to The Dome to the next switchback and follow that ridge to the rock. All approaches take between 45 minutes and an hour.

THE CRACK PRESERVE

This is a small area located on the south side of the road about a half-mile upriver from the Dome Rock parking lot. The crack-laden bluff lies up and left of a larger rock marked by a dike. Several routes have been done; one follows.

Slot Trot   5.10+   pro: RPs to #4 Friend. This follows a thin crack to a shallow offwidth.

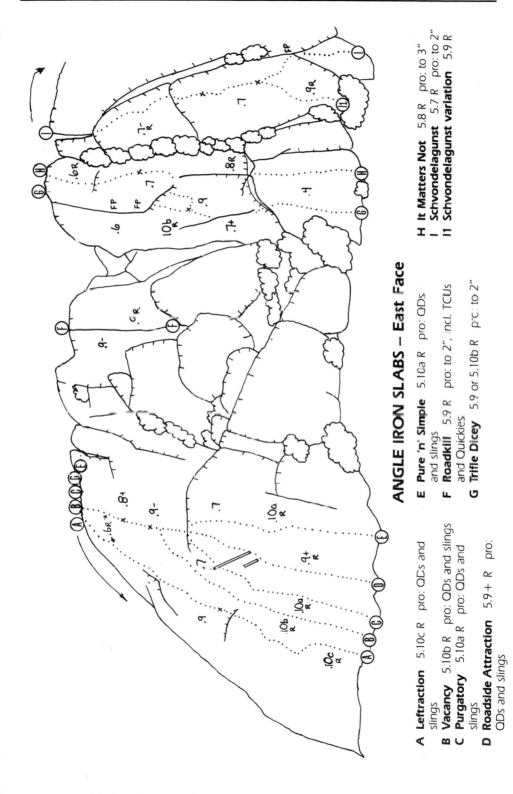

ANGLE IRON SLABS – East Face

A Leftraction 5.10c R pro: QDs and slings

B Vacancy 5.10b R pro: QDs and slings

C Purgatory 5.10a R pro: QDs and slings

D Roadside Attraction 5.9+ R pro: QDs and slings

E Pure 'n' Simple 5.10a R pro: QDs and slings

F Roadkill 5.9 R pro: to 2", incl. TCUs and Quickies

G Trifle Dicey 5.9 or 5.10b R pro: to 2"

H It Matters Not 5.8 R pro: to 3"

I Schvondelagunst 5.7 R pro: to 2"

I1 Schvondelagunst variation 5.9 R

THE BISHOP — Southeast Face

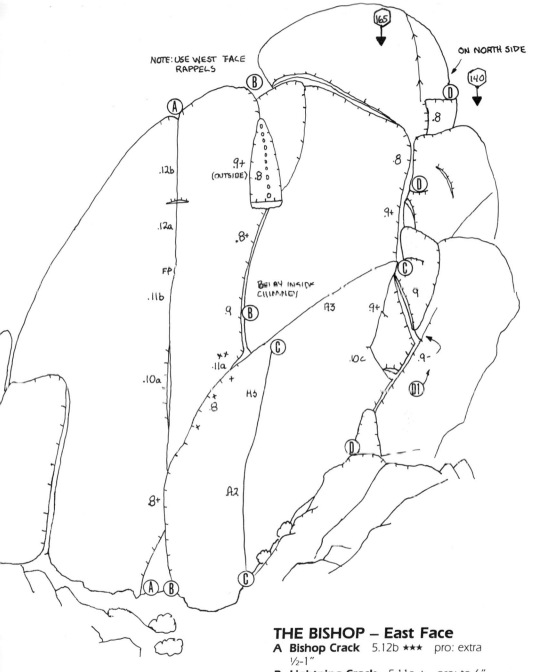

NOTE: USE WEST FACE RAPPELS

ON NORTH SIDE

165

140

.8

.8

.12b

.9+ (OUTSIDE)

.8

.8

.12a

.9+

FP

.8+

BELAY INSIDE CHIMNEY

.11b

A3

.9

.9+

.9

.10a

.9-

.11a

.10c

.8

H5

A2

8+

8+

D1

THE BISHOP – East Face

A Bishop Crack 5.12b ★★★   pro: extra ½-1"

B Lightning Crack 5.11a ★   pro: to 6"

C Aid Crack A2/A3   pro: pins

D Flounder 5.10c ★   pro: to 6"; extra 2-3"

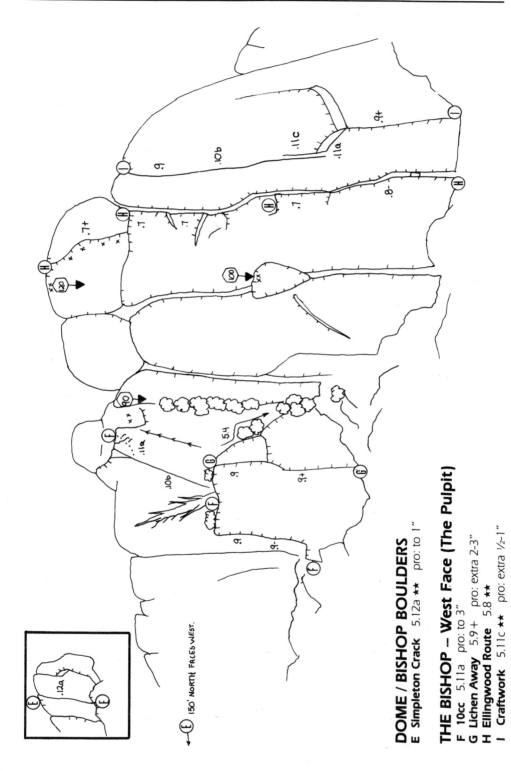

DOME / BISHOP BOULDERS
E Simpleton Crack 5.12a ★★ pro: to 1"

THE BISHOP – West Face (The Pulpit)
F 10cc 5.11a pro: to 3"
G Lichen Away 5.9+ pro: extra 2-3"
H Ellingwood Route 5.8 ★★
I Craftwork 5.11c ★★ pro: extra ½-1"

THE DOME – THE LITTLE DOME

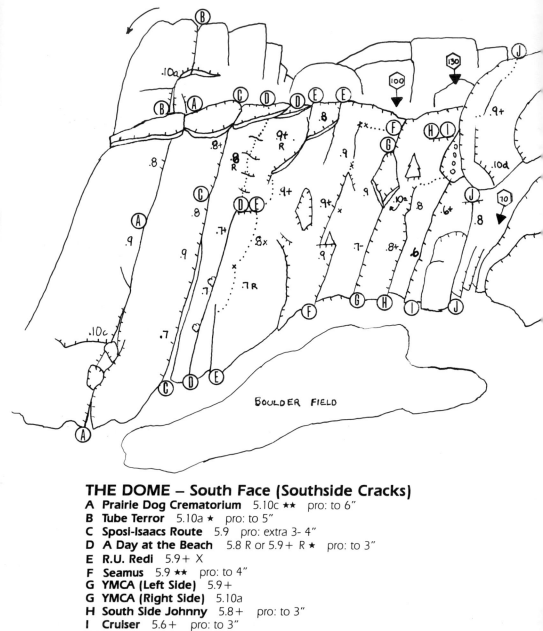

BOULDER FIELD

THE DOME – South Face (Southside Cracks)
A Prairie Dog Crematorium 5.10c ★★ pro: to 6"
B Tube Terror 5.10a ★ pro: to 5"
C Sposi-Isaacs Route 5.9 pro: extra 3- 4"
D A Day at the Beach 5.8 R or 5.9+ R ★ pro: to 3"
E R.U. Redi 5.9+ X
F Seamus 5.9 ★★ pro: to 4"
G YMCA (Left Side) 5.9+
G YMCA (Right Side) 5.10a
H South Side Johnny 5.8+ pro: to 3"
I Cruiser 5.6+ pro: to 3"
J Twist and Shout 5.10d ★ pro: extra 2- 3"

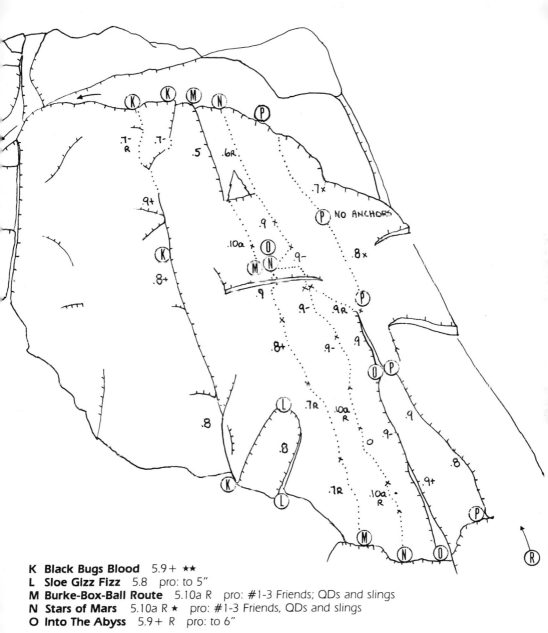

K Black Bugs Blood   5.9+ ★★
L Sloe Gizz Fizz   5.8   pro: to 5"
M Burke-Box-Ball Route   5.10a R   pro: #1-3 Friends; QDs and slings
N Stars of Mars   5.10a R ★   pro: #1-3 Friends, QDs and slings
O Into The Abyss   5.9+ R   pro: to 6"

THE DOME – Southeast Face

Descents: Rappel routes with double ropes except for **Bishop's Jagger** and **Dos Equis**.

P Higbee/Reveley Route   5.9 X   pro: to 6"

Q The Gig's Up   5.9+

R Dos Equis   5.10c A3 ★★   pro: to 2"

S Dire Straits   5.10c R ★★   pro: to 3"

T Topographical Oceans   5.10b R ★★★
    pro: #2½ Friend, #4 Rock, Qds and slings

U Bishop's Jaggers   5.9– ★★★   pro: to 4"

V Bishop's Move   5.9+

W Sea of Holes   5.11b ★★★   pro: QDs
    and slings

X Pecker Wrecker   5.11a R ★   pro: to 3"

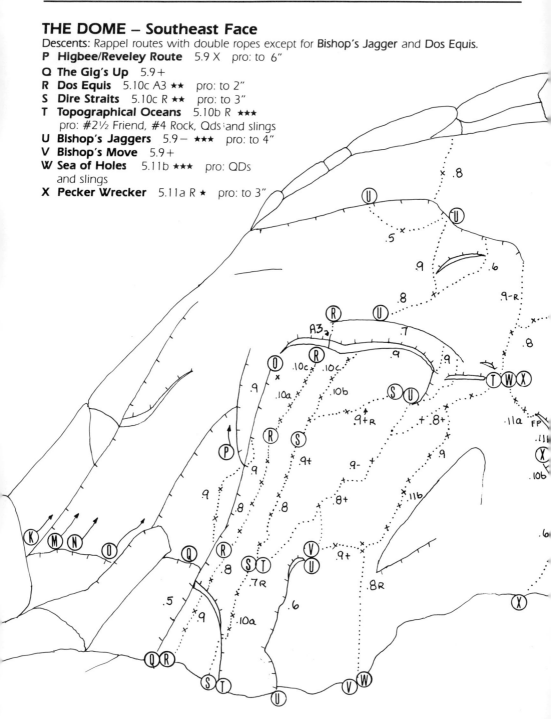

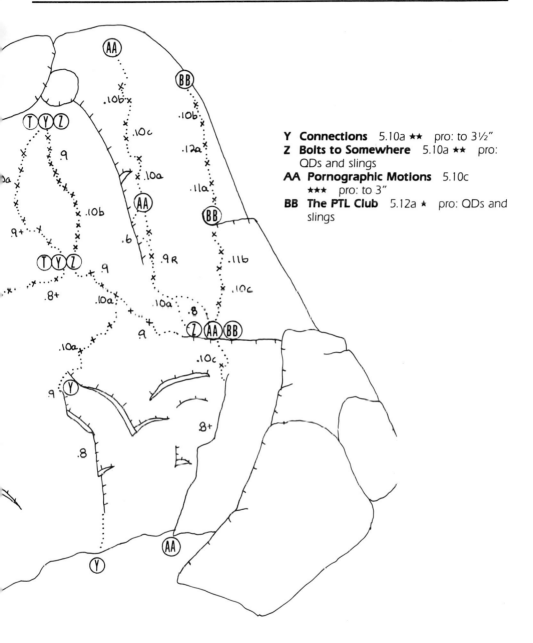

Y Connections 5.10a ★★ pro: to 3½"
Z Bolts to Somewhere 5.10a ★★ pro: QDs and slings
AA Pornographic Motions 5.10c ★★★ pro: to 3"
BB The PTL Club 5.12a ★ pro: QDs and slings

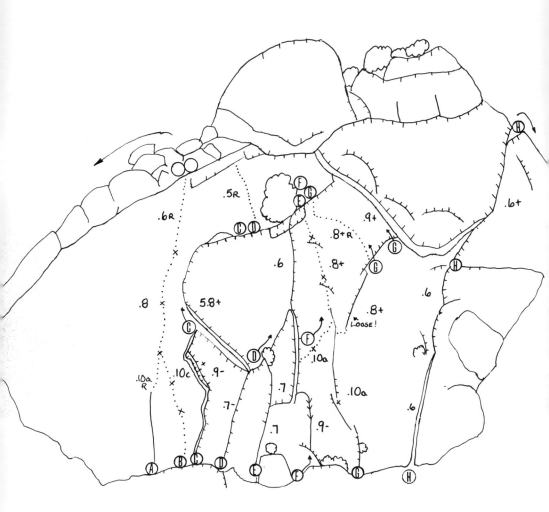

LITTLE DOME

A Ending Crack   5.10a R ★   pro: to 3"

B Beer Drinkers and Hell Raisers   5.10c ★   pro: #2-3 Friend
for belay

C Arching Way   5.9 − ★

D Flakey   5.7 − ★★   pro: extra 2- 3"

E Goofy   5.7

F Garden Party   5.10a ★   pro: keyhole hangers

G Original Sin   5.10a   pro: extra 3"; keyhole hangers

H Walking in the Rain   5.6   pro: to 5"

SUNSHINE WALL – South Face (Lower)

A **Spotlight Kid** 5.11c A1
B **Small Stuff** 5.8
C **Flakes of Wrath** 5.11 R ★★★ pro: to 3"
D **Grinder** 5.9 – pro: to 5"
E **Fred the Crack** 5.9+ ★ pro: extra 3"
F **We Scared O' de Goofa Man** 5.10a pro: to 6"
G **Buckshot** 5.10a ★★★ pro: extra 3- 4"
H **Squatters Rights** 5.10a ★★ pro: to 5"

I **Interceptor** 5.10b ★★ pro: to 6"; extra 3"
J **Strip Teaser** 5.10b ★ pro: to 6"; extra 3"
K **Gunnin' For Buddha** 5.10b ★
L **Man on Fire** 5.10a ★★
M **Arch Nemesis** 5.12b ★★★ pro: Rps to double 4"
N **Mister Skin** 5.9 ★
O **Forrest Route** 5.9 –
P **Ward Cleaver** 5.11a ★

SUNSHINE WALL (Upper)

Q **Meatcleaver** 5.10a ★★ pro: to 5"; extra 4-5"
R **Equinox** 5.11a ★★ pro: extra wires to 3"
S **What Price Glory** 5.10b ★
T **The 26th Letter** 5.8 or 5.9
U **Fallen Angel** 5.10a ★ pro: to 2½"
V **Deception Past** 5.10b ★★ pro: to 2½", incl. extra wires
W **Muddy Past** 5.9 pro: to 3"
Just a Plaything 5.12 – topropes up the face between W and Y.

X **Past Tense** 5.10a ★ pro: to 3"
Y **Standard Route** 5.11a R ★★★ pro: to 3½"
Z **The Far Reaches** 5.12c/d ★★★ pro: to 1½", extra wires
AA **Gonzo's Lament** 5.9 ★★ pro: extra 2-4"
BB **Squash** 5.11 – ★★ pro: to 3½"
CC **Squish** 5.11 – ★★★ pro: to 4"; double 4"
DD **Airborne Froth** 5.11 – R pro: to 3"

SUNSHINE WALL – South Face

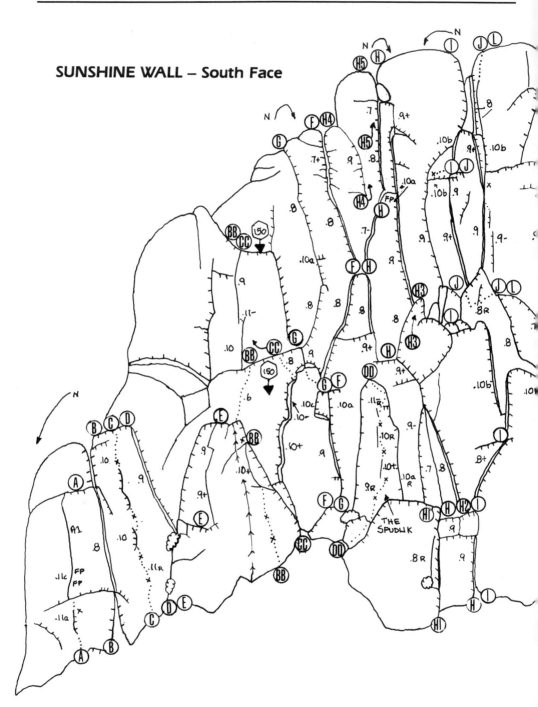

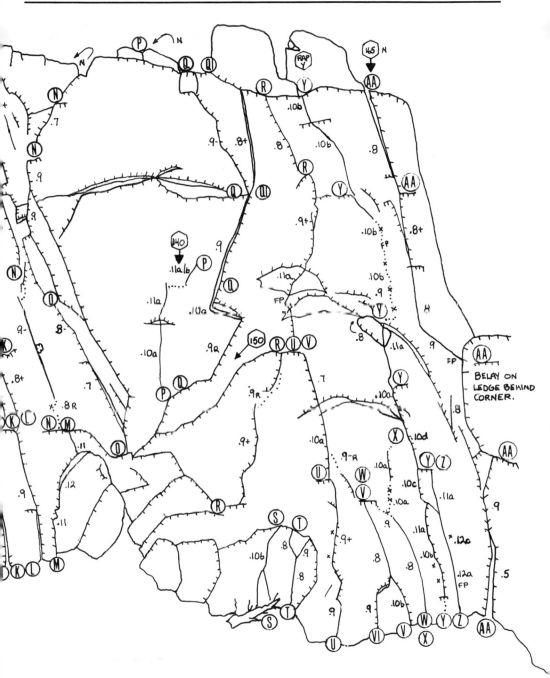

BELAY ON
LEDGE BEHIND
CORNER.

SUNSHINE
FACE ——▶

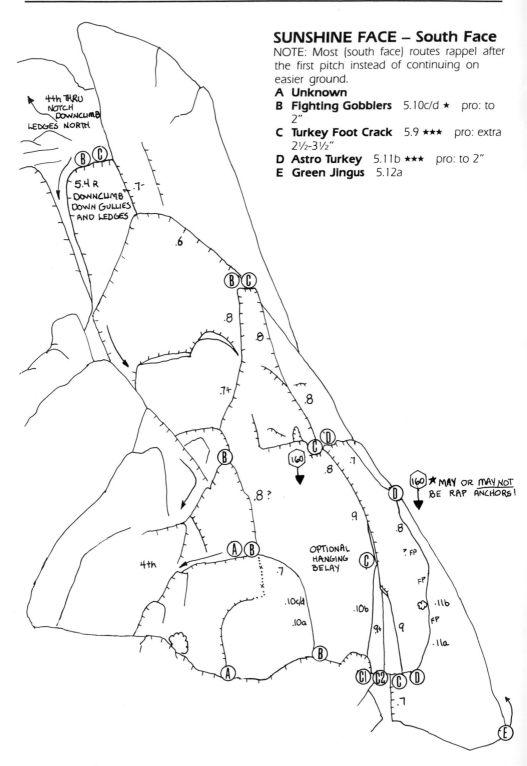

SUNSHINE FACE – South Face

NOTE: Most (south face) routes rappel after the first pitch instead of continuing on easier ground.

A Unknown

B Fighting Gobblers 5.10c/d ★   pro: to 2"

C Turkey Foot Crack 5.9 ★★★ pro: extra 2½-3½"

D Astro Turkey 5.11b ★★★   pro: to 2"

E Green Jingus 5.12a

Mike Smith, Pete Hubbel, Turkey Foot Crack, Sunshine Face

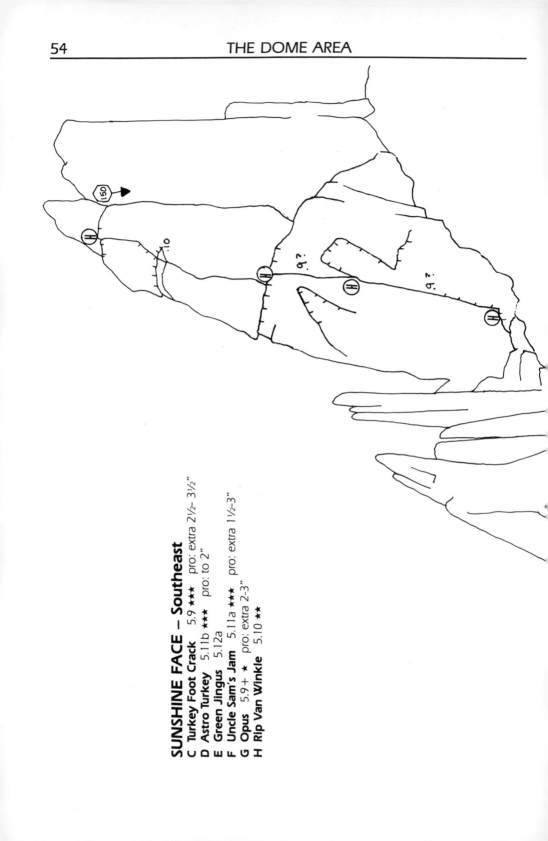

SUNSHINE FACE – Southeast
C **Turkey Foot Crack** 5.9 ★★★ pro: extra 2½- 3½"
D **Astro Turkey** 5.11b ★★★ pro: to 2"
E **Green Jingus** 5.12a
F **Uncle Sam's Jam** 5.11a ★★★ pro: extra 1½-3"
G **Opus** 5.9+ ★ pro: extra 2-3"
H **Rip Van Winkle** 5.10 ★★

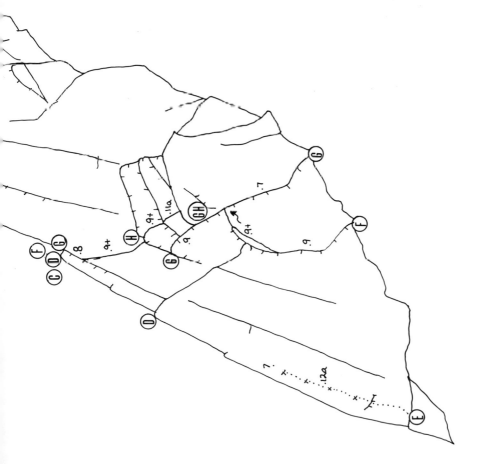

WALL OF MIRRORS

POE BUTTRESS

BLOCK TOWER

SUNSHINE WALL

THE CATHEDRAL SPIRES

This complex array of rocks has some of the best climbs in the upper part of the Platte Area. With the exception of Snake Buttress, almost all of the climbs are steep to moderately steep crack climbs. The routes range in height from 150 to 550 feet high and cover the full spectrum of sizes. Climbs on Cynical Pinnacle, Poe Buttress, and Sunshine Face tend to be very consistent in size and difficulty, while climbs on Block Tower, Sunshine Wall, the southwest face of Cynical Pinnacle and the Ice Box Wall vary a lot per pitch. Snake Buttress has only a couple of crack climbs; the majority of the routes are steep bolt-protected face climbs.

NOTE: Cynical Pinnacle is closed to climbing from May to August to protect peregrine falcon nesting sites.

ICEBOX WALL AREA

CYNICAL PINNACLE

BAD JU JU FORMATION

Access and Approach: To reach Cynical Pinnacle, Poe Buttress, Block Tower, and the Icebox Wall Areas, park at one of a couple of turnouts about 0.5 miles west of the Snake Buttress parking (described with that topo in a few pages). This parking provides the best approach to these rocks, although many people park at the large parking area a short way further up the road (at the base of the mining road approach to The Dome) and traverse back north to get to the steep drainage that goes directly off the road to a quarried area. Skirt the quarries to the southeast and follow one of a couple of trails up ridges directly below Cynical Pinnacle. For Cynical Pinnacle and the Icebox Wall, go right at a small rock outcropping to the base of the rock. For Icebox Wall, continue around the southeast nose and traverse north. To get to the climbs on the southwest face of Cynical Pinnacle and Block Tower, stay left of the outcrop. For climbs on Poe Buttress, traverse left (west) about 200' below Block Tower. Approach times vary between 35 and 45 minutes. For Sunshine Wall and the Sunshine Face see the approach information for The Dome.

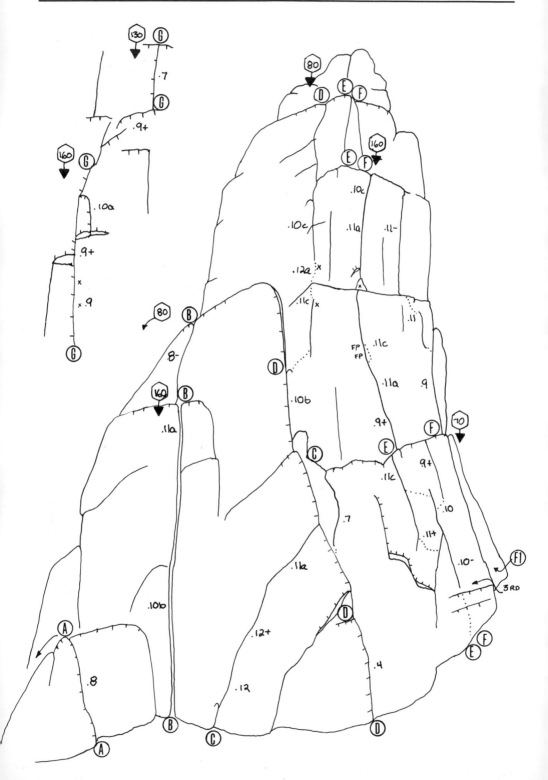

POE BUTTRESS – South Face

A Jam 5.8
B The Maelstrom 5.10d ★★★   pro: to 6"; extra 5-6"
C Brothers in Arms 5.12b/c ★★★   pro: to 2"; TCUs, larger Rollers or Quickies
D Uptown Toodleloo 5.12a ★★   pro: to 3"; extra through 1"
E Mississippi Half Step 5.11c ★★★   pro: to 3"; extra 1-2"
F Edgeofright 5.11a R ★★★   pro: to 3"; extra RPs, TCUs, Quickies
F1 variation 5.9

WALL OF MIRRORS
G Tenacity of Purpose 5.10a ★★   pro: extra 2-4"

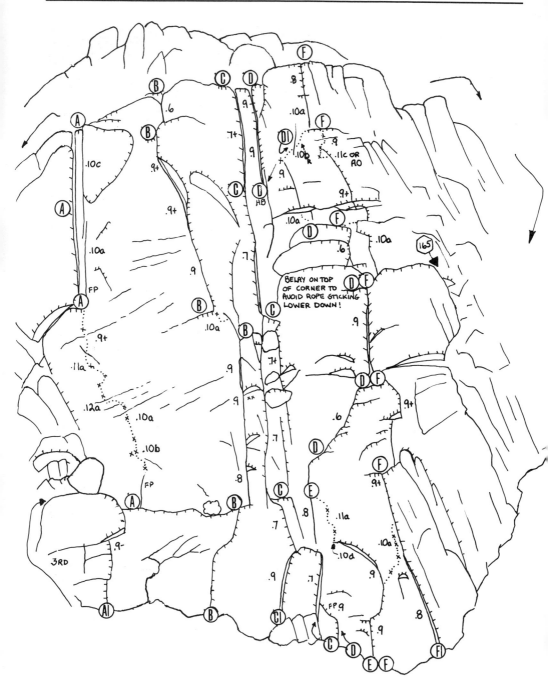

BLOCK TOWER – South Face

BLOCK TOWER

NOTE: The potential for multi-pitch 5.7-5.9 routes exists on the southeast wall, right of Queerbait.

A Mr. Mantle 5.12a ★★ pro: extra 2- 3"
B Hurt Dance 5.10a ★ pro: double 2- 3"
C Sex Dwarf 5.7+ pro: to 5"; extra 2½-3"
D Dance of Chance 5.10a ★★★ pro: extra 1½-3"
NOTE: A nice ★★★ route can be done by doing the F1 var. and 2nd and 3rd pitches of F, finishing with D; a lot of 5.9 and about 3 5.10a moves.
D1 Dance of Chance Direct 5.10b ★
E Bungi Man 5.11a ★
F Queer Bait 5.11c or 5.10a A0 ★★★

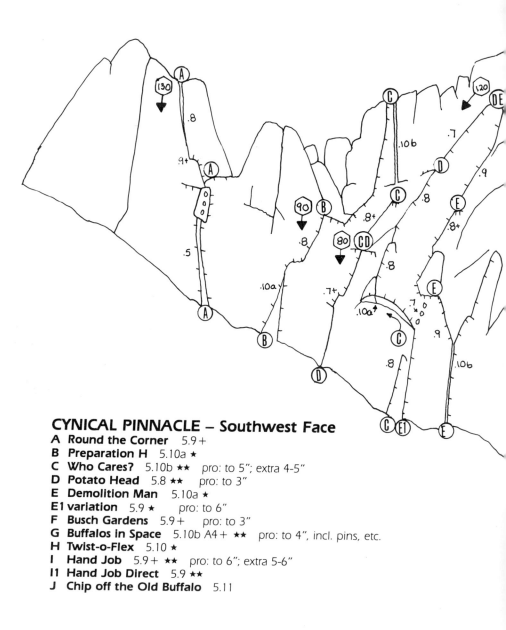

CYNICAL PINNACLE – Southwest Face

A Round the Corner 5.9+
B Preparation H 5.10a ★
C Who Cares? 5.10b ★★   pro: to 5"; extra 4-5"
D Potato Head 5.8 ★★   pro: to 3"
E Demolition Man 5.10a ★
E1 variation 5.9 ★   pro: to 6"
F Busch Gardens 5.9+   pro: to 3"
G Buffalos in Space 5.10b A4+ ★★   pro: to 4", incl. pins, etc.
H Twist-o-Flex 5.10 ★
I Hand Job 5.9+ ★★   pro: to 6"; extra 5-6"
I1 Hand Job Direct 5.9 ★★
J Chip off the Old Buffalo 5.11

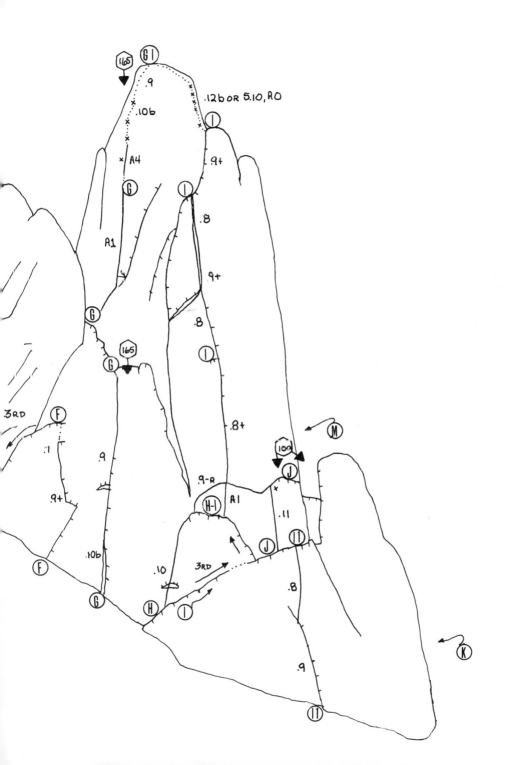

CYNICAL PINNACLE – Southeast Face

Descents: A series of 160' rappels lead off between the **Center Route** and **Turfspreader** or 165' rappels north off all routes. Do not attempt to rappel the **Center Route**; you will almost certainly lose your rope.

K Monkeys in the Forest 5.11a ★ pro: to 3"
L Breashears Finger Crack 5.11d ★★★ pro: to 3"
M Wunsch's Dihedral 5.11a ★★★ pro: extra 1-3"
N Center Route 5.9+ ★★★ pro: extra 2-4"
N1 variation 5.10a
O Rising Crescendo 5.11b ★★ pro: extra wires to 1"
P Turf Spreader (Route 66) 5.11b ★★★ pro: to 4"
Q Great Chimney 5.8+
R Class Act 5.11b ★★
S Rubber Ducky 5.9+
T Rap Crack 5.10b ★★
U CMC Route 5.8

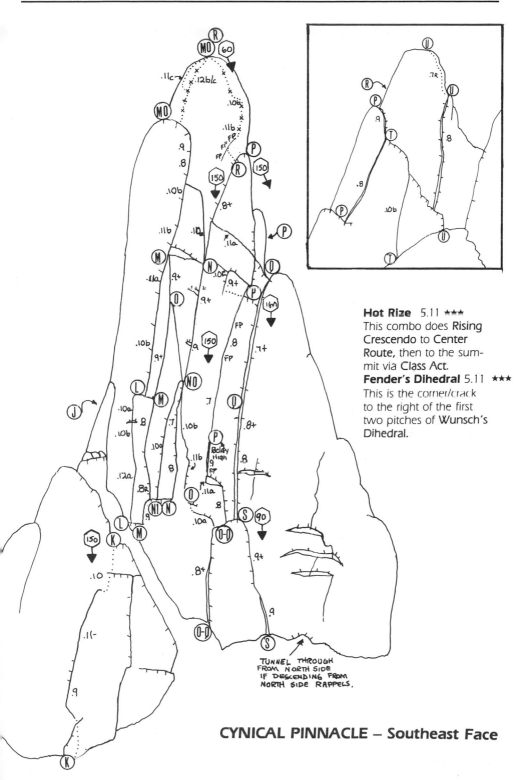

Hot Rize 5.11 ★★★
This combo does **Rising Crescendo** to **Center Route**, then to the summit via **Class Act**.

Fender's Dihedral 5.11 ★★★
This is the corner/crack to the right of the first two pitches of **Wunsch's Dihedral**.

TUNNEL THROUGH FROM NORTH SIDE IF DESCENDING FROM NORTH SIDE RAPPELS.

CYNICAL PINNACLE – Southeast Face

Melissa Ettellstein, Center Route, Cynical Pinnacle   Ken Trout

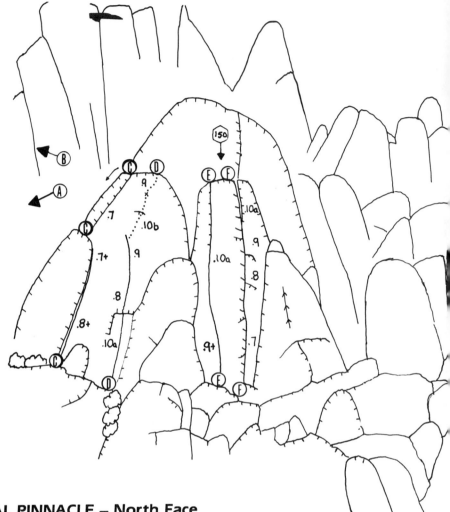

CYNICAL PINNACLE – North Face
A 5.10 Rap Crack
B Turfspreader (last pitch)

ICEBOX WALL
C Ice Age 5.8+ pro: to 5"
D Prime Line 5.10a/b ★ pro: to 3"
E Quaint Quack 5.10a ★ pro: to 4"
F Frigid Digit 5.10a ★

POWERHOUSE PINNACLE
G Emotional Rescue 5.10b ★★ pro: to 5"
H Botany Bizarre 5.9 pro: to 5"
I   Flight of the Rat 5.9+
J The Bitch 5.10c ★ pro: to 5"
Æ Round the Corner Route

THORNBIRD FACE
K Quiet Desperation 5.10c ★ pro: extra 2-
L Mr. Clean 5.9+ ★★ pro: extra 2- 3"
M Mothergrunger 5.9

BAD JU JU FORMATION
N Bad Ju Ju 5.12– ★★★ pro: extra 3- 4"

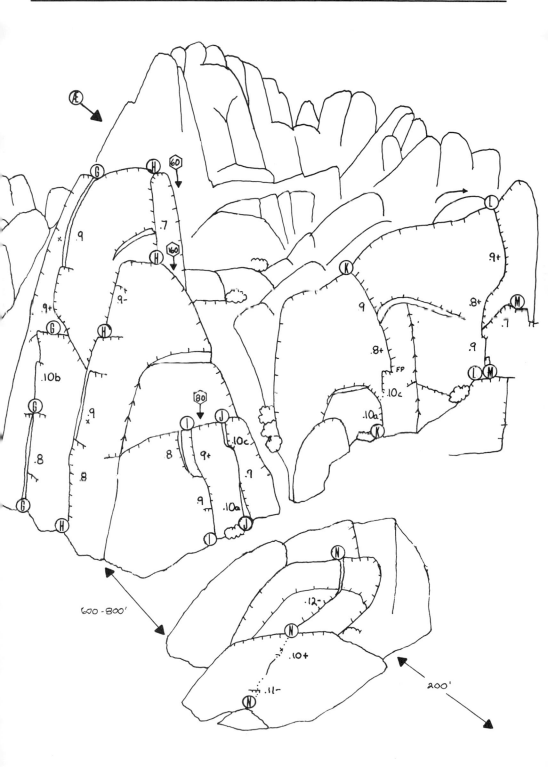

SNAKE BUTTRESS – POOP POINT

Driving west on U.S. Highway 285 from the town of Conifer, Jefferson County Road 97 (the Foxton/Reynolds Park Road) appears to the south in 0.6 miles. Follow this 8.3 miles to the junction with Jeffco 96 at the South Platte River. Turn right and Snake Buttress, Poop Point, and Poop Slab are the first rock formations above you to the west. Park at a turnout by a fence on the east side of the road. Walk back north to a drainage by a quarry and follow a path up the drainage as it leads directly toward Snake Buttress. Poop Slabs are the first rocks you come to, slightly hidden behind trees to your right (15 minutes). Poop Point is about 5 minutes farther and is directly above Poop Slab. To continue to Snake Buttress, stay on a trail to the left of these rocks to the base, about an additional 10 minutes. Bad Ju-Ju is located on a rock above and to the west of Snake Buttress (an additional 15 minutes).

Descents: From Poop Point, Poop Slabs, or Bad Ju-Ju, walk off either to the north or south; from Snake Buttress, either rappel the routes from bolts or trees or, if you've reached the top of the rock, walk off to the north.

SNAKE BUTTRESS

A Dr. Demento 5.11b ★★   pro: to 6", incl. extra 2½-3"

B Hodge Podge 5.9 ★★★   pro: to 6"

C Tronolane 5.8 R ★   pro: to 2½"

D Rude Boy 5.10c R   pro: to 1"

E Jo' Bubba 5.10a ★   pro: keyhole hangers

F Hubba-Bubba 5.10a R ★   pro: to 1"

G The Rattler 5.10d ★★★   pro: to 1"; #4 Friend for 2nd pitch belay; keyhole hangers

H The Viper 5.10b ★★   pro: to 3", keyhole hangers

I Seven Sharp 5.8 −   pro: to 3"

J Sidewinder 5.10a   pro: to 3"; keyhole hangers

K Mr. Pitiful 5.10a ★★   pro: to 2"

L Hairless 5.11b   pro: to 2"

M Geek Crack 5.10c ★   pro: to 1½"

N Illusion Chain 5.10c ★   pro: to 3"

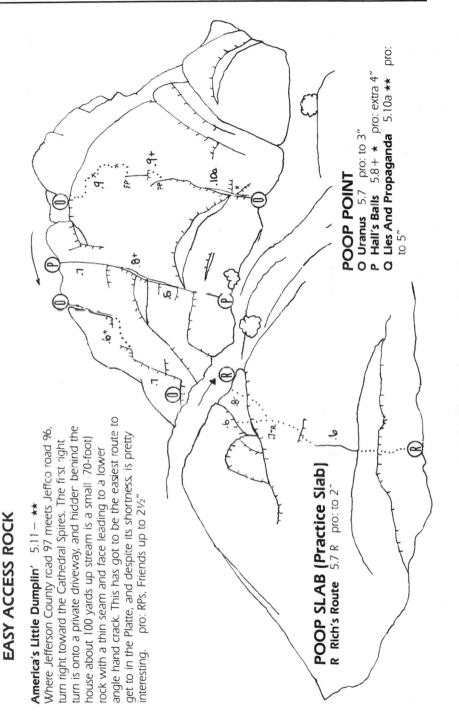

EASY ACCESS ROCK

America's Little Dumplin' 5.11 − **★★**
Where Jefferson County road 97 meets Jeffco road 96, turn right toward the Cathedral Spires. The first right turn is onto a private driveway, and hidden behind the house about 100 yards up stream is a small 70-foot rock with a thin seam and face leading to a lower angle hand crack. This has got to be the easiest route to get to in the Platte, and despite its shortness, is pretty interesting.   pro: RPs, Friends up to 2½"

POOP SLAB (Practice Slab)
R **Rich's Route**   5.7 R   pro: to 2"

POOP POINT
O **Uranus**   5.7   pro: to 3"
P **Hall's Balls**   5.8+ ★   pro: extra 4"
O **Lies And Propaganda**   5.10a ★★   pro: to 5"

Rick Dulan, Southeast Face, Chair Rocks

TOP OF THE WORLD

The scattered rocks of this area, as the name suggests, sit high above the river bottoms, with access all by one road. Most of the climbing in this area is crack climbing, with only one or two face routes in the whole area. Chair Rocks offers climbs in the 100 to 200-foot range on some of the most compact granite in this particular area. Slightly downhill from this is Spoof Rock. There hasn't been a lot of climbing done on this rock, although there is a fair amount of potential for new routes in the easier grades. Due north of Spoof Rock, Upper Gemstone offers climbs up to 200 feet high. The Slabbo has routes up to about 200 feet high, with the climbing concentrated on the east and west ends, leaving about 300 feet of untouched rock in the middle. Just below The Slabbo is Cracked Wall, with climbs — most of which contain some easy offwidth — of around a pitch in length.

The Boulder Pile, true to its name, is composed of formations 90 to 200 feet high. Although route location is somewhat hard to describe due to the steepness of the hill and the profusion of trees, this area has some very nice crack climbs in all grades and sizes. Ragnarok is the largest rock in this section, about 500 feet high and is located on the easternmost end of the ridge. Most of the climbing is concentrated on the east and southeast faces and follows prominent crack systems. The north and northeast faces are unclimbed and would offer 500-foot climbs in the 5.6 to 5.9 range.

Access and Approach:

The Top of the World Area is reached by following State Highway 126 2.6 miles south of the town of Buffalo (itself located 8.3 miles south of U.S. Highway 285 at Pine Junction) to Forest Service road #538, marked by signs to Top of the World Campground. The road forks in 1.7 miles. A right turn leads 0.4 miles to the campground. Instead, go left 1.7 miles to a left turn.

To reach Chair Rocks, follow this left turn 0.5 miles to a dead end parking area. The rocks are in straight ahead, facing south.

To reach Spoof Rock, follow the approach to the parking for Chair Rocks and follow a closed road on foot that heads west down a ridge. Ten minutes of hiking leads to Spoof Rock.

To reach Upper and Lower Gemstone, follow the approach to Spoof Rock for about 100 feet, looking for a faint animal trail that heads due north. Take this trail, staying beneath all the rock formations on the top of the ridge for 20-30 minutes. This puts you directly above Upper Gemstone. To reach Lower Gemstone, skirt the upper rock on the south. Lower Gemstone is about 250 yards downhill, an additional 10 minutes.

THE CHESSMEN

THE KINGPIN

A Three Stooges 5.10c ★★ pro: extra 2-3"

B Parabolic Flight 5.8+ A4 pro: pins?

PARKING LOT ROCK

C Latch Hand 5.9+ pro: to 3"

THE PAWN

D Slit 5.10a ★ pro: to 6"; extra 4-5"

E First Aid 5.8 A4 pro: pins?

F Short n' Sweet 5.9 ★

THE HIGH CHAIR

G Buckbo 5.10a ★★ pro: to 5"

H Handbo 5.8 pro: to 4"; extra 2-3"

CHAIR ROCK

Descend the routes on the south side of Chair Rock in any of three ways: Exit west and downclimb a short chimney from Suntan Ledge; or follow Trails of Tropical Lotions, Toot Suite, or Destination Unknown to the next ledge and a rappel west; or summit out and walk off. The rating on all routes is dependent on the finish.

I The Anti-Christ (Thin Ice) 5.12c/d ★★★ pro: to 3"; double RPs, small TCUs, Quickies

J Last Tango 5.9+ pro: to 6"; extra 5-6"

K Handcrack 5.9+

L Trails of Tropical Lotions 5.9+ ★

M Right Stuff 5.8+

N Stuff'n Fuckit 5.8

O Toot Suite 5.11a ★★★

P Low Pressure 5.11a ★★

Q Destination Unknown 5.9 ★

R Blues for Allah 5.7+ ★★ pro: extra 3"

S Secret Journey 5.10c/d ★★

T Angel Eyes 5.10a pro: to 5"; extra 4"

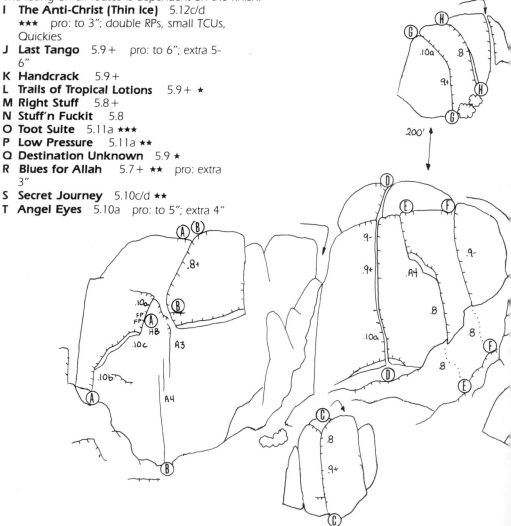

THE KNIGHT – Southwest Face

U Richart-Spaulding Route 5.8 pro: to 6"

V Huston-Johnson Route 5.8+ pro: to 6"

W The Sandwich 5.9+ pro: to 5"

X Chamber Music (Fender Route) 5.10a ★ pro: to 5"; extra 4"

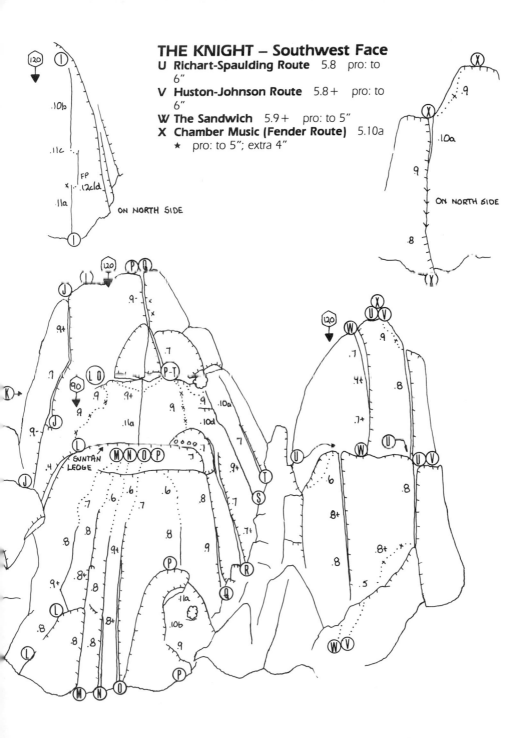

THE CHESSMEN

SPOOF ROCK

A Scab Labor 5.9+ ★ pro: to 3½"
B Whiney the Pooh 5.8−

C Punchline 5.7 ★ pro: to 6"
D Newlywed 5.8+ pro: to 5", extra 2-3"

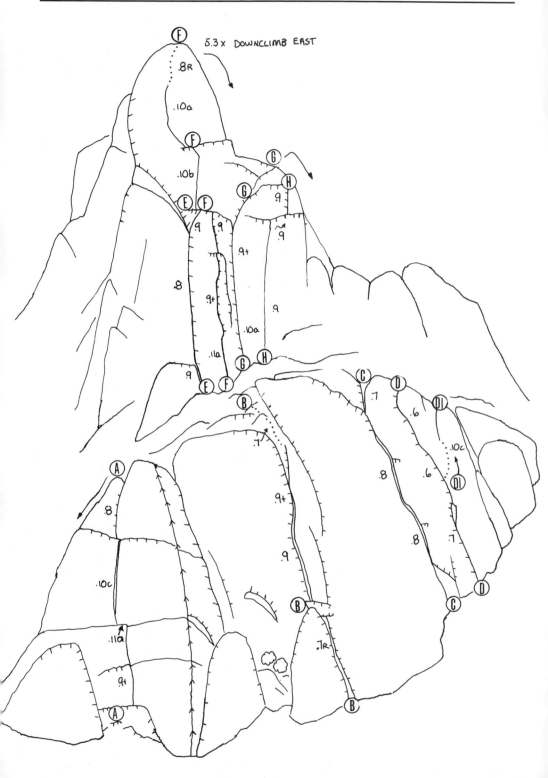

GEMSTONE (Lower)

A Just Say No 5.11a ★★★ pro: extra 1-3"

B Corporate Cowboy 5.9+ pro: to 6"; extra 4"

C 5 Weird 5.8

D Piece of Cake 5.7 ★ pro: to 5"; extra 4"

GEMSTONE (Upper)

E Agent Orange 5.9 ★ pro: extra 3"

F Group Therapy 5.11a ★★ pro: extra 2-3"

G Sloppy Joe 5.10a ★ pro: extra 2-3"

H If 6 was 9 5.9 ★★ pro: extra 3"

CRACKED WALL

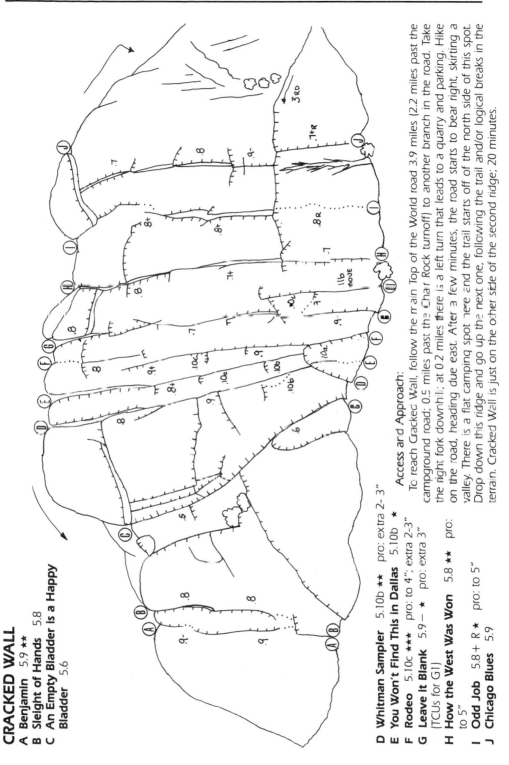

CRACKED WALL

A Benjamin 5.9 ★★
B Sleight of Hands 5.8
C An Empty Bladder is a Happy
    Bladder 5.6

D Whitman Sampler 5.10b ★★   pro: extra 2- 3"
E You Won't Find This in Dallas 5.10b ★
F Rodeo 5.10c ★★★   pro: to 4"; extra 2-3"
G Leave it Blank 5.9 – ★   pro: extra 3"
    (TCUs for G1)
H How the West Was Won 5.8 ★★   pro:
    to 5"
I Odd Job 5.8+ R ★   pro: to 5"
J Chicago Blues 5.9

Access and Approach:

To reach Cracked Wall, follow the main Top of the World road 3.9 miles (2.2 miles past the campground road; 0.5 miles past the Char Rock turnoff) to another branch in the road. Take the right fork downhill; at 0.2 miles there is a left turn that leads to a quarry and parking. Hike on the road, heading due east. After a few minutes, the road starts to bear right, skirting a valley. There is a flat camping spot here and the trail starts off of the north side of this spot. Drop down this ridge and go up the next one, following the trail and/or logical breaks in the terrain. Cracked Wall is just on the other side of the second ridge; 20 minutes.

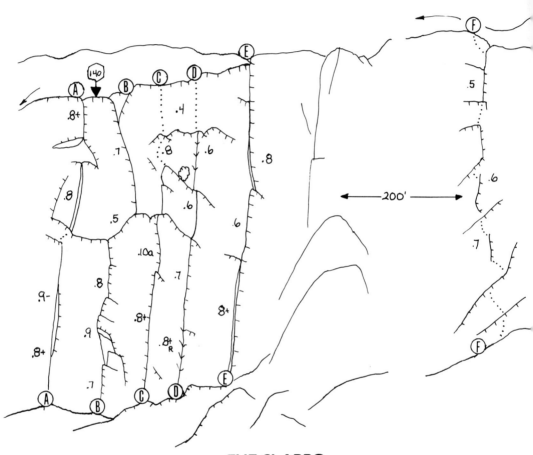

THE SLABBO

Access and Approach:

To reach The Slabbo and Ragnarok, follow the main Top of the World road 3.9 miles (2.2 miles past the campground road; 0.5 miles past the Chair Rock turnoff) to another branch in the road. Go left, up a rough uphill road for another 0.5 miles or so until the road bears sharply left and downhill. Park here in a turnout. The Slabbo is directly beneath you and slightly east; 5 minutes.

A Whining Dog 5.9− ★
B Kentucky Long Rifle 5.9
C Hand Jive II 5.10a ★ pro: TCUs
D The Pogue 5.8+ R
E Slime Mold 5.8+ pro: to 5"
F Fair Game 5.7 ★★ pro: to 3"

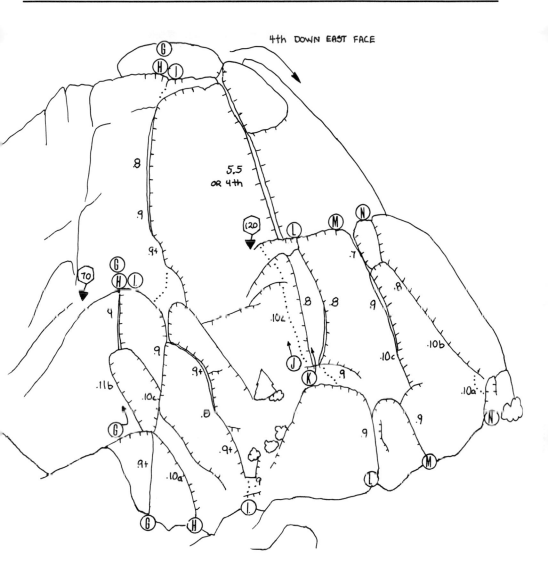

4th DOWN EAST FACE

G **Crank Corner** 5.11b ★★ pro: to 5";
extra 3-4"
H **Whiplash Smile** 5.10c ★★ pro: extra
2- 4"
I **My Pet Monster** 5.9+ ★★★ pro: ex-
tra 2-4"
J **5.10 Face**
K **5.8 var.**
L **Boulderer's Delight** 5.9 ★
M **Heinous Anus** 5.10c ★★ pro: to 6"
N **Hosemonster** 5.10b ★★ pro: to 3½";
extra 2½-3"

THE SLABBO

Pete Hubbel, Heinous Anus, The Slabbo

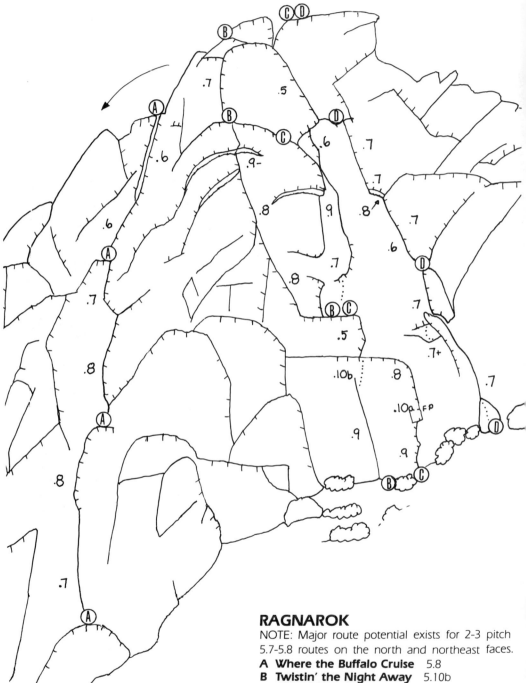

RAGNAROK

NOTE: Major route potential exists for 2-3 pitch 5.7-5.8 routes on the north and northeast faces.

A Where the Buffalo Cruise   5.8

B Twistin' the Night Away   5.10b

C Chasin' the Elements   5.10a

D Fun Climb #101 ★★★   5.8   (This is one of the best multi-pitch 5.7 routes in the Platte; the 5.8 section is 10' long.)

RAGNAROK

Access and Approach:

To reach the Ragnarok and End of the World Areas, park as for The Slabbo and drop off the road directly to the east, staying about halfway up the north side of the ridge and beneath the back side of The Slabbo. Go past the saddle (a good spot to approach the climbs on the east part of The Slabbo). At the first deep valley angle uphill to a break in the ridge; the back side of Ragnarok is directly ahead. The End of the World Area is immediately south. For Ragnarok, continue past these valleys and underneath the unclimbed north and northeast faces of Ragnarok. When you end up on the east end of the ridge, go straight uphill to the east face of Ragnarok. About 30 minutes.

THE BOULDER PILE

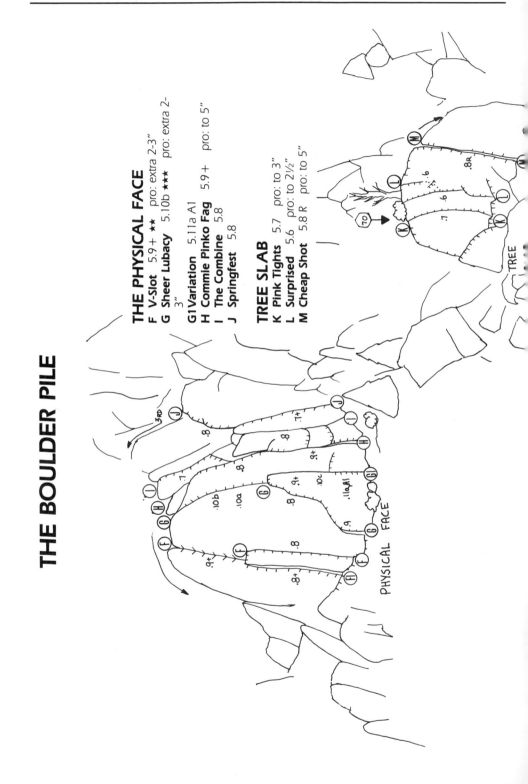

THE PHYSICAL FACE

F V-Slot 5.9+ ★★ pro: extra 2-3"
G Sheer Lubacy 5.10b ★★★ pro: extra 2-3"
G1 Variation 5.11a A1
H Commie Pinko Fag 5.9+ pro: to 5"
I The Combine 5.8
J Springfest 5.8

TREE SLAB

K Pink Tights 5.7 pro: to 3"
L Surprised 5.6 pro: to 2½"
M Cheap Shot 5.8 R pro: to 5"

PHYSICAL FACE

TREE

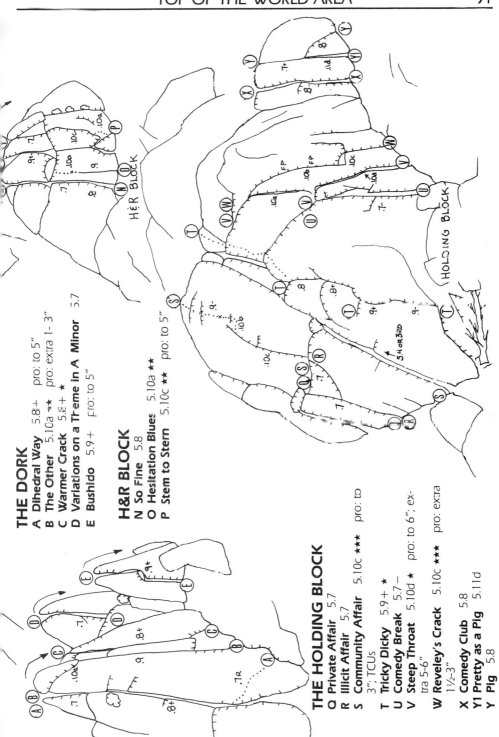

THE DORK

A Dihedral Way 5.8+ pro: to 5"
B The Other 5.10a ★★ pro: extra 1-3"
C Warmer Crack 5.8+ ★
D Variations on a Theme in A Minor 5.7
E Bushido 5.9+ pro: to 5"

H&R BLOCK

N So Fine 5.8
O Hesitation Blues 5.10a ★★
P Stem to Stern 5.10c ★★ pro: to 5"

THE HOLDING BLOCK

Q Private Affair 5.7
R Illicit Affair 5.7
S Community Affair 5.10c ★★★ pro: to 3", TCUs
T Tricky Dicky 5.9+ ★
U Comedy Break 5.7−
V Steep Throat 5.10d ★ pro: to 6"; extra 5-6"
W Reveley's Crack 5.10c ★★★ pro: extra 1½-3"
X Comedy Club 5.8
Y1 Pretty as a Pig 5.11d
Y Pig 5.8

THE BOULDER PILE

Approach:

To reach The Boulder Pile, continue past Cracked Wall, heading east. For climbs on The Physical Face, go left and uphill until you are even with the base of the rock, then scramble east. For all the other rocks, the trail cuts across the base of the Boulder Pile at a little less than half-height. It is not well marked. Approach time depends on the particular rock. It takes about 20 minutes to get to The Aerie and Weasel Ranch area from Cracked Wall, 40 minutes total from the car.

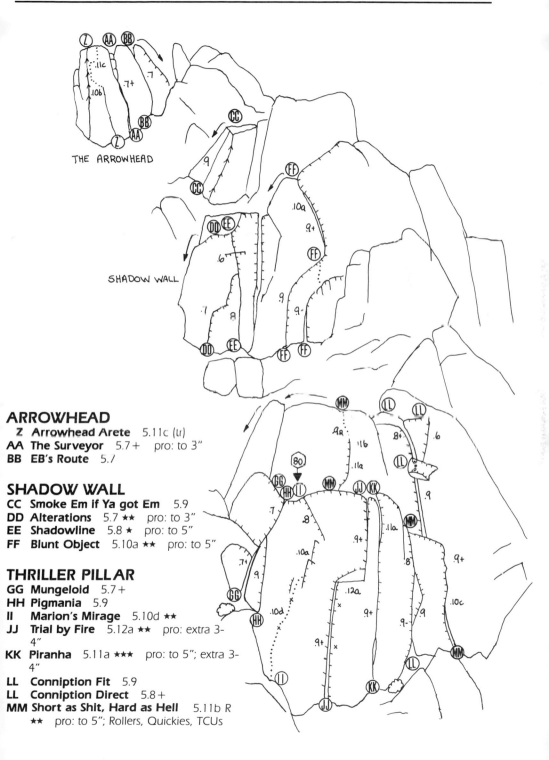

THE ARROWHEAD

SHADOW WALL

ARROWHEAD
Z **Arrowhead Arete** 5.11c (tr)
AA **The Surveyor** 5.7+ pro: to 3"
BB **EB's Route** 5.7

SHADOW WALL
CC **Smoke Em if Ya got Em** 5.9
DD **Alterations** 5.7 ★★ pro: to 3"
EE **Shadowline** 5.8 ★ pro: to 5"
FF **Blunt Object** 5.10a ★★ pro: to 5"

THRILLER PILLAR
GG **Mungeloid** 5.7+
HH **Pigmania** 5.9
II **Marion's Mirage** 5.10d ★★
JJ **Trial by Fire** 5.12a ★★ pro: extra 3-4"
KK **Piranha** 5.11a ★★★ pro: to 5"; extra 3-4"
LL **Conniption Fit** 5.9
LL **Conniption Direct** 5.8+
MM **Short as Shit, Hard as Hell** 5.11b R
　　★★ pro: to 5"; Rollers, Quickies, TCUs

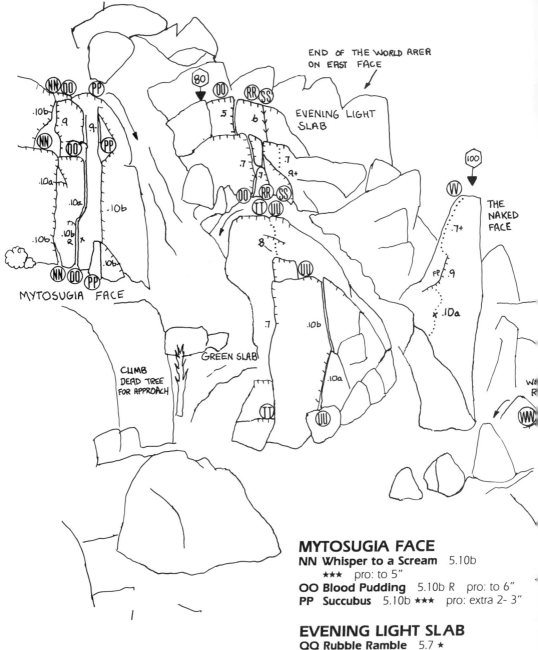

MYTOSUGIA FACE
NN Whisper to a Scream   5.10b
   ★★★   pro: to 5"
OO Blood Pudding   5.10b R   pro: to 6"
PP   Succubus   5.10b ★★★   pro: extra 2- 3"

EVENING LIGHT SLAB
QQ Rubble Ramble   5.7 ★
RR   Evening Light   5.7 ★★
SS   Monkey See, Monkey Do   5.9+

GREEN SLAB
TT   Omnique   5.8 ★★
UU Astral Pig   5.10b ★   pro: to 5"; extra
   3½-5"

THE AERIE (Weasel Ranch)

VV The Naked Face 5.10a R ★★
WW Weasels Rip My Flesh 5.10c
   ★★★ pro: extra 2-3"
XX Shuwfalo 5.8
YY Feeding Frenzy 5.9 ★
ZZ Weasels in Lust 5.8
A The Weasel 5.9
B Spookshow 5.9 ★★
B1 Horrorshow 5.10d ★★★
C Belay Slave 5.9
D Small Loans, Easy Payments 5.10a
   ★★ pro: to 5"
E Varicose Veins 5.8 or 5.9 ★ pro: extra
   3-4"
F Ides of March 5.10b ★★ pro: to 5";
   extra 4-5"
G Nuclear Waste 5.9 ★ pro: to 5"; extra
   2-3"

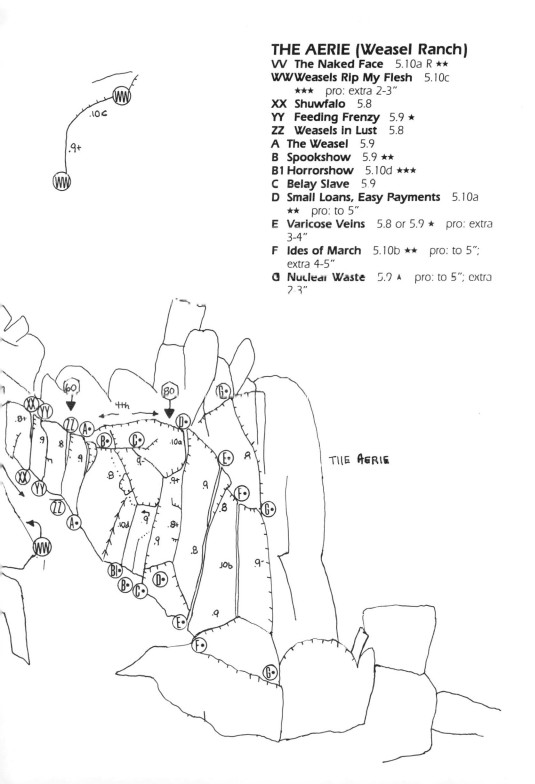

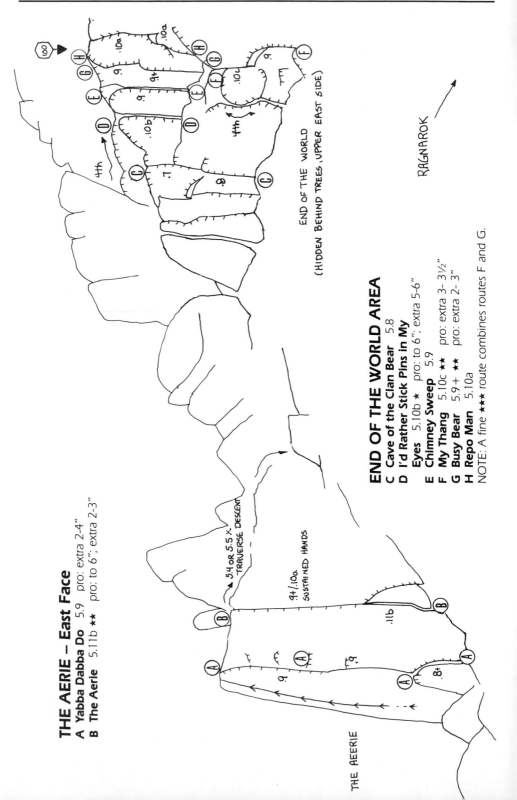

THE AERIE – East Face

A Yabba Dabba Do 5.9   pro: extra 2-4"
B The Aerie 5.11b ★★ pro: to 6"; extra 2-3"

END OF THE WORLD AREA

C Cave of the Clan Bear 5.8
D I'd Rather Stick Pins In My
   Eyes 5.10b ★ pro: to 6"; extra 5-6"
E Chimney Sweep 5.9
F My Thang 5.10c ★★ pro: extra 3- 3½"
G Busy Bear 5.9+ ★★ pro: extra 2- 3"
H Repo Man 5.10a

NOTE: A fine ★★★ route combines routes F and G.

Pete Hubbel, I'd Rather Stick Pins in My Eyes, Boulder Pile

MALAY ARCHIPELAGO

This area consists of scattered domes and slabs ranging in height from 100 to 400 feet, all within easy access of the road. Most of the climbing consists of bolt-protected face climbing, although crack climbs are also found here. Jazz Dome offers some of the easiest climbing, while the climbs on Atlantis Slab are some of the hardest in this area.

Access and Approach:

From the junction of North Turkey Creek Road and Hwy. 285, follow 285 towards Aspen Park and Conifer. 0.6 miles past Conifer, take Jefferson County road 97 (the Foxton/Reynolds Park Road) 8.3 miles to the junction with Jeffco 96, at the river.

Jazz Dome is reached by turning southeast (left) on 96; in 2.5 miles the cliff is on your left. Park at a turnoff on the right, next to the Platte River, and approach the rock with a drainage/trail from the farthest house to the upper (north) side of the rock (10 minutes). **Descents:** for routes from the southeast side, a 165-foot rappel leads from bolts; an 80-foot rappel from a tree on the right side is the descent for the remaining routes.

Dome Rock and the Dome Rock Slabs are located on the south side of the Platte, 0.8 miles past Jazz Dome and directly above the town of Dome Rock. Dome Rock Slabs are the slabs immediately west of the prominent Dome Rock. Cross the river wherever reasonable west of town and go straight uphill to The Slabs or traverse left to Dome Rock (20 minutes). **Descents:** From The Slabs, descend west. For Dome Rock, descend either side.

Atlantis Slab and Gilligan's Island are located 4.8 miles past Dome Rock and 2.4 miles past the (abandoned) South Platte Hotel. Park at a turnout at the mouth of a small valley. Atlantis Slab is closest to the road on the west side. Gilligan's Island is slightly uphill. (Some climbs on the southwest side of Java Dome can be approached from here if you stay high and above the deadfall and boulders.) Follow the trail, bearing left below some rocks (5-10 minutes). **Descents:** For Atlantis Slabs, rappel all routes, either from bolts or trees. Walk off either to the north or south from the top of Gilligan's Island.

Redemption Rock, Java Dome, and Bali Dome are located a tenth of a mile further down the road from the parking for Atlantis Slab and Gilligan's Island. A trail leads up and left from a parking turnout. Redemption Rock is the first rock on the right that offers any climbing; Java Dome and Bali Dome are about 10 minutes past this point. **Descents:** For Redemption Rock, walk off ledges to the south; Java Dome, rappel the routes from bolts; Bali Dome, Rappel the routes or walk off/downclimb to either the east or west.

Half Dome is located 1.6 miles past the parking area for Atlantis Slab. Park in a turnout on the north side of the Platte River and follow a trail to the base of the rock (5 minutes). **Descent:** Walk off east or west.

It should be noted that the entire Malay Archipelago area will be under water should Two Forks Dam be built.

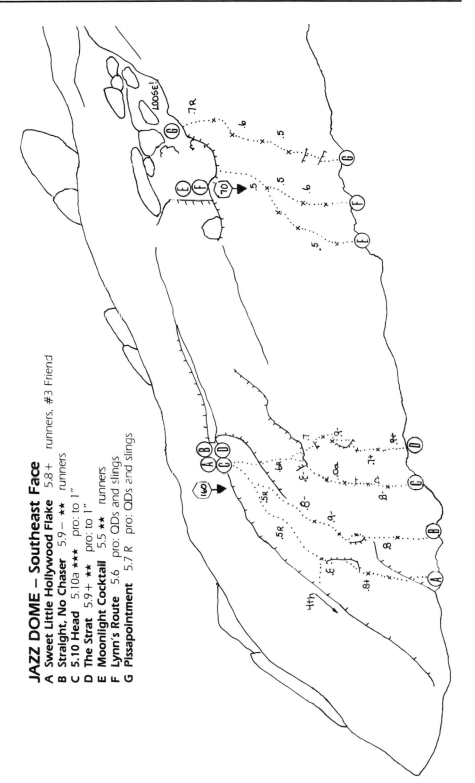

JAZZ DOME – Southeast Face

A **Sweet Little Hollywood Flake** 5.8+ runners, #3 Friend

B **Straight, No Chaser** 5.9– ★★ runners

C **5.10 Head** 5.10a ★★★ pro: to 1"

D **The Strat** 5.9+ ★★ pro: to 1"

E **Moonlight Cocktail** 5.5 ★★ runners

F **Lynn's Route** 5.6 pro: QDs and slings

G **Pissapointment** 5.7 R pro: QDs and slings

DOME ROCK

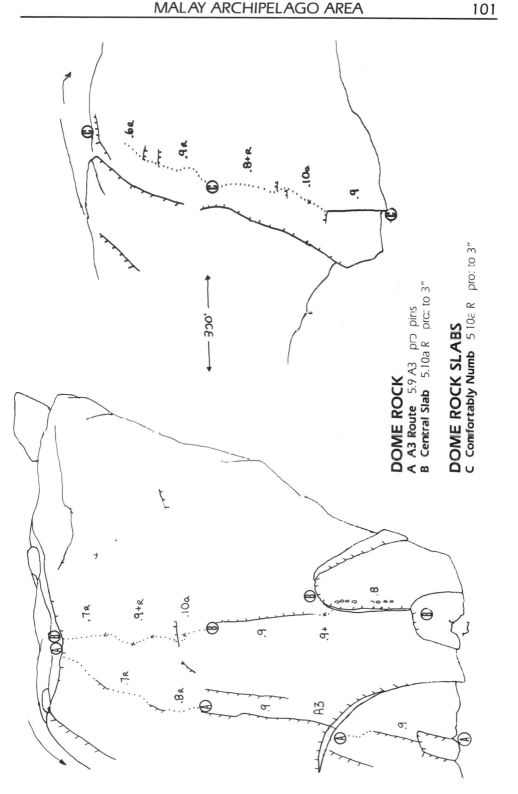

DOME ROCK
A A3 Route 5.9 A3 pro pins
B Central Slab 5.10a R pro: to 3"

DOME ROCK SLABS
C Comfortably Numb 5.10a R pro: to 3"

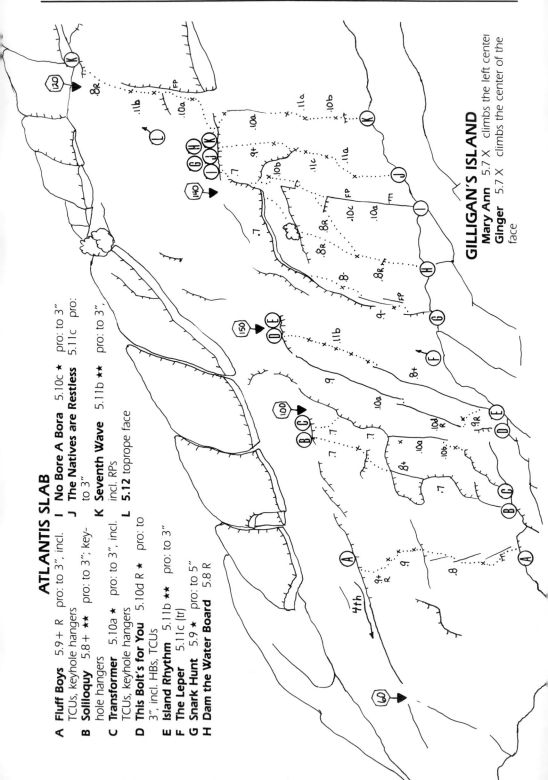

ATLANTIS SLAB

A Fluff Boys 5.9+ R pro: to 3", incl. TCUs, keyhole hangers

B Soliloquy 5.8+ ★★ pro: to 3", key-hole hangers

C Transformer 5.10a ★ pro: to 3", incl. TCUs, keyhole hangers

D This Bolt's for You 5.10d R ★ pro: to 3", incl. HBs, TCUs

E Island Rhythm 5.11b ★★ pro: to 3"

F The Leper 5.11c (tr)

G Snark Hunt 5.9 ★ pro: to 5"

H Dam the Water Board 5.8 R

I No Bore A Bora 5.10c ★ pro: to 3"

J The Natives are Restless 5.11c pro: to 3"

K Seventh Wave 5.11b ★★ pro: to 3", incl. RPs

L 5.12 toprope face

GILLIGAN'S ISLAND

Mary Ann 5.7 X climbs the left center

Ginger 5.7 X climbs the center of the face

ATLANTIS SLAB

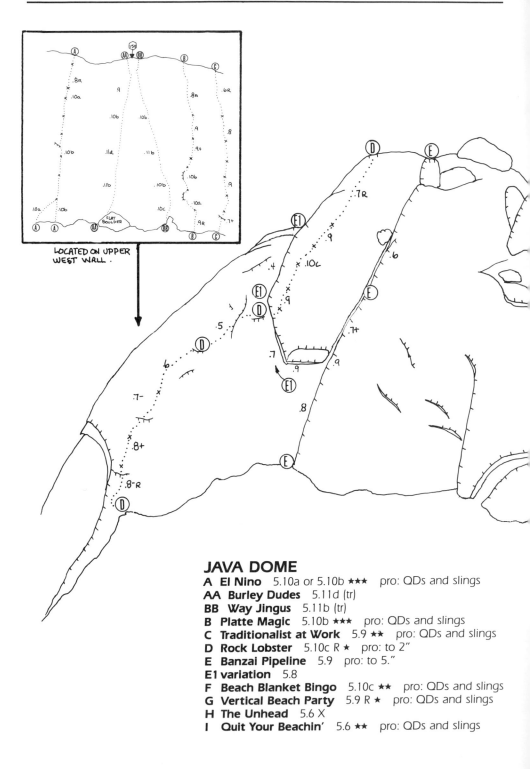

LOCATED ON UPPER
WEST WALL .

JAVA DOME
A El Nino 5.10a or 5.10b ★★★   pro: QDs and slings
AA Burley Dudes 5.11d (tr)
BB Way Jingus 5.11b (tr)
B Platte Magic 5.10b ★★★   pro: QDs and slings
C Traditionalist at Work 5.9 ★★   pro: QDs and slings
D Rock Lobster 5.10c R ★   pro: to 2"
E Banzai Pipeline 5.9   pro: to 5.''
E1 variation 5.8
F Beach Blanket Bingo 5.10c ★★   pro: QDs and slings
G Vertical Beach Party 5.9 R ★   pro: QDs and slings
H The Unhead 5.6 X
I Quit Your Beachin' 5.6 ★★   pro: QDs and slings

BALI DOME
J Pee Wee's First Bolt   5.7+ ★   pro: QDs and slings
K Island Express   5.9 R ★   pro: QDs and slings
L Good Left Hand   5.7 R   pro: to 3"; 180' pitch

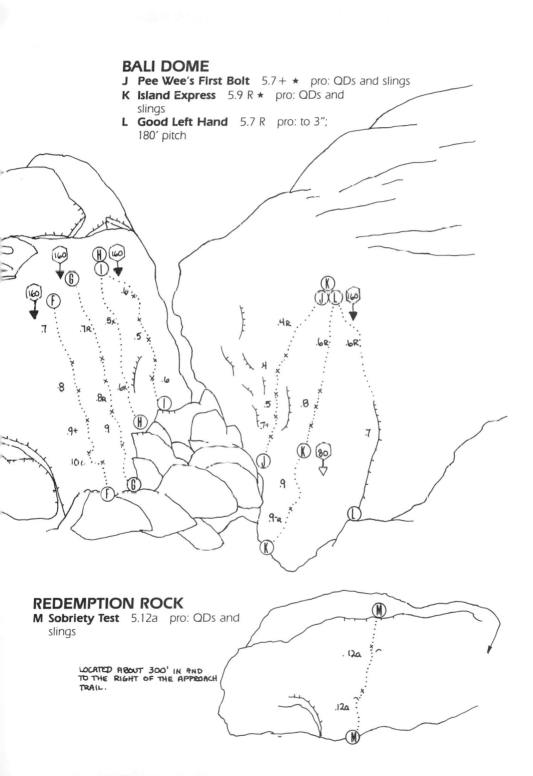

REDEMPTION ROCK
M Sobriety Test   5.12a   pro: QDs and slings

LOCATED ABOUT 300' IN AND TO THE RIGHT OF THE APPROACH TRAIL.

JAVA DOME – BALI DOME

HALF DOME

A **Tin Can Alley**   5.6+ R   pro: to 3"; keyhole hangers
B **The Tube**   5.9+ R   pro: to 6"
C **Party Time**   5.8 ★   pro: extra 2-3"

NODDLE HEAD AREA

The climbing on the Noddle Heads consists mostly of crack climbs of all difficulties and sizes. The height of the climbs varies from 150 to 350 feet. There are some face climbs on the third Noddle Head that, although of good quality, tend to be sparsely bolted. This area has some potential for new routes, especially on the northeast face of the Fourth Noddle Head. This is a semi-remote area with some very nice views as it sits up high on a ridge overlooking a large part of the Platte.

Access and Approach:

The easiest approach from the Denver metro area to this area is via Sedalia, located 10 or 15 miles out of town on U.S. Highway 285 (South Santa Fe Drive). From Sedalia, drive west on State 67 to the small town of Sprucewood. Continue south 3½ or 4 miles to a sharp turn with a pulloff and a gate. This is not especially well marked, but is at the end of most of the switchbacks and before the road begins to drop downhill. The Noddle Heads are visible due west. Park and follow the faint road west past the fence for about 45 minutes. On the ridge before you get to the Noddle Heads is a junction with a dirt bike trail; continue bearing west, crossing under power lines instead of following the dirt bike trail north.

To get to Deep Creek Dome, continue about a half mile south on Highway 67 past the Noddle Heads parking to the next drainage. This is Deep Creek. Follow the drainage east, bearing south near the top of the ridge. Deep Creek Dome is about 20 minutes from the road, and the described climb takes the most obvious break in the west face.

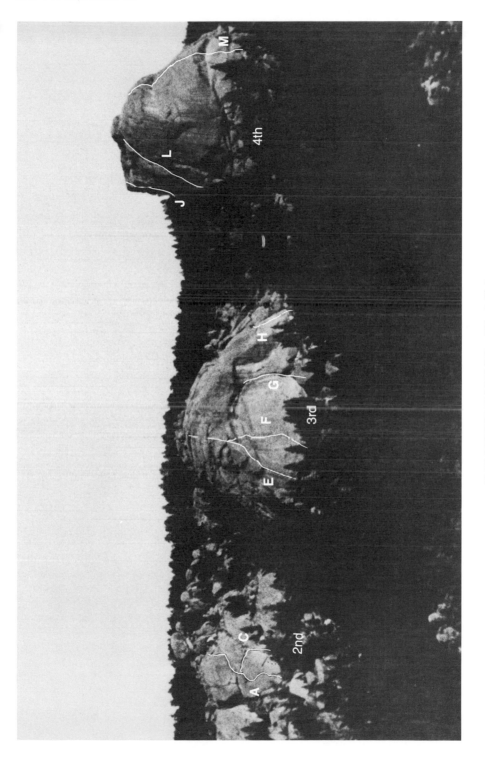

THE NODDLE HEADS – West Side

SECOND NODDLE HEAD

A Spinal Tap 5.8+ ★ pro: to 6"
B Bullets for Bonzo 5.9+ (tr)
C Spinal Block 5.8+ ★★ pro: to 6"

THIRD NODDLE HEAD

E Gone with the Wind 5.9 R pro: to 3"
F Intoxication 5.10b R ★★ pro: to 3"
G Once Is Enough 5.10c ★★ pro: to 5"
H New Creations 5.10b ★★★ pro: to 2½"
I Noodle Head 5.10a pro: to 3"

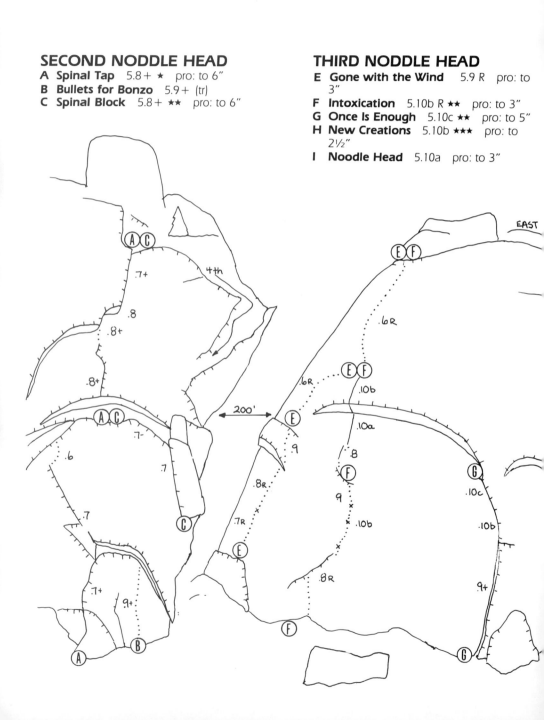

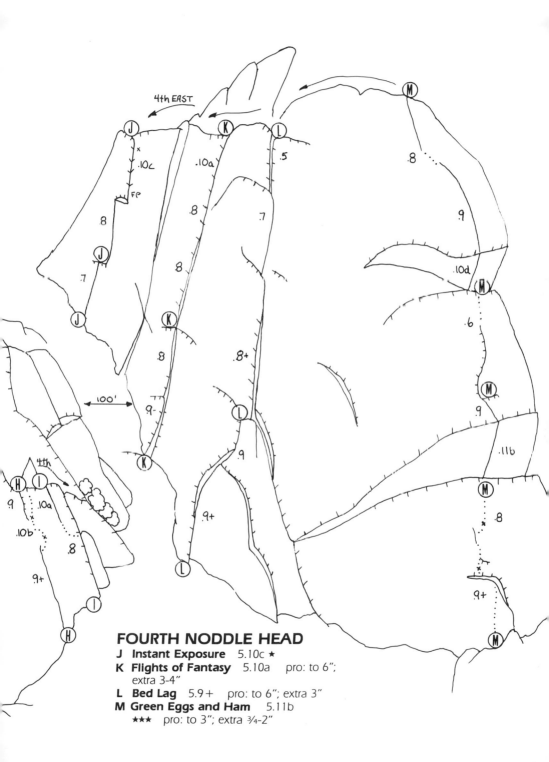

FOURTH NODDLE HEAD

J Instant Exposure 5.10c ★

K Flights of Fantasy 5.10a pro: to 6";
   extra 3-4"

L Bed Lag 5.9+ pro: to 6"; extra 3"

M Green Eggs and Ham 5.11b
   ★★★ pro: to 3"; extra ¾-2"

FIRST NODDLE HEAD

N **Sounds of a Desperate Man** 5.10b

★ pro: extra 3"

FOURTH NODDLE HEAD – East Face

O **Die Too High** 5.8+
P **Too High to Die** 5.8+ ★★

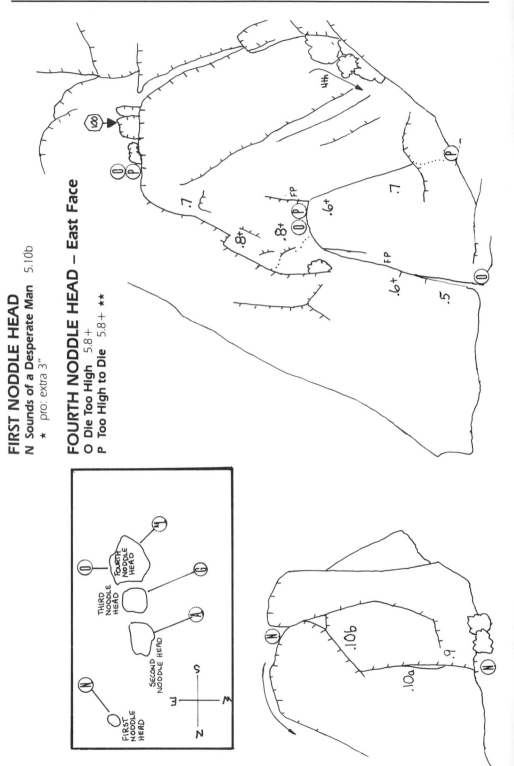

DEEP CREEK DOME

A On Butterfly Wings Rising 5.9 R

pro: to 6", extra 5-6"

JACKSON CREEK AREA

This area consists of scattered domes and rock faces ranging in size from 200 to 600 feet high that lie along a long north-south running valley on the eastern edge of the foothills. All are located within a few minutes' approach from the road. The best rock and climbing is on the smaller rocks at the northern end of the Jackson Creek Road, though Devil's Head, the largest formation in the area, with routes up to 600 feet long, is located at the far southern end of the valley. The granite on Devil's Head, however, is not up to the standard South Platte quality. The climbing consists of partially discontinuous cracks, and because of the sparse information available at the time of publication, is not included in this book. There is an amazing potential for new routes throughout this Jackson Creek Area.

Access and Approach:

From U.S. Highway 285 at Sedalia (located 10 or 15 miles south of the Denver metro area on Santa Fe Drive or about 8 miles north of Interstate 25 at Castle Rock) turn west on State Highway 67. Almost immediately, turn south on State 105 (Perry Park Road) and follow this 5 or 6 miles to Route 38 (Jackson Creek Road). This is followed west, always going straight at each of several intersections, and eventually dropping down into the Jackson Creek Valley.

The Taj Mahal is located directly west of a sharp curve 10.5 miles from the Perry Park Road. Approach the rock from a drainage on its northern side, then bear west. Approach time: about 15-20 minutes.

Jackson Creek Dome is beyond Taj Mahal about a mile, on the east side of the road. The existing climbs are on the west face. Approach: 15 minutes.

Spire Rock is located just a little north of Jackson Creek Dome and just west of a turnout on the west side of the road. The climb is on the east face. The approach takes about three minutes from the car.

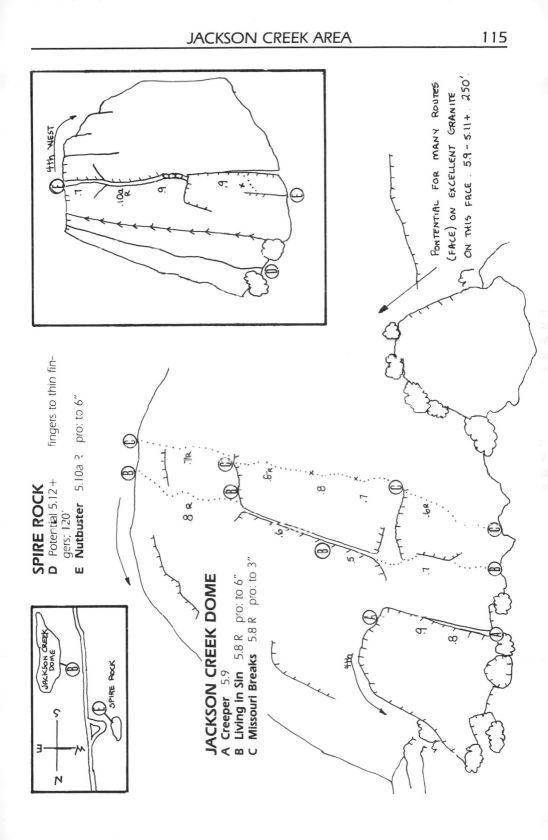

POTENTIAL FOR MANY ROUTES (FACE) ON EXCELLENT GRANITE ON THIS FACE. 5.9 - 5.11+ . 250'

4th WEST

SPIRE ROCK
D Potential 5.12+   fingers to thin fingers; 120'
E Nutbuster   5.10a ?   pro: to 6"

JACKSON CREEK DOME
A Creeper   5.9
B Living In Sin   5.8 R   pro: to 6"
C Missouri Breaks   5.8 R   pro: to 3"

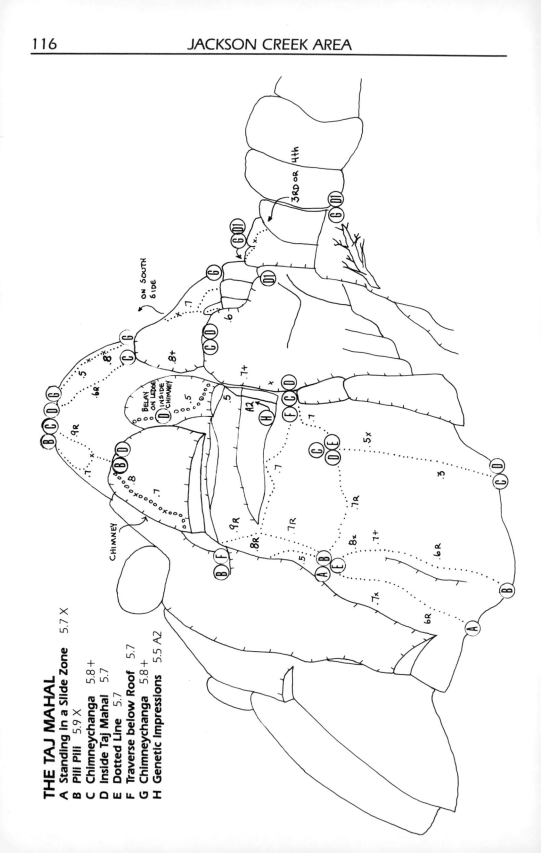

THE TAJ MAHAL
A Standing in a Slide Zone   5.7 X
B PIII PIII   5.9 X
C Chimneychanga   5.8+
D Inside Taj Mahal   5.7
E Dotted Line   5.7
F Traverse below Roof   5.7
G Chimneychanga   5.8+
H Genetic Impressions   5.5 A2

BUFFALO CREEK AREA

This area consists of short drives to rock outcrops 100 to 550 feet high. Most of the approaches are short (assuming you follow the directions), seldom more than 25 minutes. Almost all of the climbing is crack climbing with the occasional bolt used to connect the cracks. Humphrey's Dome has a wide array of climbs, both crack and face, and is about 425 feet high. The Hidden Valley Area is a ridge about a mile long with a number of formations on it of up to 250 feet. Although some climbing has been done on the ridge, the rock tends to be more broken than usual for Platte granite and is not as consistent in difficulty. Climbers who want to put up new routes in the 5.8 and under range should check this area out. The Castle and Dildo Rock offer climbs that rival some of the best in the Platte, with climbs of up to 600 feet. Although only a few routes are listed, climbs have been done on these rocks as far back as the late 1960s. Asshole Rocks offer some nice climbs in the 5.7 to 5.11 range. These are mostly crack climbs 100 to 250 feet high, and the approach is one of the shortest in this area.

Little Scraggy Dome, a west facing dome about 500 feet high, lies in the valley due west of Asshole Rocks. It has one classic crack and face climb in the center and plenty of room for harder face routes to either side. Refugee Rock is tucked away in a valley east of Asshole Rocks. At present it has only one route on it because the approach is somewhat brutal. With some cleaning, there is some potential for hard one-pitch routes here.

Skinner Mountain is the last of the rocks in this area. It is about 350 feet high and has climbs on both the east and south faces. The climbs on the south side tend to be harder, with the exception of **Wally World**. The cracks on the east tend to be slightly dirty but with additional ascents would clean up nicely.

The town of Buffalo is located at the junction of the Foxton Road (2.4 miles west of the Cathedral Spires and Dome areas) and State Highway 126 (8.3 miles south of U.S. 285 at Pine Junction). Buffalo is a starting point of reference for the approach descriptions that will accompany the topos in The Buffalo Creek Area.

Mark Drier, Nazi's Demise, Asshole Rock

HUMPHREY'S DOME

Access and Approach:

To reach Humphrey's Dome drive south on Highway 126 0.4 miles to the Bailey/Wellington Lakes Road (a right turn). Drive 3.1 miles along this road; Humphrey's Dome is seen off to the right. Park and follow drainages, passing a forest ranger's cabin, until you are about even with the east side of the rock. Only then should you traverse west to the base. About 20 minutes. The rock is not of the best quality.

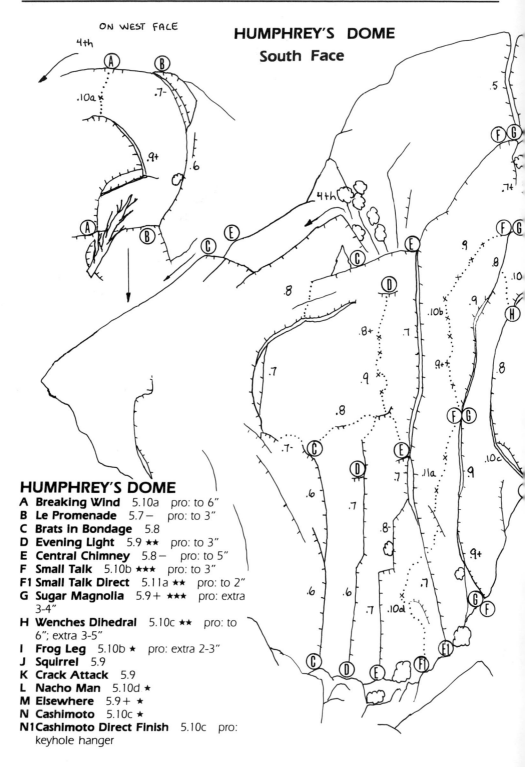

ON WEST FACE

HUMPHREY'S DOME
South Face

HUMPHREY'S DOME
A Breaking Wind   5.10a   pro: to 6"
B Le Promenade   5.7 –   pro: to 3"
C Brats in Bondage   5.8
D Evening Light   5.9 ★★   pro: to 3"
E Central Chimney   5.8 –   pro: to 5"
F Small Talk   5.10b ★★★   pro: to 3"
F1 Small Talk Direct   5.11a ★★   pro: to 2"
G Sugar Magnolia   5.9+ ★★★   pro: extra 3-4"
H Wenches Dihedral   5.10c ★★   pro: to 6"; extra 3-5"
I   Frog Leg   5.10b ★   pro: extra 2-3"
J   Squirrel   5.9
K Crack Attack   5.9
L Nacho Man   5.10d ★
M Elsewhere   5.9+ ★
N Cashimoto   5.10c ★
N1 Cashimoto Direct Finish   5.10c   pro: keyhole hanger

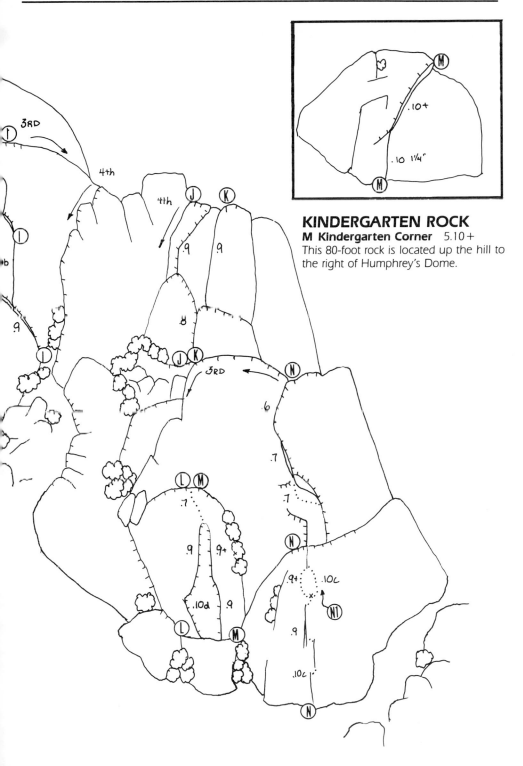

KINDERGARTEN ROCK
M Kindergarten Corner   5.10+
This 80-foot rock is located up the hill to
the right of Humphrey's Dome.

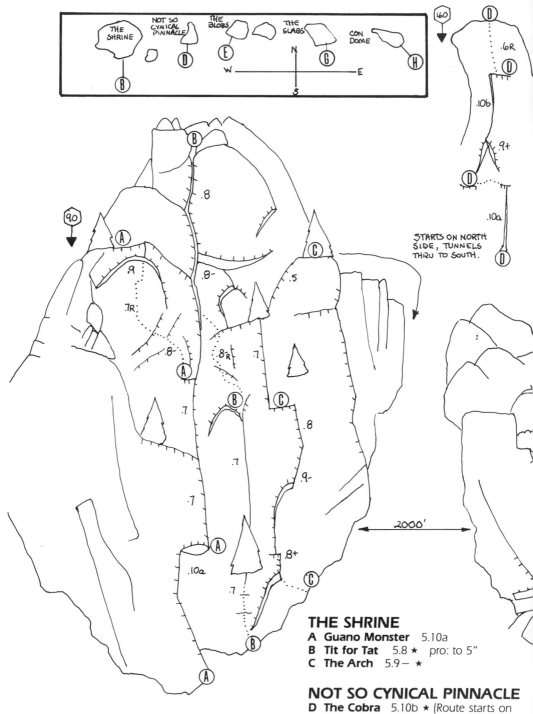

THE SHRINE
A Guano Monster 5.10a
B Tit for Tat 5.8 ★ pro: to 5"
C The Arch 5.9 − ★

NOT SO CYNICAL PINNACLE
D The Cobra 5.10b ★ (Route starts on
north side, then tunnels through to
south.)

HIDDEN VALLEY AREA

This is a ¾ mile-long ridge that faces south in the valley behind Humphrey's Dome. There is a lot of potential for easy routes here. Follow the directions to Humphrey's Dome, but continue past the east side of the dome. Follow ridges, staying out of valleys, and head roughly towards the break in the ridge between the rocks (40 minutes past Humphrey's).

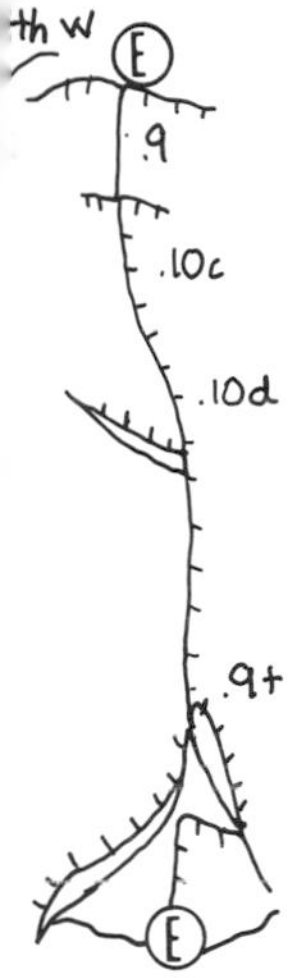

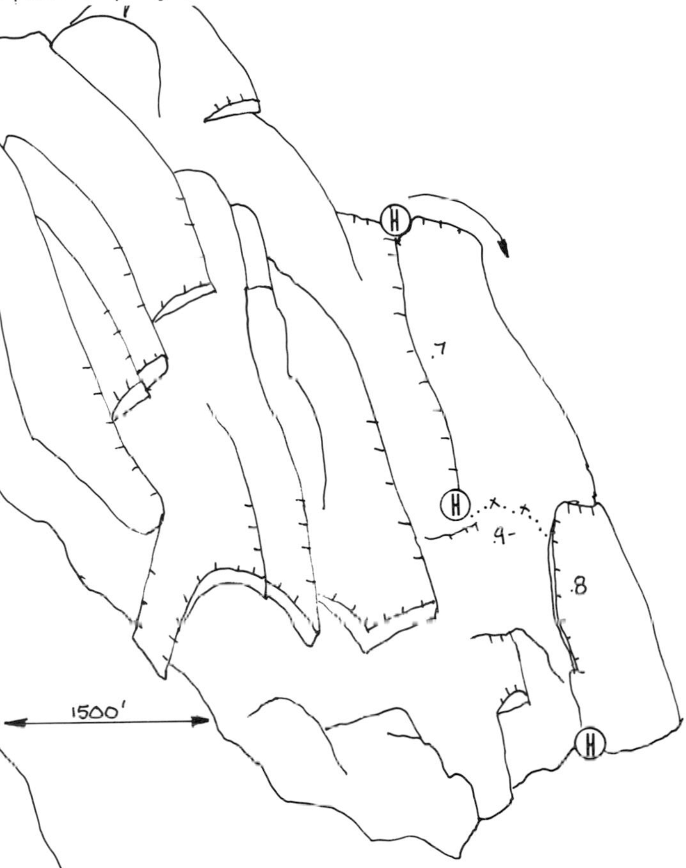

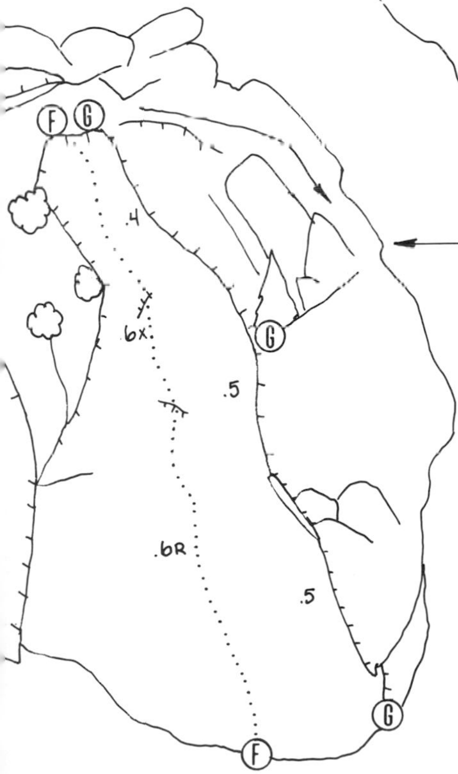

1500'

THE BLOBS

E The Last Hurrah   5.10d (tr) ★★   pro: to 4"; extra 2-3"

THE SLABS

F Easy Does It   5.6 X
G Face Route #425   5.5 ★★

CON DOME

H Trojan Trauma   5.9 −

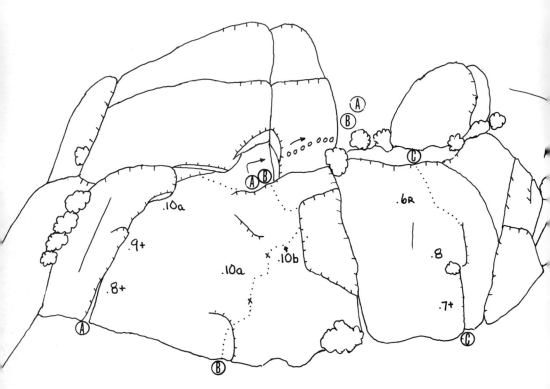

GNOME DOME

To reach Gnome Dome, take State Highway 126 4.3 miles south of Buffalo to a (right) junction with Forest Service road #550. 1.8 miles west on #550 (if coming from the west, 3.3 miles from the junction of #543 and #550), a turn north should be taken for about 100 yards to a small dip in the road. Gnome Dome is located at the bottom of the valley to the east, facing due west. 5 minute approach.

    A Fat Head 5.10a ★
    B Leave My Monkey Alone 5.10b ★ pro: to 3"
    C Fat Freddy's Crack 5.8 R

THE CASTLE – DILDO ROCK

Access and Approach:

The Castle and Dildo Rock are located above the west side of Wellington Lake. Drive south of Buffalo on Highway 126 0.4 miles to the Bailey/Wellington Lake Road (a right turn). 4.8 miles along this road leads to the Tramway Picnic Ground, and another 0.9 miles leads to the junction of Forest Service Roads #550 and #543. Bear right here, following signs to Wellington Lake, Redskin Campground and Bailey. After 0.4 miles #543 and #550 fork (#550 continuing on to Bailey in another 11 miles). Take road #543 on past Green Mountain Campground to Wellington Lake (3.2 miles). The approach to the rocks takes up to 1½ hours; the landowner charges a small access fee. Forest Service road #560 meets #543 at the lake. This is followed to the Wigwam Creek Area after about 9 miles.

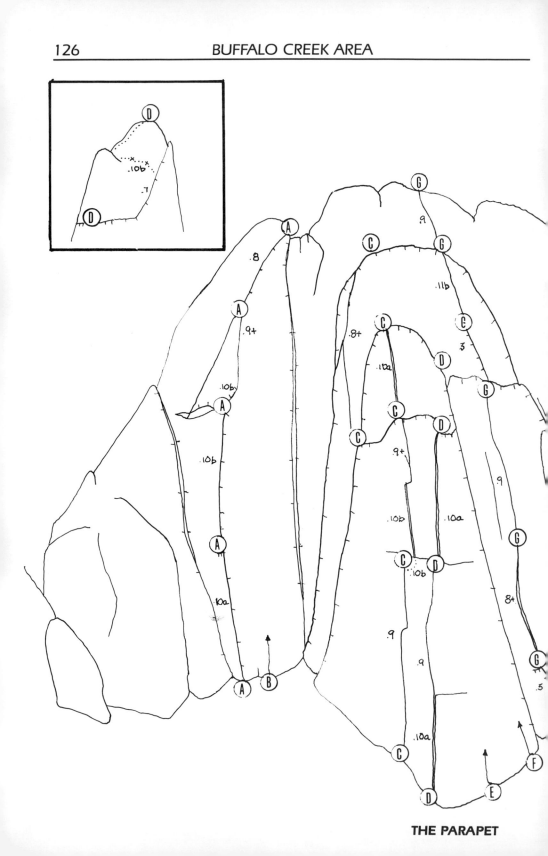

THE PARAPET

THE CASTLE
A Name unknown 5.10b
B Name unknown 5.11+
C Throne Room 5.10b ★★★ pro: to 5-6"; extra thin to hands
D Dungeon 5.10b ★★ pro: extra 3- 5"
E Schmauser/Bohannon Route 5.11c pro: extra thin to hands
F Dalke-Jennings Route 5.?
G Castle Directissima 5.11b/c

Many other routes exist on the Castle formation. Art and Earl Wiggins are known to have put up some of the earliest in 1972-74, the exact whereabouts of which are unknown. Greg Dewitt and partner also put up a mixed free and aid route about 1983, location also unknown.

FOREST

LITTLE SCRAGGY DOME

Access and Approach:

To reach Little Scraggy Dome, take State Highway 126 4.3 miles south of Buffalo to a (right) junction with Forest Service road #550. 2.2 miles west on #550 (if coming from the west, 2.9 miles from the junction of #543 and #550) a south-bearing road should be taken as far as possible, usually to a field just before crossing the second small stream. Follow the road another 250 yards and Little Scraggy Dome is on the left, five minutes from the road.

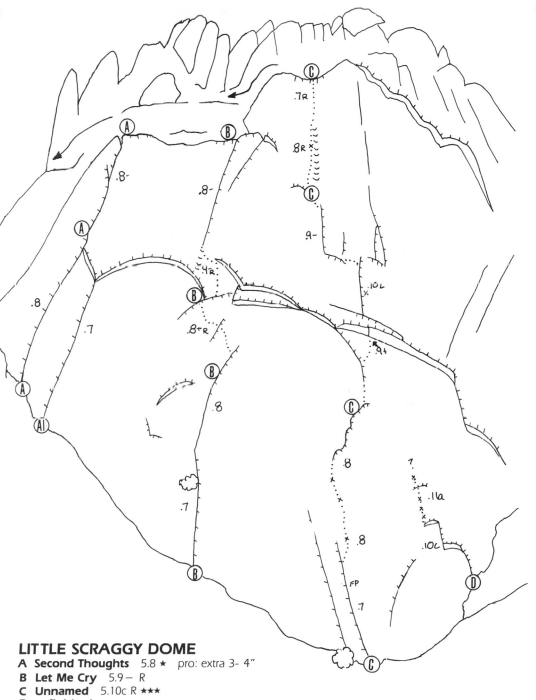

LITTLE SCRAGGY DOME
A Second Thoughts   5.8 ★   pro: extra 3- 4"
B Let Me Cry   5.9– R
C Unnamed   5.10c R ★★★
D unfinished

ALMOST ASSHOLE ROCK – Southwest Face

Access and Approach:

To reach Asshole and Almost Asshole Rocks, take State Highway 126 4.3 miles south of Buffalo to a (right) junction with Forest Service road #550. 0.3 miles west on #550 (if coming from the west, 4.8 miles from the junction of #543 and #550), take a south-trending road. Continue bearing right at the next two junctions, driving mostly southwest and uphill. Drive as far as you can and park. Asshole Rock is the largest rock in the area and faces almost due north. drop down in to the valley below Asshole for the climbs on the north and northeast faces. This is about a 25 minute hike. For the climbs on the south face, bear left of the valley and stay left of Asshole Rock to the saddle, then traverse. Almost Asshole Rock is to the northwest of Asshole Rock and is best approached via the valley that runs under Asshole Rock. Stay on the south-facing side and then traverse uphill. About 15 minutes from the car. (This rock can also be approached from where you park for Little Scraggy Dome. Just head due east over a couple of ridges; about 15 minutes.)

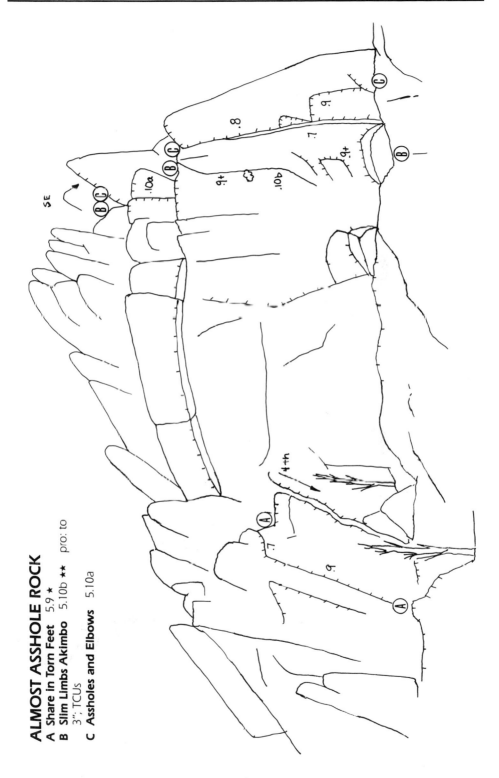

ALMOST ASSHOLE ROCK
A Share in Torn Feet   5.9 ★
B Slim Limbs Akimbo   5.10b ★★   pro: to 3", TCUs
C Assholes and Elbows   5.10a

ASSHOLE ROCK – Northeast Face

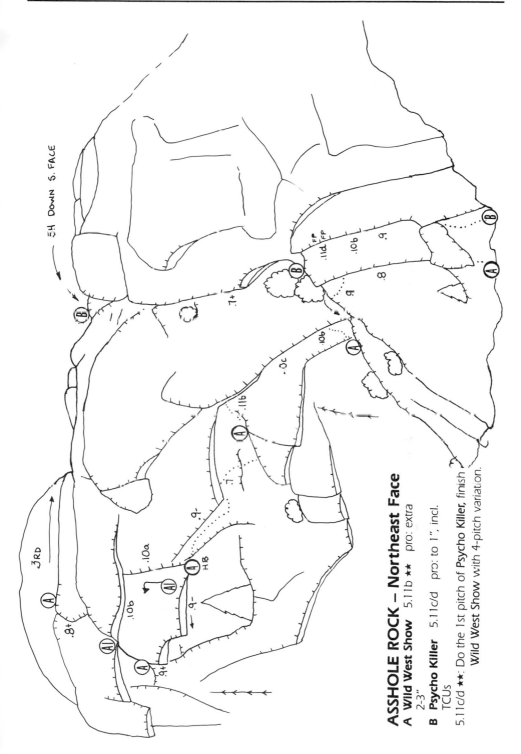

ASSHOLE ROCK – Northeast Face

A Wild West Show 5.11b ★★ pro: extra 2-3"

B Psycho Killer 5.11c/d pro: to 1", incl. TCUs

5.11c/d ★★: Do the 1st pitch of Psycho Killer, finish Wild West Show with 4-pitch variation.

ASSHOLE ROCK – South Face
A Mister Sol   5.10c ★★   pro: to 3"; key-
hole hangers
B Parallax   5.11c ★   pro: to 5", incl.
TCUs
C Anything Goes   5.11b/c ★   pro: to 3"
D Cardiac Crack   5.9+ ★★★   pro: to 4";
extra 3-4"
E Southern Exposure   5.6 A3 ★★   pro:
to 3", incl. pins
F Laughing Stock   5.10d   pro: to 5",
incl. extra 5"
G Worst Error   5.11a   pro: to 6", incl. ex-
tra 5"
H Inflatulation   5.8+   pro: to 6"

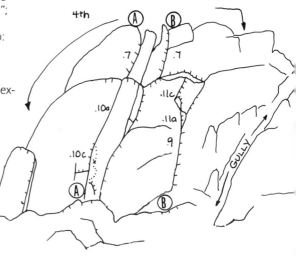

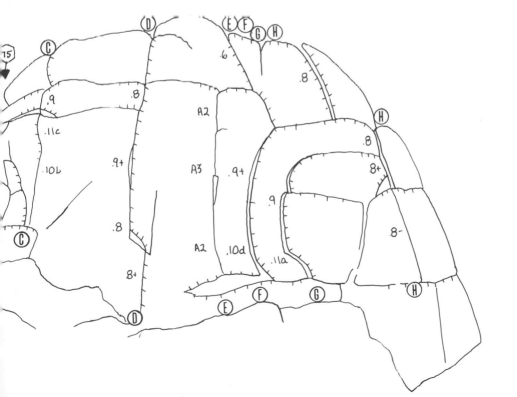

BIG BUTT – Southeast Face

DA BUTTS ROCKS

Approach:

    To reach Big Butt and Little Butt, approach as for Asshole Rock, but at the second fork bear left. (It should be said that one can see the rocks throughout the drive in, but that it is easy to get lost trying to find the closest road approach. Pay attention to where you leave the car!) Ideally, park well off the road at the top of a small ridge located in a logging area. Big Butt is the formation visible on top of the ridge just south of the parking area, about 10 minutes away. Little Butt faces a little northeast, directly across the boulder-strewn valley from Big Butt and about 5 minutes away.

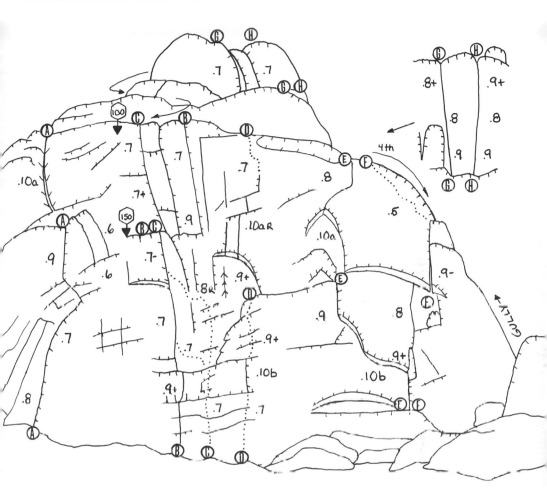

BIG BUTT
A Buttkicker 5.10a ★
B Roll Dem Bones 5.9+ ★★
C Ho De Do 5.7+ ★★★
D Dumb de Dumb Dumb 5.10b R   pro: TCUs
E Nazi's Demise 5.10b ★★   pro: extra 2-. 3"
F Smegma Burns 5.9+ ★
G Hymen Trouble 5.9
H Urine Trouble 5.9+

LITTLE BUTT – Northeast Face

A Showcase 5.11a ★★★ pro: to 5", extra 3-4"
B Cloudwalk 5.7+ A4 pro: pins, Crack n ups

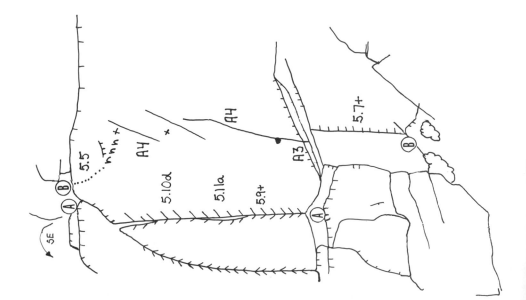

REFUGEE ROCK

To reach Refugee Rock drive 1.7 miles south of the junction of State Highway 126 and Forest Service road #550 to a west-running dirt road. Take this about 100 yards and park. Follow a trail by a stream, heading west until the undergrowth gets very thick. Cross the stream at this point and head south into an open valley. Refugee Rock sits at the southern end of this valley and high up on the side of the ridge, about 1 hour of uphill hiking.

There is much potential here for routes in the 5.9-5.12 range.

A Kneeknocker 5.9+ pro: to 3"; extra 2- 3"

SKINNER MOUNTAIN

NOTE: Routes E, F, and G are good routes for their grade,
although somewhat dirty; additional
traffic should clean them nicely.

A Attitude Adjustment   5.9+ R ★
B Easy Out   5.7 R
C Central Corner   5.10a ★★   pro: extra 1- 3"
D Wally World   5.5 ★★
E Route To Baga   5.9 ★
F Vegomatic   5.8
G Eastern Front   5.7 ★

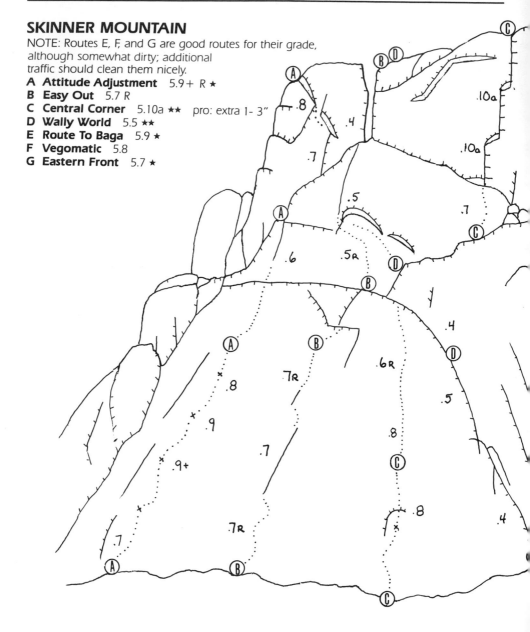

Access and Approach:

Skinner Mountain is located just above and to the west of Kelsey Campground, located 5.9
miles south of Buffalo on State Highway 126. Approach from the southeast; about 15 minutes.
The Grovel Pit is a little north of the campground and lower on the ridge. Approach to the
northwest, up the ridge that holds the western part of the campground; 15 minutes.

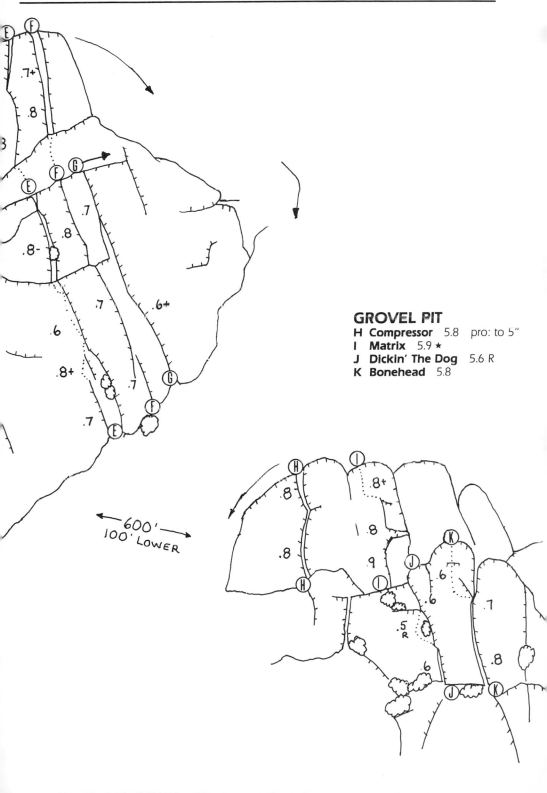

GROVEL PIT
H Compressor 5.8   pro: to 5"
I Matrix 5.9 ★
J Dickin' The Dog 5.6 R
K Bonehead 5.8

SKINNER MOUNTAIN

WIGWAM CREEK AREA

This area is perhaps the most alpine of any of the areas covered in this book. Most of the climbing takes place between 7000 and 9500 feet, so the weather can impact the climbing experience more so than in the lower areas. Little Wigwam is probably the least spectacular of any of the rocks here and is one of the least explored. There is potential for more routes here up to about 300 feet high in a very pretty valley. Wigwam Dome, The Sun, and The Moon offer crack and face climbs up to 600 feet high. The area is mostly known for the beautiful Tuolumne-type face climbing up steep water grooves. This beautiful little valley has been pretty trashed out by irresponsible car campers; let's clean it up.

About six miles of nice trail hiking beyond these rocks lead to Wigwam Tower and Keystone Buttress. These rocks, located at the northern edge of the Lost Creek Wilderness Area, provide climbs up to 500 feet high in a remote setting. The climbing here is crack climbing with the exception of the aid routes which are mostly bolt ladders.

Access and Approach:

From Deckers drive west on State Highway 126 2.0 miles to Road #211. There is a sign at this junction listing Cheesman Reservoir, Lost Valley Ranch, Mully Gulch, etcetera. After 1.5 miles there is a turnout on the right and a rock is visible due south. This is Little Wigwam Dome. Another ½ mile past the parking for Little Wigwam Dome is another junction. Turn right here at the Lost Valley Ranch sign and drive 1.1 miles to yet another junction. Turn right again, following the signs to the Wigwam Creek Trailhead, Wellington Lake and Flying G Ranch. One and a half miles past this turn the road forks at a Flying G Ranch/Wellington Lake sign. Bear right here (towards Wellington Lake) and after 4.1 miles turn left on road #545 at the Wigwam Creek Trailhead sign. At a point 0.8 miles past the turn the road forks; bear right and 0.4 miles farther is the parking. For climbs on Wigwam Dome, The Sun and The Moon, follow the trail west for about 2 miles (35-45 minutes) to an aspen grove and turn right to the rocks. For climbs on Wigwam Tower and Keystone Buttress, continue 6 miles past Wigwam Dome. To get to the climbs on Bear Tooth Spire and Rock Island hike due south from the parking, about 30 minutes, depending on approach.

LITTLE WIGWAM DOME

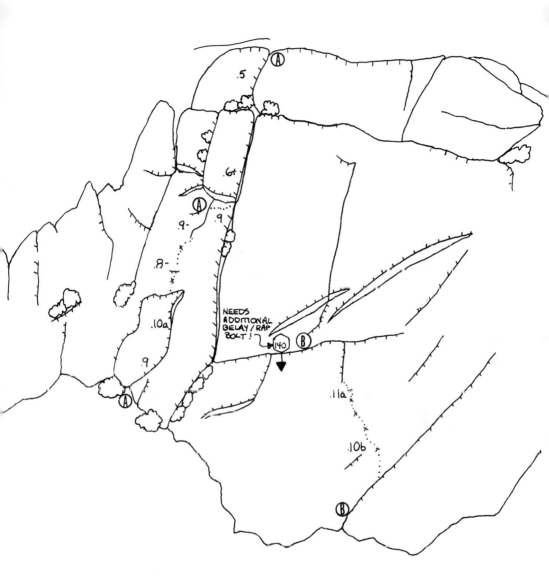

LITTLE WIGWAM DOME

A Sloe Moe 5.10a ★   pro: extra 2-3"
B Why Me? 5.11a ★   pro: to 3"

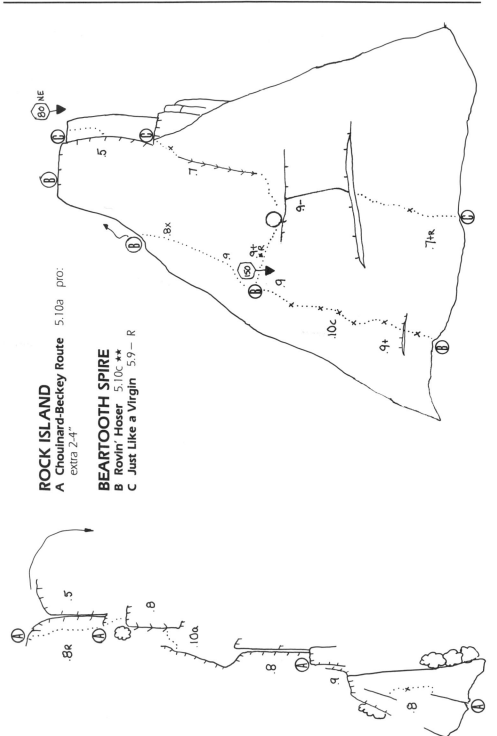

ROCK ISLAND

A Choulnard-Beckey Route 5.10a pro: extra 2-4"

BEARTOOTH SPIRE

B Rovin' Hoser 5.10c ★★
C Just Like a Virgin 5.9 – R

ROCK ISLAND – BEAR TOOTH SPIRE

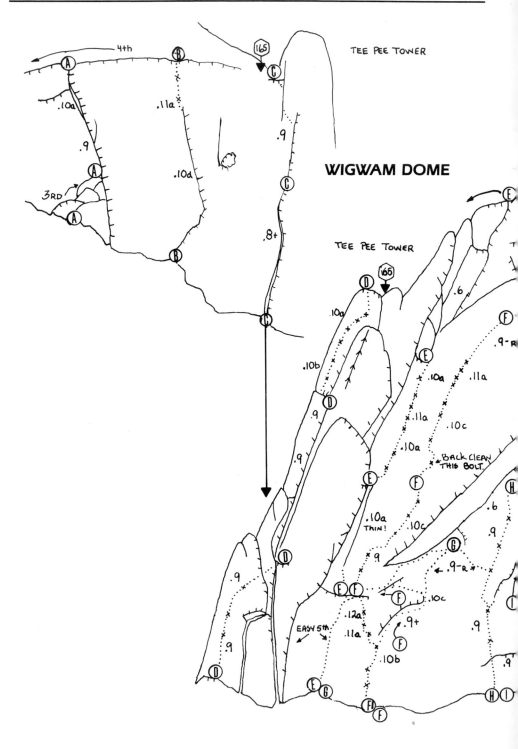

WIGWAM DOME

TEE PEE TOWER

TEE PEE TOWER

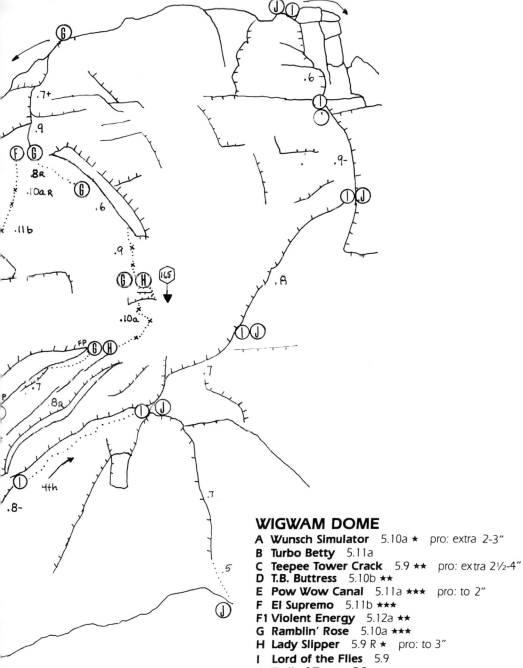

WIGWAM DOME

A Wunsch Simulator 5.10a ★ pro: extra 2-3"
B Turbo Betty 5.11a
C Teepee Tower Crack 5.9 ★★ pro: extra 2½-4"
D T.B. Buttress 5:10b ★★
E Pow Wow Canal 5.11a ★★★ pro: to 2"
F El Supremo 5.11b ★★★
F1 Violent Energy 5.12a ★★
G Ramblin' Rose 5.10a ★★★
H Lady Slipper 5.9 R ★ pro: to 3"
I Lord of the Flies 5.9
J Trail of Tears 5.9

WIGWAM DOME – South Face

THE MOON – THE SUN

THE MOON

A One Small Step   5.9+ R   pro: to 3"
B Luna-C   5.10b R ★   pro: to 3"
C Lunar Kreep   5.7
D Dark Side of the Moon   5.9+ R   pro: to 3"

THE SUN

E Halogen Angels   5.10b R ★★★   pro: to 3"
F Machination   5.10a R   pro: to 3"
G Better Lock Next Time   5.10b ★★★   pro: extra 2-3½"
H Sketch Book   5.12a A0 ★   pro: extra ¾-1½"

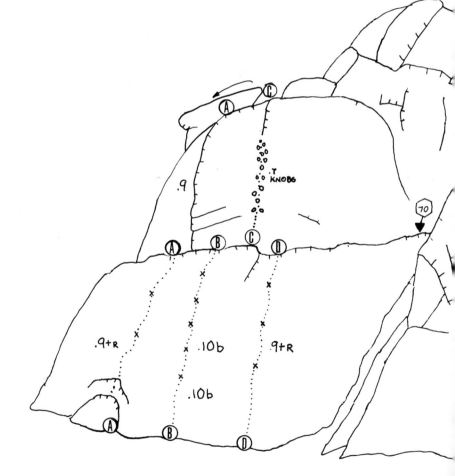

THE MOON

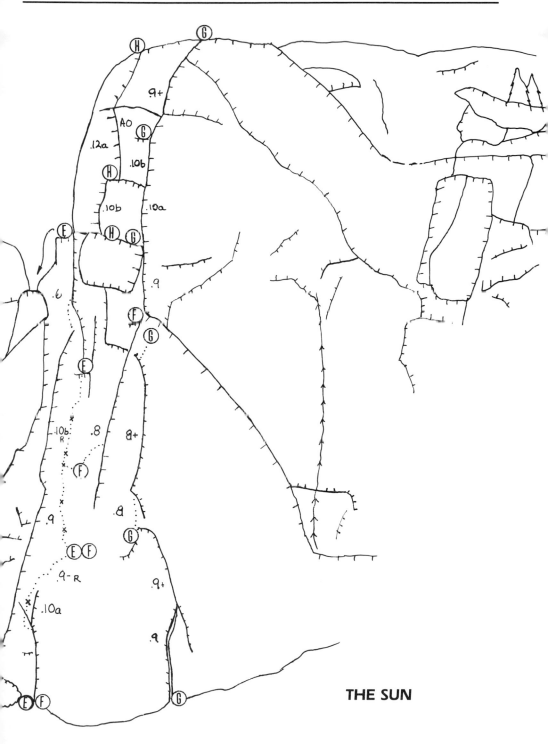

THE SUN

WIGWAM TOWER　　　　Doug Werme

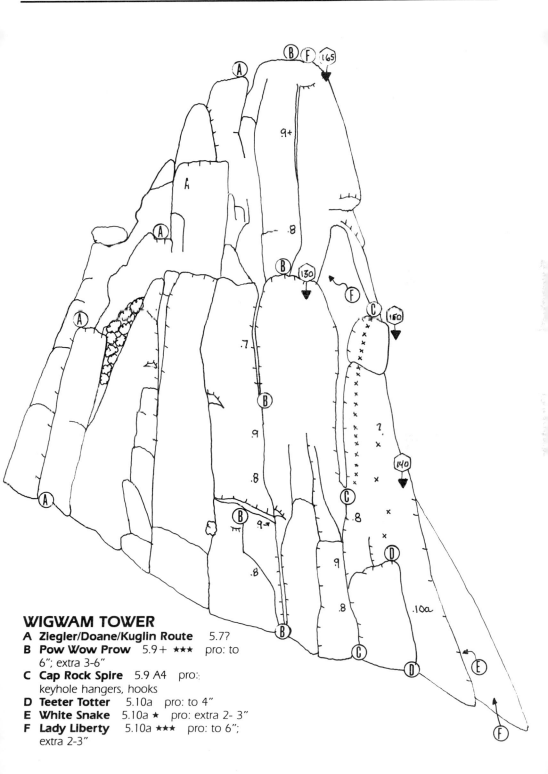

WIGWAM TOWER
A Ziegler/Doane/Kuglin Route   5.7?
B Pow Wow Prow   5.9+ ★★★   pro: to
6"; extra 3-6"
C Cap Rock Spire   5.9 A4   pro:
keyhole hangers, hooks
D Teeter Totter   5.10a   pro: to 4"
E White Snake   5.10a ★   pro: extra 2- 3"
F Lady Liberty   5.10a ★★★   pro: to 6";
extra 2-3"

Doug Werme

WIGWAM TOWER – KEYSTONE BUTTRESS

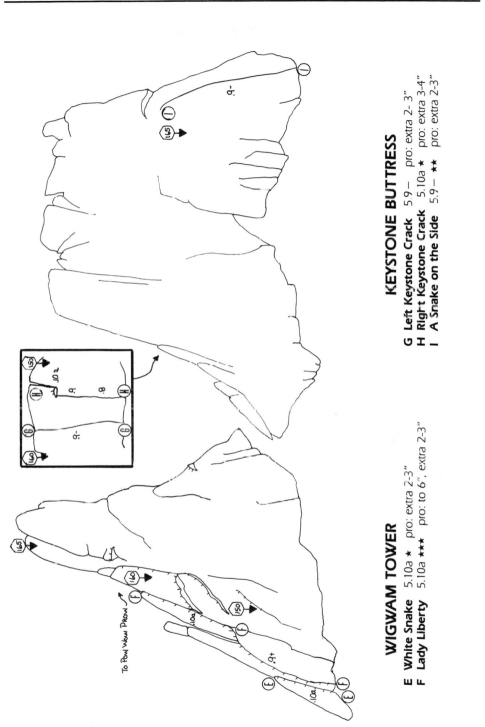

KEYSTONE BUTTRESS

G Left Keystone Crack 5.9 –   pro: extra 2- 3"
H Right Keystone Crack 5.10a ★   pro: extra 3-4"
I A Snake on the Side 5.9 – ★★   pro: extra 2-3"

WIGWAM TOWER

E White Snake 5.10a ★   pro: extra 2-3"
F Lady Liberty 5.10a ★★★   pro: to 6", extra 2-3"

BIG ROCK AREA

These scattered rocks are located in a broad area to the west of Cheesman Reservoir and at the northern edge of the Lost Creek Wilderness Area. With a couple of notable exceptions, these rocks usually provide face climbing up to 500 feet high. The area also boasts probably the largest rock in the Platte Area, Big Rock Candy Mountain, 1,300 feet high and harboring some of the longest face climbs in the state.

Helen's Dome is actually a massif comprised of three separate rocks: Helen's Dome, Acid Rock, and Sheep Rock. These rocks are known for face climbing on steep, knobby granite. The climbs on Acid Rock tend to be both crack and face climbs. Most of the climbs are about 300 feet long. Helen's Dome is about 600 feet high, but most parties generally do the first two pitches and then rap off rather than do 300 feet of 5.5. Rainy Day Rock is located about a five minute approach east from Goose Creek Campground. and has both crack and face climbs from 5.7 to hard 5.11. It is about 300 feet high.

Sunshine Dome is the largest formation in this area, next to Big Rock, at about 900 feet high, and the climbing consists of mixed crack and face climbing. The Couch Potatoes have mostly one to two pitch slightly runout face climbs and the Flagship offers crack climbs up to 450 feet high. Across the valley and about a half mile south of Sunshine Dome is Big Rock Candy Mountain. The next valley south of Big Rock contains Longwater Dome, about 400 feet high and host to only one route.

Big Rock Candy Mountain has no easy route to the summit. The long, often wet central gully between the west and east buttresses is said to be easy 5th class, though it is clearly long and unaesthetic. The routes that have been done on the west side involve all face climbing that varies in steepness from slab to vertical. The coarse granite provides plenty of edges and pinch holds, making for sequential face climbing. The job of the first ascent party is especially arduous since bolts must protect the entire length of the route. Possibilities for shorter routes (2-3 pitches) can be found on the south face in the form of overhanging cracks.

Access and Approach:

From the town of Deckers, drive west 2.8 miles on State Highway 126 to a junction with #211. There is a sign at this junction listing Cheesman Reservoir, Lost Valley Ranch, and Molly Gulch. Follow this for 2 miles to another junction. Continue straight here, following signs to Goose Creek, JVL Lost Valley Ranch, and the Goose Creek Trailhead. 5.1 miles past this sign is Molly Gulch Campground. Helen's Dome and surrounding rocks are located east, just across the stream from the campground. The approach takes about 20 minutes to the base of Helen's Dome.

Continue past Molly Gulch Campground another 0.3 mile to another junction. Again, follow the sign to Goose Creek Campground, found 3.1 miles after this right turn. Park here for Rainy Day Rock. The rock is about 15 minutes' walk to the east of the campground.

To get to Sunshine Dome and the rocks in that area, continue past Goose Creek Campground another 2.8 miles to a road on the left that passes through a fence. Go left here, drive 0.7 miles to a fork, go left again, and in an additional 0.6 miles there is a right turn that goes uphill. Take this 0.3 miles to the top of the ridge. To approach all of the climbs except for the climbs on the Couch Potatoes take a faint trail north off the eastern end of the ridge. At the first valley go part way up the next ridge and traverse the ridge to the east and north to the rocks. This approach puts you at the base of Renaissance Slab.

To get to Sunshine Dome, it is best to make a circuitous boulder-hopping and bushwacking approach from far to the left, near **The Infidel**. The way is not obvious, and defies exact description. Nevertheless, at best, it takes 45 minutes to an hour. Some people have found that it is more straight-forward — though not necessarily faster — to do one of the routes on Renaissance Slab. For climbs on the Flagship, traverse uphill and left below the slab. To get to the climbs on the Couch Potatoes, walk back west from the parking area, drop down off the ridge to the north on a horse trail and follow it around to the rocks, first bearing north, then east. Both of these approaches take about 35 to 45 minutes. Allow 1½ hours for the approach to Sunshine Dome no matter if you climb the slab or hike.

Big Rock Candy Mountain is approached from the west by following the directions to the Sunshine Dome Area; this entails crossing the South Platte River, a dangerous undertaking during spring runoff. (An approach to Big Rock is possible from the east, beyond the road to Turkey Rocks, though it is reportedly rough and circuitous.) Instead of going left at the turn to Sunshine Dome, continue past this road an additional 0.9 miles. (From Colorado Springs, this point is reached by taking Highway 24 one mile west of Lake George. Turn north on the Tarryall Road and follow this for 6.4 miles. A right turn here, on road #211 leads 8.5 miles to the two-track road described below) Take a left turn onto this two-track road. The road branches after about 2 miles or so, but stay straight and drive to the top of a ridge, bald from a previous forest fire. From this point, hike due east downhill to the river, cross over (about knee to mid-thigh deep during late summer and fall) and hike due north to the base of the rock. This approach takes about an hour and involves hiking back down after the climb and then back up to your car. To get to the dome on the west side of the river (across the river from Big Rock), just hike north from the river. This Dome is called Tick Dome and has a few climbs on it. It looks better from Big Rock than it does up close.

SHEEP ROCK

ACID ROCK

BABY HELEN

HELEN'S DOME

L

D   E F   K

B

HELEN'S DOME AREA

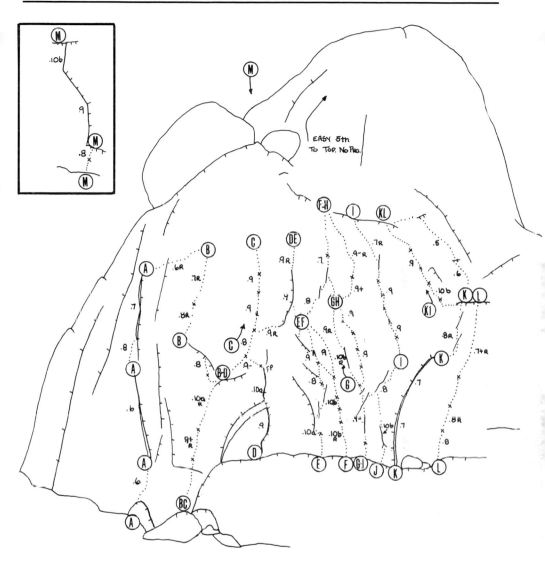

HELEN'S DOME – Southwest Face

A Moss Toss 5.8 R

B On the Bus 5.10a R   pro: misc to 3"

C Electric Koolaid Acid Test   5.10a R
★★ pro: runners

D Borderline Boulevard 5.10b ★★ pro:
to 3"

E Buffalo Tears 5.10a ★★★ pro: to 3"

F Buffalo Soldier 5.10b R ★ pro: to 3"

G Beam Me Up Scotty 5.10a R
★★★ pro: RPs to 3"

H Pebble Beach 5.10a X This weaves
an indistinct and unprotected line to belay H.

I Fools Gold 5.9+ ★★ pro: to 3"

J 5.10 5.10 (tr)

K Face Value 5.9

K1 Face Value Direct 5.10b ★★

L Spree 5.8 R pro: runners

M Hokahey 5.10b ★

Descents Rappel any of the center routes. Two double- rope rappels or 5.5 to the top and a
walk off south.

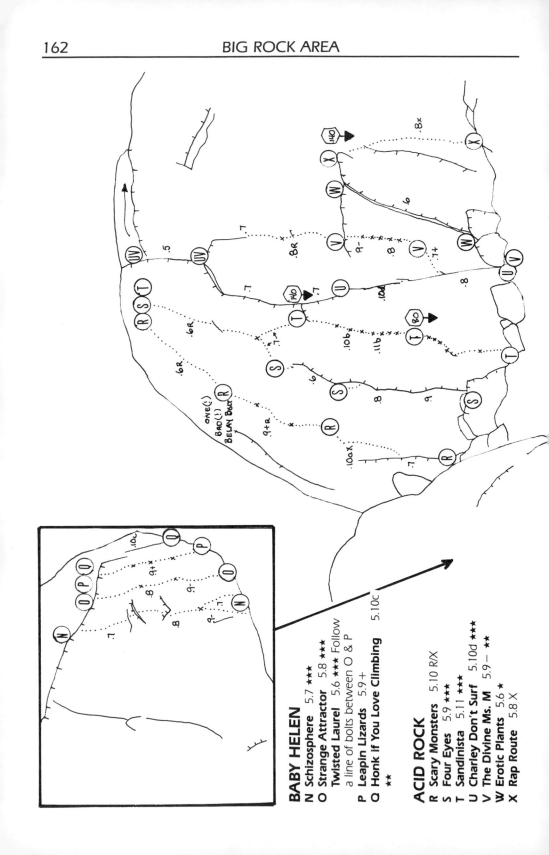

BABY HELEN

N **Schizosphere**   5.7 ★★★
O **Strange Attractor**   5.8 ★★★
   Twisted Laurel   5.6 ★★★ Follow
   a line of bolts between O & P
P **Leapin Lizards**   5.9+
Q **Honk If You Love Climbing**   5.10c
  ★★

ACID ROCK

R **Scary Monsters**   5.10 R/X
S **Four Eyes**   5.9 ★★★
T **Sandinista**   5.11 ★★★
U **Charley Don't Surf**   5.10d ★★★
V **The Divine Ms. M**   5.9 – ★★
W **Erotic Plants**   5.6 ★
X **Rap Route**   5.8 X

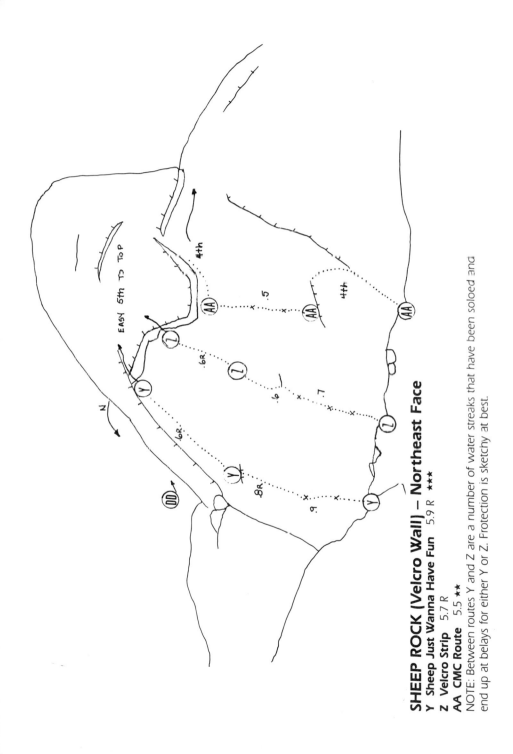

SHEEP ROCK (Velcro Wall) – Northeast Face
Y Sheep Just Wanna Have Fun 5.9 R ★★★
Z Velcro Strip 5.7 R
AA CMC Route 5.5 ★★
NOTE: Between routes Y and Z are a number of water streaks that have been soloed and end up at belays for either Y or Z. Protection is sketchy at best.

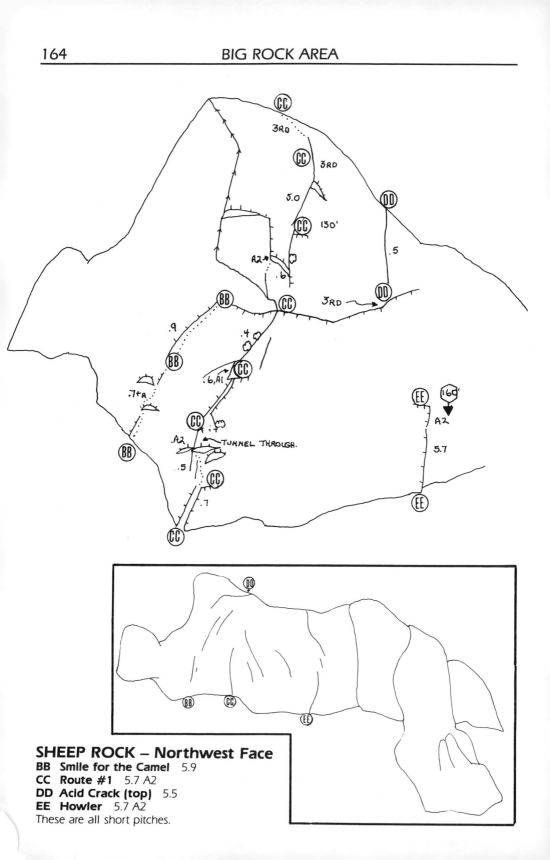

SHEEP ROCK – Northwest Face
BB   Smile for the Camel   5.9
CC   Route #1   5.7 A2
DD   Acid Crack (top)   5.5
EE   Howler   5.7 A2
These are all short pitches.

Ken Trout and Marvin Porter, Thunder Thigh, Couch Potatoes Karen Trout

RAINY DAY ROCK

A **Crackola** 5.6+

A1 **Crackola Direct** 5.8–

B **Natural Disaster** 5.11 – X   pro: 5 Tri-cams, RPs to 3"

C **Toad Strangler** 5.10a ★★   pro: to 3"

D **Buffalo Bullion** 5.10b/c ★★   pro: to 2½"

E **7-Up** 5.7+ ★   pro: to 3"

E1 **8-Up** 5.8+

F **Never Had It Never Will** 5.9+
  ★   pro: to 2"

G **Shinola** 5.9 R or 5.10b R   pro: to 3"

H **Shits And Grins** 5.11b   pro: to 3"

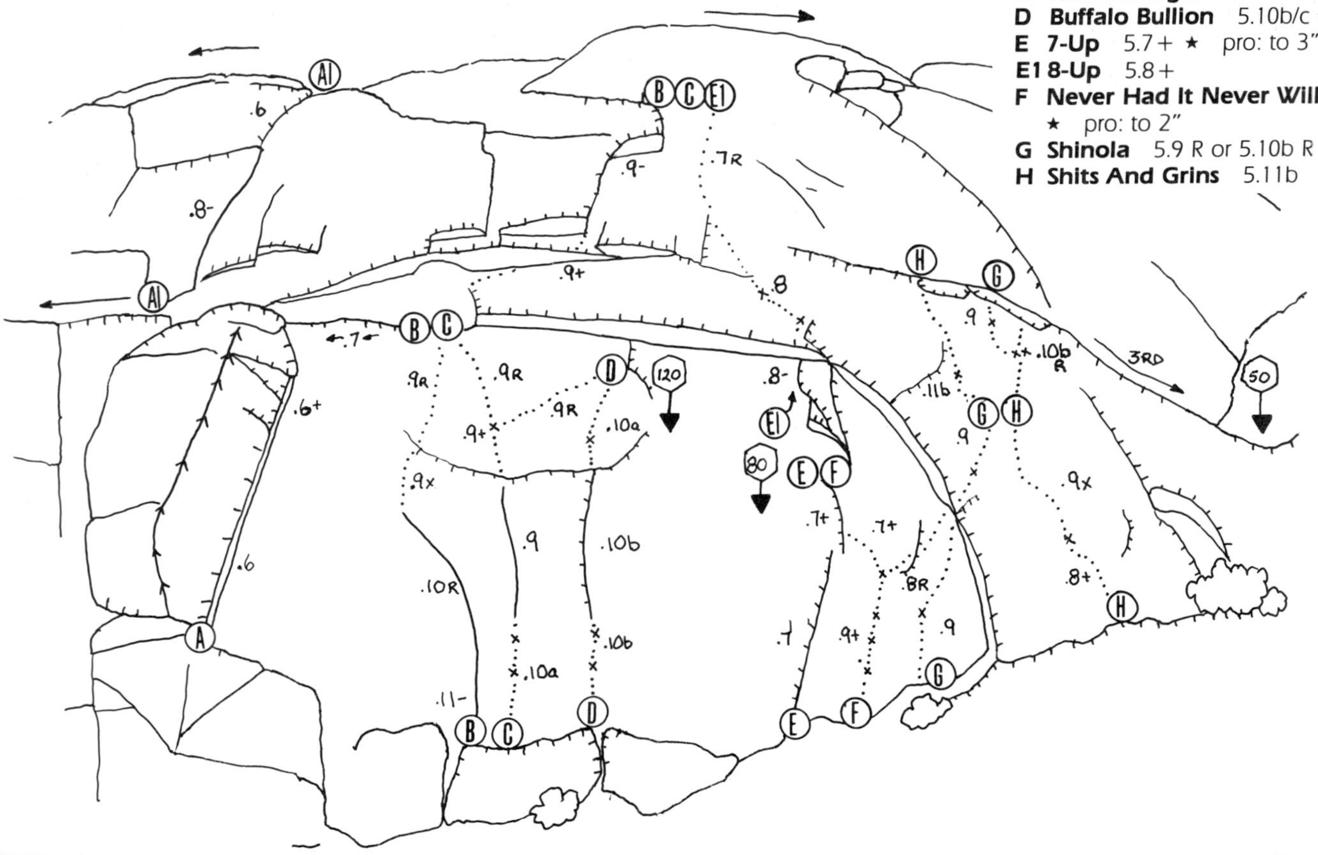

RAINY DAY ROCK – South Face

THE COUCH POTATOES
A Potato Peel 5.10b X 190' pitch
B Top rope 5.10
C Crash Diet 5.9 X
D Power Loungers 5.10a R
E Thunder Thigh 5.9+ R ★★
F Sweat Therapy 5.9+ ★★★
G Potato Pancakes 5.9
G1No Mistake or Pancake 5.9 R   pro: to 1½"
H Gong with the Wind 5.8+

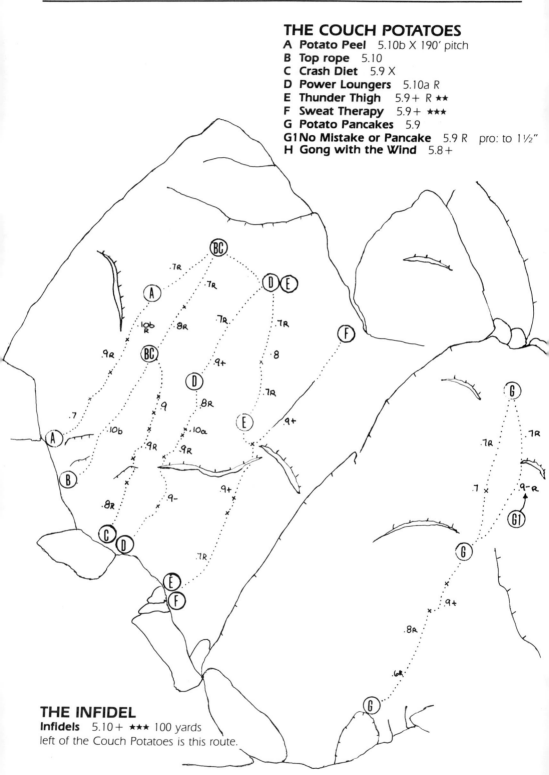

THE INFIDEL
Infidels 5.10+ ★★★ 100 yards
left of the Couch Potatoes is this route.

THE FLAGSHIP
I Bong for Glory   5.9 –   pro: to 6"; extra 4"
J Sorcerer's Apprentice   5.10c ★★★   pro: extra 2-3½"

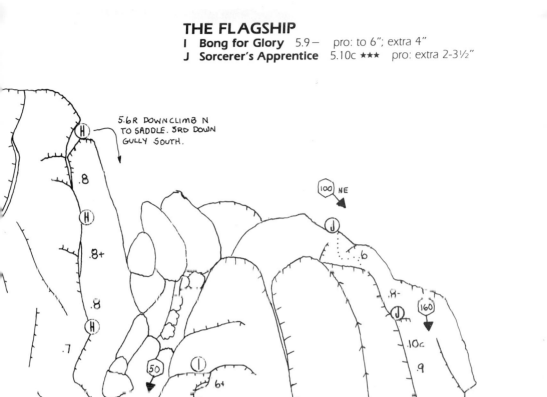

COUCH POTATOES – FLAGSHIP – RENAISSANCE SLAB – SUNSHINE DOME

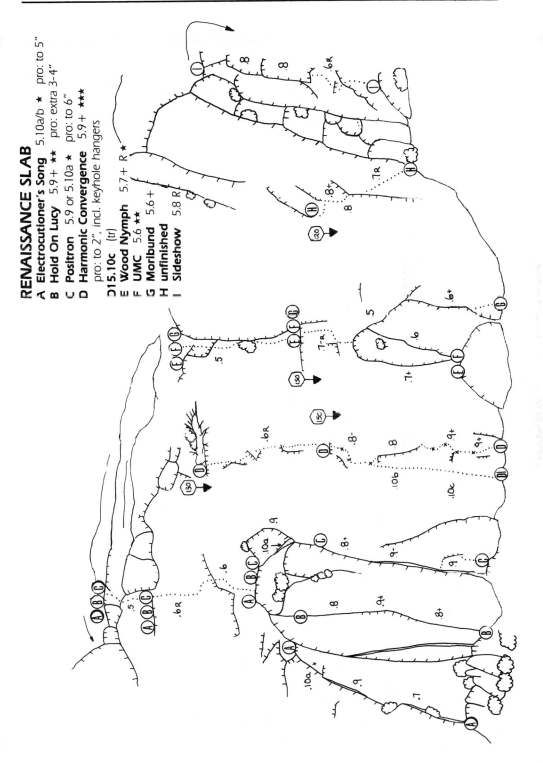

RENAISSANCE SLAB

A **Electrocutioner's Song** 5.10a/b ★ pro: to 5"
B **Hold On Lucy** 5.9+ ★★ pro: extra 3-4"
C **Positron** 5.9 or 5.10a ★ pro: to 6"
D **Harmonic Convergence** 5.9+ ★★★
   pro: to 2", incl. keyhole hangers
D15.10c (tr)
E **Wood Nymph** 5.7+ R ★
F **UMC** 5.6 ★★
G **Moribund** 5.6+
H **unfinished**
I **Sideshow** 5.8 R

Ken Trout and Robby Baker, Shining Path, Sunshine Dome *Kirk Miller*

SUNSHINE DOME

SUNSHINE DOME
A French Curve   5.10b ★★   pro: extra 2-3½"
B Heart of Darkness   5.12b ★★★   pro: many RPs, small
Friends, Stoppers, #3½" & 4 Friends
C Shining Path   5.11a ★★★   pro: to 4"
D Tree Route   5.11b ★★   pro: extra 2- 3"
E Sunshine Route   5.9 − R ★
E1 Variation   5.10a
F Narrow Escape   5.10a ★★★   pro: many extra 2-4"
G Sunrise Ridge   5.7 + R ★   pro: to 5"
H Easy Sun   5.7 + R   pro: to 5"

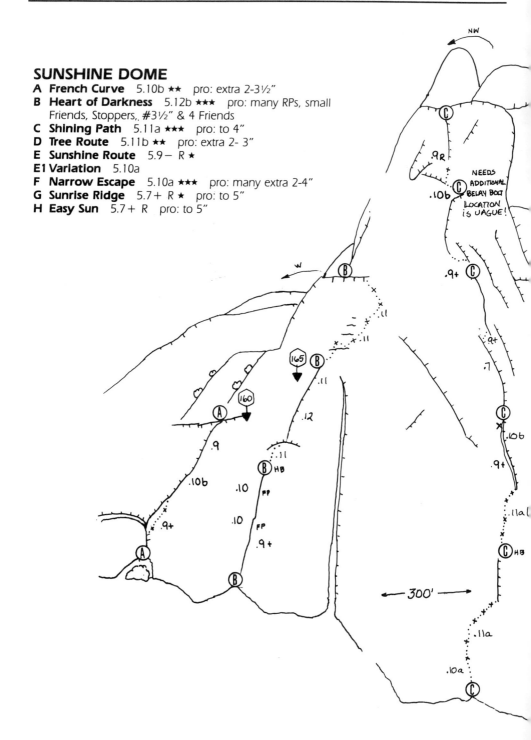

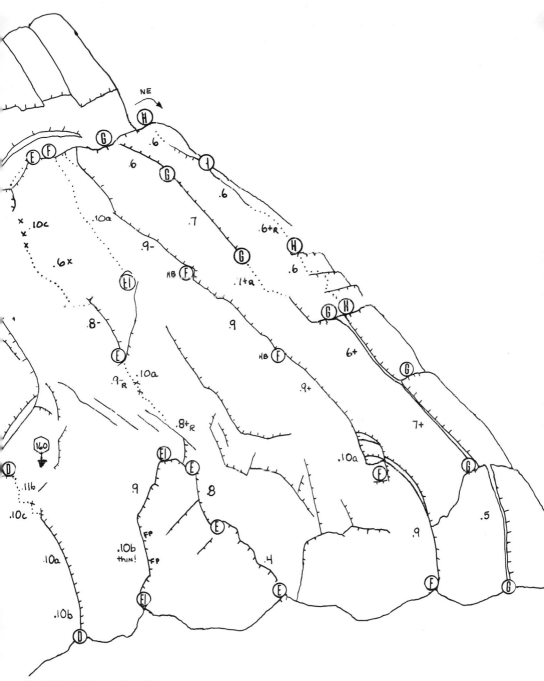

SUNSHINE DOME

LONGWATER DOME

A Barracuda   5.11+ R ★★
There is a 4WD approach to within a 30 minute-walk of
the Dome by way of the Turkey Rock area. There is also
another 5.11 route on the dome, whereabouts unknown.

TICK DOME

This is the interesting-looking dome across from Big Rock.
Upon closer examination, however, the rock has borne
only poor quality routes. The two central crack systems
have been climbed, both 5.9, as well as at least one
route down on the smaller buttress to the east.

BIG ROCK CANDY MOUNTAIN – Southwest Faces

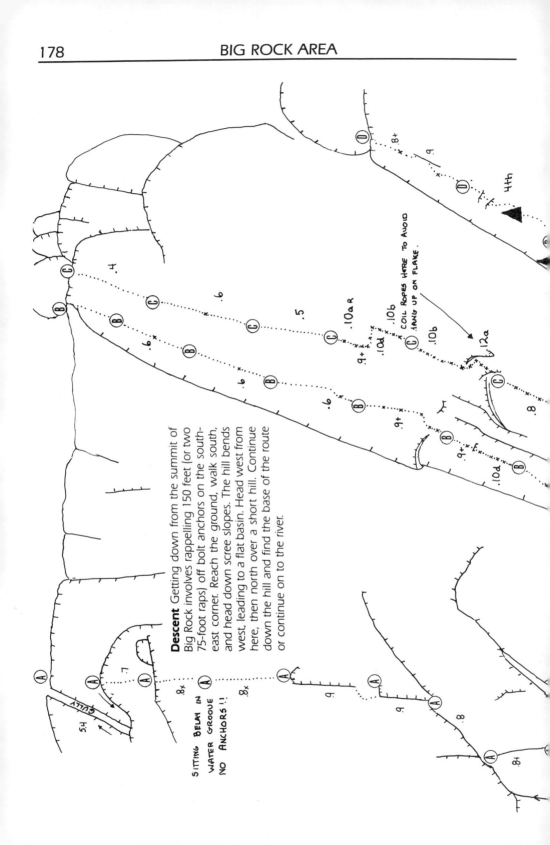

Descent Getting down from the summit of Big Rock involves rappelling 150 feet (or two 75-foot raps) off bolt anchors on the south-east corner. Reach the ground, walk south, and head down scree slopes. The hill bends west, leading to a flat basin. Head west from here, then north over a short hill. Continue down the hill and find the base of the route or continue on to the river.

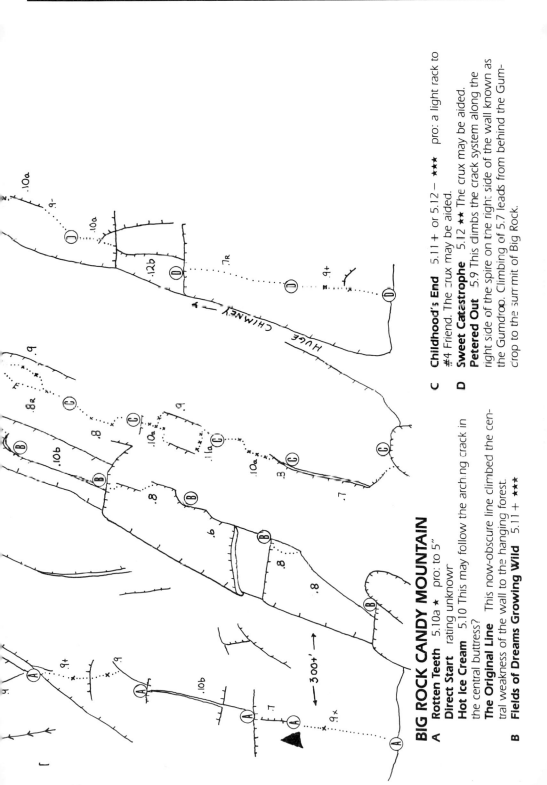

BIG ROCK CANDY MOUNTAIN

A Rotten Teeth 5.10a ★ pro: to 5"
Direct Start rating unknown
Hot Ice Cream 5.10 This may follow the arching crack in the central buttress?
The Original Line This now-obscure line climbed the central weakness of the wall to the hanging forest.

B Fields of Dreams Growing Wild 5.11+ ★★★

C Childhood's End 5.11+ or 5.12− ★★★ pro: a light rack to #4 Friend. The crux may be aided.

D Sweet Catastrophe 5.12 ★★ The crux may be aided.
Petered Out 5.9 This climbs the crack system along the right side of the spire on the right side of the wall known as the Gumdrop. Climbing of 5.7 leads from behind the Gumdrop to the summit of Big Rock.

TURKEY ROCK AREA

Located about 40 miles northwest of Colorado Springs (near Westcreek, Colorado) is some of the best climbing on the entire Front Range: The Turkey Rock Area. The rock is much like the pink feldspar granite of Veedawou, Wyoming, but without the jagged, flesh-ripping crystals. Most of the climbs are on south faces, giving a fun-in-the-sun atmosphere to this secluded crag spot.

The unique geometric symmetry of the south face of Turkey Tail is rivaled by few crags. Vertical cracks cut through ceilings, while the profile is outlined by sharp aretes. The crag has some of the best crack climbing in the state. The latest craze on the crag has been ascending the aretes (with bolt protection).

The area is filled with aesthetic cracks ranging in difficulty from 5.7 to 5.12. The cracks eat nuts and Friends, giving a safe feeling to most climbs. Variety is found in the area, from pure crack climbs to steep, edge-covered faces. The two techniques are often combined on many thin crack routes. The quality of the course-grained rock is near-perfect. Tape is advised for several crack climbs, depending on one's technique and pain threshold.

The crack lines are nearly climbed out and the future development is to be found on the faces. 5.9 and 5.10 faces are common, and usually involve runouts off natural protection. Drilling on lead has taken place, but requires much aid on 5.11 + or harder. **Brush Turkey** (5.12a) and **Future Chic** (5.13) were established with aid to drill bolts, while **Infraction** (5.12b) and **I Turkey** (5.11d) were brilliant products of the European style (bolting on rappel after top-rope rehearsal). This style of climbing has not been accepted in the area and has been stifled by the subsequent chopping of these two routes.

Perhaps the reason for so much objection to rappel-bolting (and just bolting) is in reaction to what was once a nearly bolt-free area. Cracks were the focus since development started in the early 70s. A few aid lines went up (some in the late 60s) and involved A1 nail-ups that were slow and repetitious. The use of nuts and jamming techniques saw the birth of free climbing here. Steve Cheyney and Kurt Rasmussen were the first to pioneer several of the classic 5.8 to 5.10− routes. Rasmussen is remembered for his boldness of **Reinhold Messner's Delight** (5.9 X) and the unrepeated **Little Feat** (5.10 X). Jim Dunn led the development of hard crack climbs on Turkey Tail and The Rightovers, climbing such classics as **Whimsical Dreams** (5.11b), **Turkey Turd** (5.11c), **For Turkey's Only** (5.12a offwidth) and **Rufus** (5.11d).

Earl Wiggins climbed with Dunn and pioneered several of his own fine lines, such as **Vanishing Point** (5.10d) and **Finger Lickin' Good** (5.10d). He is most noted for his free-soloing achievements like the first free-solo of **Whimsical Dreams** (5.11b), climbed at the peak of his soloing career.

Most of the routes that Dunn, Wiggens, Cheyney and others climbed were protected with Chouinard stoppers and Hexentrics. Fixed pegs and bolts were not generally placed to make a first ascent.

The year 1978 saw a major change in first ascent tactics with the free climb of **Journey to Ixtlan** (5.12a), an old aid line that required pitons. Leonard Coyne, Peter Mayfield, and Henry Lestor pre-protected with aid to place two bolts and a peg, allowing desperate finger-tip underclings and laybacks around two overhangs. The entire route involves a pitch of 5.12a, one of 5.10d, and then finishes with the crux pitch of **Rufus** (5.11d), making the most sustained route in the area today.

That same year, Coyne attempted to free climb the prominent overhanging dihedral on The Rightovers. Dunn had climbed the route using aid at the top. One bolt was placed, but a nut above protected the actual crux. In 1980, Mark Rolofson and Eric Geurrein made the first free ascent of the line, dubbed **Back to the Zodiac** (5.11d). (The ¼" bolt placed by Coyne was deemed unnecessary, and, in fact, was pulled in a fall by Mark Milligan in 1987, resulting in a 45-foot fall, underscoring the need to place ⅜" bolts when a bolt is needed.)

Visiting Brit John Allen established two 5.12 classics in 1981 that are some of the most strenuous routes even today. **Shear Shark Attack** (5.12b) and **Beauty and the Beast** (5.12c) had both been previously attempted. Allen succeeded on **Beauty and the Beast** after taking 10-20 falls in an afternoon.

Natural lines continued to be plucked, one of the most notable being Andy Parkin's **Dogs of Furniture** (5.12a R), a route involving thin stemming protected by tiny RPs.

In 1983 Harrison Dekker made the first free ascent of a 50-foot aid pitch, calling the climb **Jello Party** (5.12c). The climb involved the most technical sequence of vertical face moves in the entire South Platte region for its day. Two pegs protected the crux moves and five days of attempts were required. After this, new route activity dropped off for a couple years.

Activity resumed again in 1986, with several notable ascents being made. Dale Goddard led the pursuit of pioneering the faces by establishing **The Infraction** (5.12b) with Will Gadd. This brilliant face climb was pre-protected by five bolts (placed on rappel) and the result was uproar from several old-time Colorado Springs locals. A petition to have the route chopped, left to be signed at a local mountain shop, was signed by only three people, and the route remained intact until the following fall. The spring of 1986 also saw the birth of the brilliant arete climb called **I Turkey** (5.11d), established by Mark Sonnefield, Bill Myers, and John Steiger using a rappel to place three bolts and a peg. Both routes were chopped in the fall of 1986 by an unknown local, who acted without the weight of common consensus but who nonetheless has stifled the creation of further routes put up with European tactics.

Also in 1986, Goddard made the first ascent of **History Lesson** (5.12c), which ascends a thin discontinuous crack to a bulging face, protected by a bolt placed from a hook placement. Jonny Woodward climbed the continuation of the thin crack on **Dogs of Furniture** to produce a pitch of at least 5.12b. This was one of the only extreme routes put up in 1986 without bolts.

The arete left of **Jello Party** was finally established as a lead climb to produce the exciting **Brush Turkey** (5.12a). This arete had been previously top-roped by Harrison Dekker in 1984. Harvey Miller placed three bolts with aid, and Bob Robertson made the first lead. Ironically, this route remains intact from the local route choppers ostensibly because it was placed from the ground up, even though the resulting route is much inferior to **The Infraction** because of the poor ¼" bolts, the unnatural (bathooking) aid ascent, and the fact that the first bolt was placed next to a perfect #5 RP placement.

In 1987 Charlie Fowler established the area's hardest climb, **Future Chic** (5.13) that ascends the overhanging arete left of **Journey to Ixtlan**. Where natural protection was lacking, aid was used to pre-protect the crux. (There is some doubt that aid was not used during the final ascent.)

Access and Approach:

From Colorado Springs, drive west on U.S. Highway 24 to Woodland Park and drive 14 miles north on State Highway 67 to the town of Westcreek. If coming from the north, from U.S. 285, about 32 miles of driving on State Highway 126 leads to Deckers. Nine miles south of Deckers is Westcreek. From Westcreek, State Road 68 branches south from Highway 67 and after 1.2 miles a right turn west leads along Highway 68 (by this time known as Stump Road) to an access road under Sheep's Nose. Parking is located 0.3 miles up this road. For Turkey Rocks continue past the access road for Sheep's Nose and after another mile (3.7 miles from Westcreek) a right turn is taken (on Road #360) to Big Turkey Campground, located just northeast of the crags. From here the rocks are a 15-minute hike away. It is best to approach from either the campground or slightly to the west (which is directly below the north faces). The road which leads to these parking spots is usually snowed over in winter and is muddy and icy in early spring. The months of April to November are best for these crags.

It is also possible to drive to the base of the short hill on which the south faces of these rocks sit. This is tempting, especially in winter, but is not advised because it involves crossing private property; the landowner is not sympathetic. Water is available at the campground, though it contains some rust.

SHEEP'S NOSE

Sheep's Nose, located a few miles before the Turkey Rock massif, is known for fine, delicate face climbs and thin cracks of generally a non-strenuous nature. The occasional bolt or pin supplements natural protection provided by wired nuts. The arms will get pumped on only a few climbs on Sheep's Nose. On a sunny day it can be thought of as a relaxing outing for those used to overhanging rock. Sheep's Nose is often popular on warm winter days, when the road to Turkey Rock is snowed over.

The east face has routes as long as five pitches. The most frequently climbed classic is **Lost in Space Direct** (5.9−), offering a combination of face and thin cracks. The **Ozone Direct** (5.10a) gives the route a better finish. Several harder starts are possible to add to the difficulty as well.

For the more adept climber, the **Golden Fleece** (5.10d) is recommended, particularly when combined with **Assassination Slabs** (5.11b) and/or **For Wimps Only** (5.11a).

Of the many worthwhile one or two-pitch routes, **Seamis** (5.11a), **Ten Years After** (5.9), **Psycho Babble** (5.12− R), and **Sheep's Dare** (5.10b) are most recommended.

SHEEP'S NOSE – Southeast Face

SHEEP'S NOSE

A Ten Years After 5.9 ★★★ pro: to 3". Lieback
B Ten Years After (var.) 5.9
C Seamis 5.11a ★★ pro: RPs, wires
D Time to Space 5.9 − ★ pro: wires
E Chinook 5.9+ ★ pro: wires
F Evening Stroll 5.7 ★ pro: to 2½"
G Hard Monkeys 5.8 pro: wires, some medium

HIDDEN

H Harpoon the Manta Ray 5.10d pro: RPs, wires, some Friends
I Psycho Babble 5.12a ★ pro: #½-1½ Friends, RPs
J Jah Sport 5.12a ★
K Sheep with a Silver Tail 5.10b
L Sheer Sheep Attack 5.11c ★ pro: some nuts and Friends useful
M 5.9 Dihedral 5.9
N An Apostle or Two 5.10d ★ pro: wires
O The Arch 5.9 A2
P Old Man Route 5.9
Q Leaning Corner 5.10b ★ pro: wires. Thin/stem
R The Pimp 5.11a fingers
S Space Cadet 5.11a roof
T For Wimps Only 5.11a ★ face
U Lost in Space Direct 5.9 − ★★★ pro: wires, #1-3 Friends

V Friction 5.9 ★ pro: mostly wires
W Sparse 5.9 X ★ pro: some nuts
X Virgin Wool 5.9 overhang
Y 100% Wool 5.9 overhang
Z Golden Fleece 5.10d ★★★ pro: wires, #1-3 Friends. Thin stemming corner
AA When Sheep are Nervous 5.9 ★
BB When Sheep are Safe 5.9 ★ pro: wires, medium Friends
CC Ozone Direct 5.10a ★★ pro: wires, medium nuts or Friends
DD Ozone (var.) 5.9+ ★
EE The Men from Wyoming 5.9
FF Assassination Slab 5.11b ★★ (combined with **Golden Fleece** ★★★) pro: RPs, Stoppers. Slab/face

SHEEP'S NOSE

GG Sheep and Wolves Clothing 5.9 R/ X   pro: wires, Friends?

HH Lamb's Prey 5.9 − ★   pro: wires, #1-3 Friends. Thin crack/face

II   Direct Line 5.9 + R ★

JJ   Sheep's Dare 5.10b ★★   pro: wires, #1- 3 Friends

KK Mr. Salty and the Crunch Crowd 5.10a ★   pro: mainly wires

LL   Complications 5.11a   pro: wires, some Friends. Face

MM Army Route 5.9 −

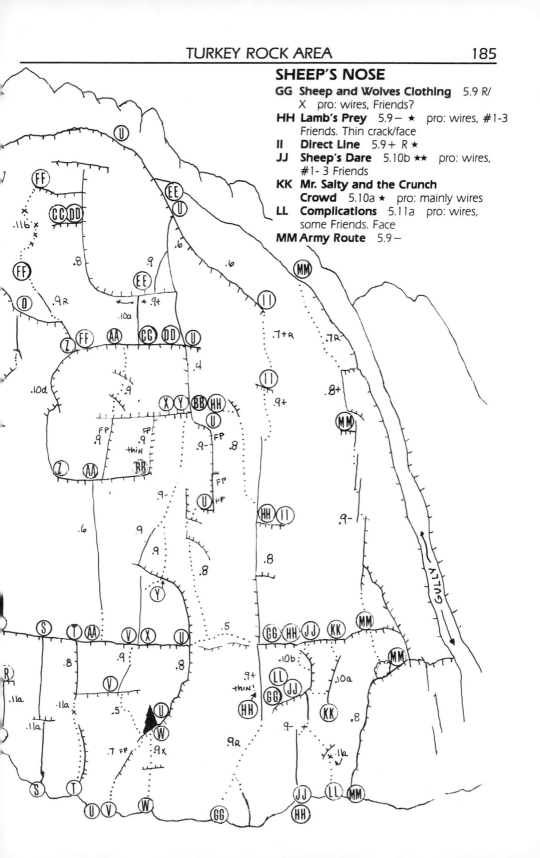

Gary Issacs, Whimsical Dreams, Turkey Tail Dan Hare

TURKEY ROCK – South Face

TURKEY ROCK – South Face

A Direct Hit 5.9 R ★★★   pro: RPs, wires, TCUs.
Vertical face

B Direct Hit (var.) 5.10b

C Southern Comfort 5.9 ★★★   pro: wires

D Beginners Route 5.7 ★   pro: medium to 3"

E Route 902 5.7+ ★   pro: medium to 3½"

F Northern Comfort 5.9 R ★★   pro: mostly
small wires

G Little Feat 5.10b X

H Dash and Triangle 5.7

I Messner's Delight 5.9 X ★★★   pro: to 3½".
Offwidth/face

J Gobbler's Grunt 5.9− ★★★   pro: small to
medium; one 3"

J1 Gobbler's Grunt (var.) 5.9 ★★ Hands

K Second Coming 5.8 ★★   pro: to 3½"

K1 Second Coming (original start) 5.8

L Roof Variation 5.11b/c ★

M Safety Buffalo 5.10a ★   pro: to 3½". Face

N Spring Turkey 5.11a ★★   pro: RPs to 3½".
Face

O The Pro 5.11 A2 (unfinished)

P Turkey Shoot 5.9− ★★★   pro: to 3½".
Hands

Q Turkey's Dare 5.9 ★   pro: to 3½". Offwidth

R Glen's Pancake 5.8

S Nightime Madness 5.7 ★★   pro: to 3½".
Hands/chimneys

S1 Nightime Madness (var.) 5.8

T Turkey's Forever 5.9 ★ Hands

U Chopping Block 5.7 ★★ pro: to 3½".
Hands/offwidth/chimney
V Pillar Variation 5.8+ Offwidth/chimney

W Jump Start 5.9
X Vanishing Point 5.10d ★★★ pro: wires,
some medium. Fingers
Y Stewart's Crack 5.8
Z Manimal One 5.10b R/X
AA Great White Crime 5.11a ★★★ pro:
wires, medium nuts. Thin crack and face
BB Satyr's Asshole 5.10a ★★★
pro: to 3½". Offwidth
CC Straw Turkey 5.10a ★★★
pro: to 2½", mainly
wires. Fingers/hands/face
DD Brain Cramps 5.9+
EE The Eastern Front 5.8−
FF The Fiend 5.9 ★
GG No Block Route 5.9 R/X
HH Hallucinogenic Blues 5.9
II Uncle John 5.8
**JJ Little Eddie Webster's
Little Overhang** 5.10d
KK Big Edward's Big Overhang 5.11a
LL Casual Elegance 5.9
This is a hard to find route on the upper
right side that starts as a hand crack
and goes to offwidth at the top.
MM Turkey Shit 5.9−
Undercling a flake on an overhanging
wall and go left in to an offwidth.
NN Mariposa 5.10b
This is a finger to hands crack
that overhangs and is a little awkward.
OO Face by the Fallen Tree 5.6
Just left of a north-pointing fallen
tree is an easy finger crack.

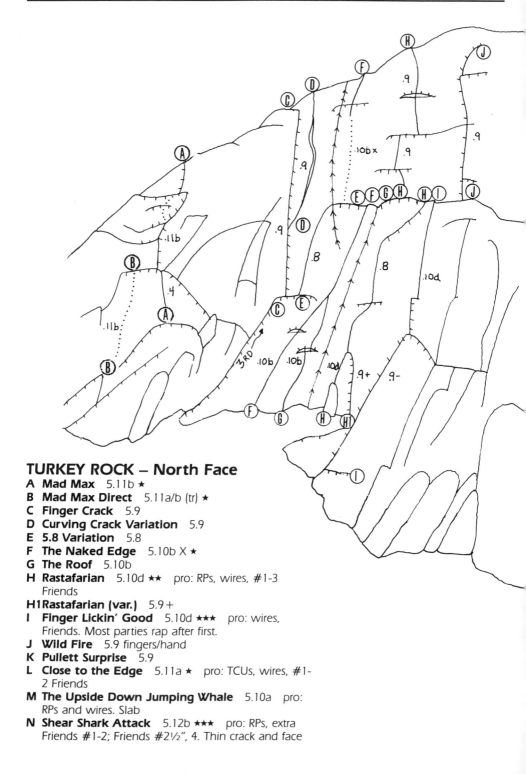

TURKEY ROCK – North Face

A Mad Max 5.11b ★
B Mad Max Direct 5.11a/b (tr) ★
C Finger Crack 5.9
D Curving Crack Variation 5.9
E 5.8 Variation 5.8
F The Naked Edge 5.10b X ★
G The Roof 5.10b
H Rastafarian 5.10d ★★ pro: RPs, wires, #1-3
   Friends
H1Rastafarian (var.) 5.9+
I Finger Lickin' Good 5.10d ★★★ pro: wires,
   Friends. Most parties rap after first.
J Wild Fire 5.9 fingers/hand
K Pullett Surprise 5.9
L Close to the Edge 5.11a ★ pro: TCUs, wires, #1-
   2 Friends
M The Upside Down Jumping Whale 5.10a pro:
   RPs and wires. Slab
N Shear Shark Attack 5.12b ★★★ pro: RPs, extra
   Friends #1-2; Friends #2½", 4. Thin crack and face

O Wellflare 5.11a ★ pro: TCUs, wires, #1-3 Friend
P The Go Between 5.11a pro: RPs, wires
Q Tofonarecker 5.8
R Dogs of Furniture 5.12a R ★★ pro: RPs, wires, #1-2 Friend (#3-4 useful at start). Stemming
R1 Dogs of Furniture (var.) 5.12b
S Slab Center 5.9+ ★
T History Lesson 5.12c ★ pro: RPs, wires
U Mobius Trip 5.8 R ★★
V Look Ma, No Hands 5.8
W The Unic Horn 5.8
X The Golden Crack 5.9

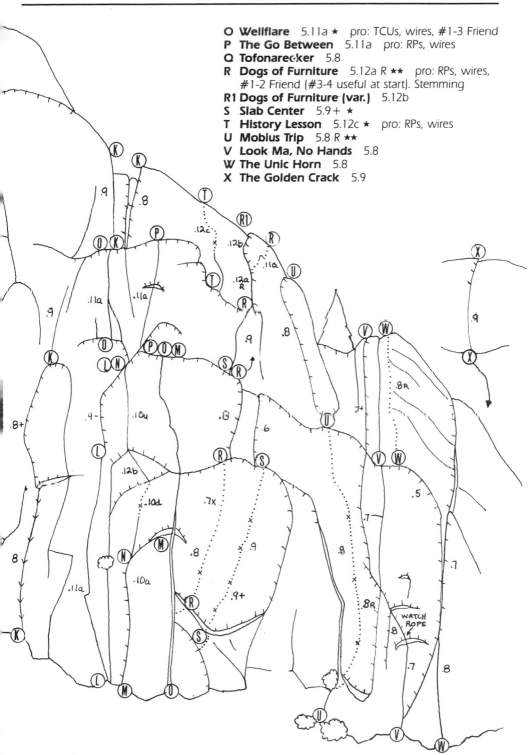

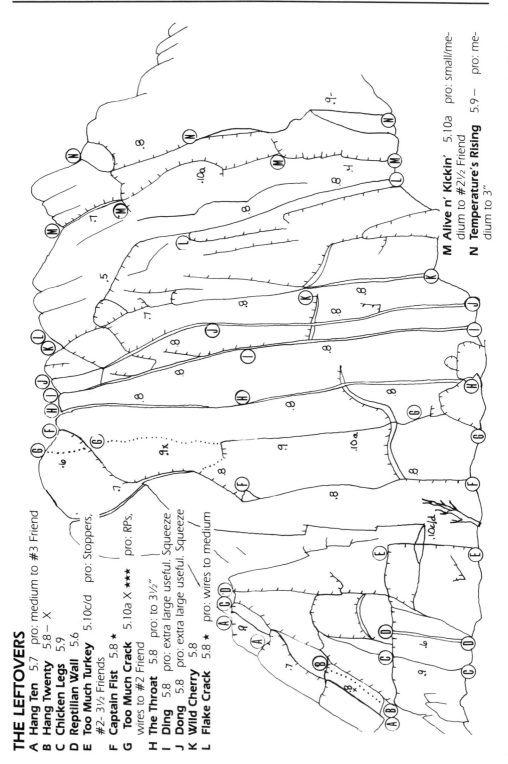

THE LEFTOVERS

A Hang Ten 5.7 pro: medium to #3 Friend
B Hang Twenty 5.8 – X
C Chicken Legs 5.9
D Reptilian Wall 5.6
E Too Much Turkey 5.10c/d pro: Stoppers, #2- 3½ Friends
F Captain Fist 5.8 ★
G Too Much Crack 5.10a X ★★★ pro: RPs, wires to #2 Friend
H The Throat 5.8 pro: to 3½"
I Ding 5.8 pro: extra large useful. Squeeze
J Dong 5.8 pro: extra large useful. Squeeze
K Wild Cherry 5.8
L Flake Crack 5.8 ★ pro: wires to medium

M Alive n' Kickin' 5.10a pro: small/me-dium to #2½ Friend
N Temperature's Rising 5.9 – pro: me-dium to 3"

TURKEY PERCH (H-M)

TURKEY TAIL (A-II)

THE RIGHTOVERS (G-M)

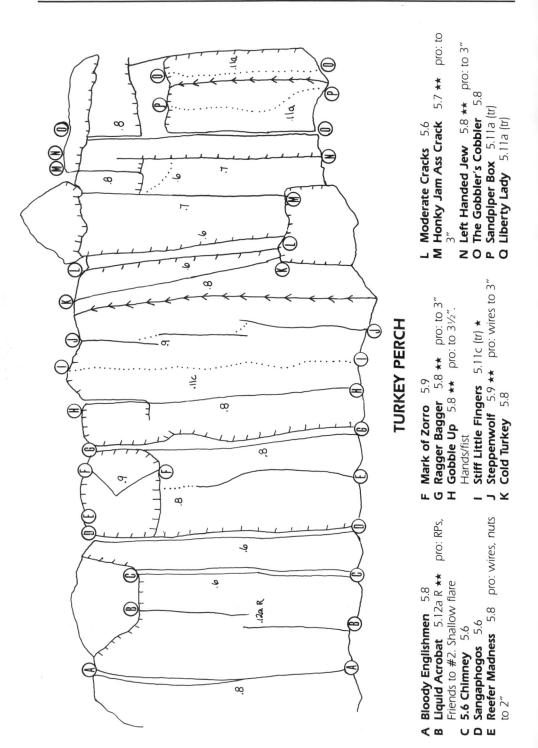

TURKEY PERCH

A Bloody Englishmen 5.8
B Liquid Acrobat 5.12a R ★★   pro: RPs,
    Friends to #2. Shallow flare
C 5.6 Chimney 5.6
D Sangaphogos 5.6
E Reefer Madness 5.8   pro: wires, nuts
    to 2"

F Mark of Zorro 5.9
G Ragger Bagger 5.8 ★★   pro: to 3"
H Gobble Up 5.8 ★★   pro: to 3½".
    Hands/fist
I Stiff Little Fingers 5.11c (tr) ★
J Steppenwolf 5.9 ★★   pro: wires to 3"
K Cold Turkey 5.8

L Moderate Cracks 5.6
M Honky Jam Ass Crack 5.7 ★★   pro: to
    3"
N Left Handed Jew 5.8 ★★   pro: to 3"
O The Gobbler's Cobbler 5.8
P Sandpiper Box 5.11a (tr)
Q Liberty Lady 5.11a (tr)

TURKEY TAIL – South Face

A Piece of Cake 5.11c ★ pro: #2-2½ Friends; thin hand roof crack

B Vegetable 5.8

C Bald Turkey 5.10d ★ pro: RPs, wires to #3 Friend. Thin

D Bitchin' Hot Mineral 5.10b ★ pro: RPs, small nuts, #1-4 Friends. Thin crack/ stemming

E The Flakes 5.8 (tr)

F Dark Meat 5.8 ★ pro: to 3½". Hand/ offwidth/squeeze

G Turkey's Delight 5.7 pro: emphasis on medium to 3½". Chimney

H Rasmussen's Crack 5.10b ★★★ pro: wires to #2 Friend. Thin crack to vertical face

I Hummingbird Way (Snively's Crack) 5.8 ★★ pro: to 3½"; offwidth

I1 Direct Finish 5.9 ★ pro: 4½" useful; offwidth

J Wild Turkey 5.10c ★ pro: to 3½; lie-back

K I Turkey 5.11d ★★ pro: 3 bolts and a pin were chopped

L Whimsical Dreams 5.11b ★★★ pro: RPs, wires, TCUs, #1-3 Friends; fingers/ hand

M Dekker Route 5.11a pro: small to 3"; face crux

N In Search of Unicorns 5.6 A2 ★ pro: RPs, wires, Friends to #3½; Lost Arrow or Crack n Up

O Wudamudafuka 5.11a ★★ pro: thin to #1½ Friend; upper pitches are offwidth

P For Turkeys Only 5.11d ★★ pro: to 6"; offwidth

Q Drumstick Direct 5.10d ★★★ pro: small/medium Stoppers; several #1-4 Friends. hand/fist

R Second Helpings 5.10b pro: wires to #4 Friend; undercling

S Turkey's Turd 5.11c ★★★ pro: RPs, wires, two each Friends #1-2, one each #2½-4 Friends. Finger/hand

T Squeeze Chimney 5.8 pro: to 3½", slings; squeeze

U Brush Turkey 5.12a ★★ pro: RPs, wires #2- 2½ Friends

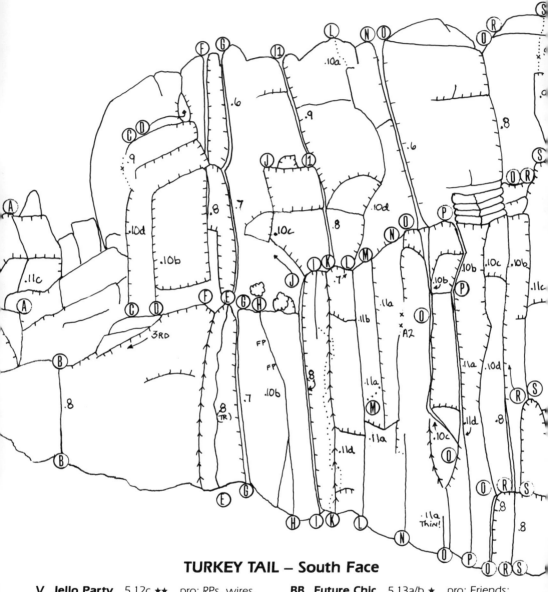

TURKEY TAIL – South Face

V Jello Party 5.12c ★★ pro: RPs, wires, TCUs, #1½ Friend. Face

W Spider Lady 5.9 ★ pro: to 3"

X Sidewinder 5.10a ★★ pro: medium to 5"; hands, offwidth, chimneys

Y Wisecrack 5.11c ★★ pro: #6 Stopper, #2 and 2½ Friend; thin hands roof crack

Z Snake 5.9 ★ pro: to 6"; offwidth

AA Wishful Thinking 5.9+ ★ pro: to 6"; offwidth

BB Future Chic 5.13a/b ★ pro: Friends; crack to overhanging arete

CC Hong Out 5.8+ ★

DD Journey to Ixtlan 5.12a ★★★ pro: RPs, wires, TCUs, Friends to #3; undercling/layback crux

EE Rufus 5.11d ★★ pro: wires, RPs, TCUs, Friends #1-4

FF Beauty and the Beast 5.12c ★★ pro: RPs, Stoppers, TCUs, #1-4 Friends

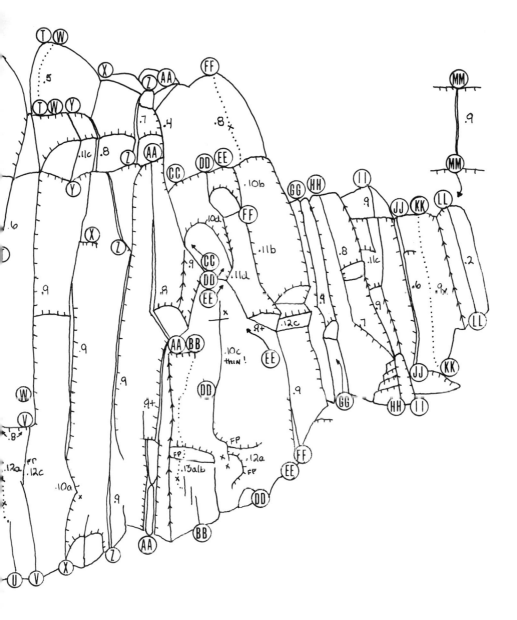

GG Double Trouble 5.9
HH Turkey in the Straw 5.8
II Cheap Trick 5.11c ★ pro: RPs, wires, #1-3 Friends

JJ 5.6 Easy Offwidth pro: to 3½"
KK 5.9 Face (tr)
LL Easy Crack 5.2
MM East Side Story 5.9

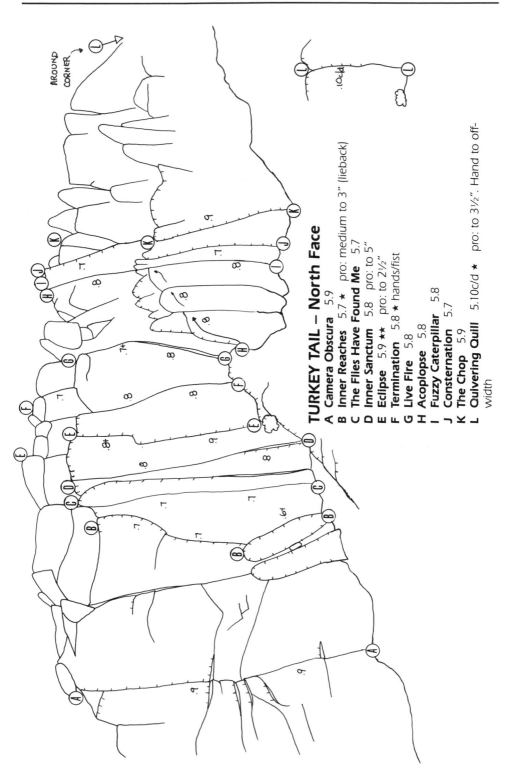

TURKEY TAIL – North Face

A Camera Obscura 5.9

B Inner Reaches 5.7 ★ pro: medium to 3" (lieback)

C The Flies Have Found Me 5.7

D Inner Sanctum 5.8 pro: to 5"

E Eclipse 5.9 ★★ pro: to 2½"

F Termination 5.8 ★ hands/fist

G Live Fire 5.8

H Acoplopse 5.8

I Fuzzy Caterpillar 5.8

J Consternation 5.7

K The Chop 5.9

L Quivering Quill 5.10c/d ★ pro: to 3½". Hand to off-width

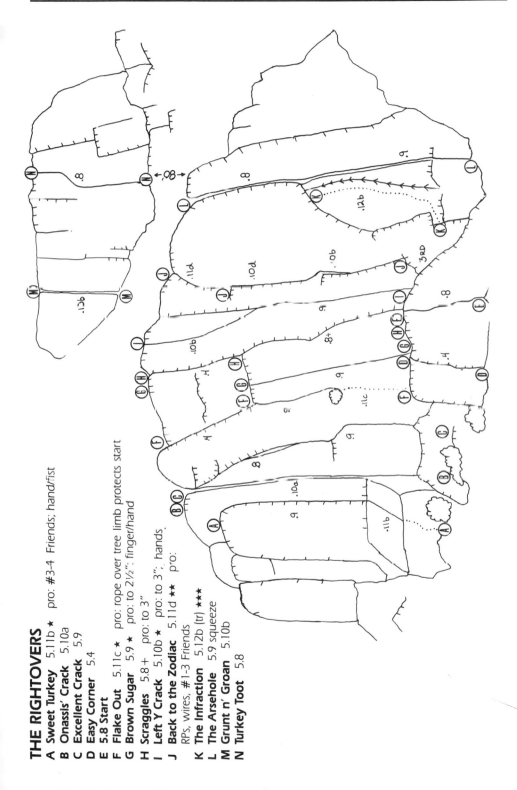

THE RIGHTOVERS

A Sweet Turkey 5.11b ★   pro: #3-4 Friends; hand/fist
B Onassis' Crack 5.10a
C Excellent Crack 5.9
D Easy Corner 5.4
E 5.8 Start
F Flake Out 5.11c ★ pro: rope over tree limb protects start
G Brown Sugar 5.9 ★ pro: to 2½"; finger/hand
H Scraggles 5.8+ pro: to 3"
I Left Y Crack 5.10b ★ pro: to 3"; hands
J Back to the Zodiac 5.11d ★★ pro:
    RPs, wires, #1-3 Friends
K The Infraction 5.12b (tr) ★★★
L The Arsehole 5.9 squeeze
M Grunt n' Groan 5.10b
N Turkey Toot 5.8

TARRYALL AREA

This rock is located on the southern end of the Lost Creek Scenic Area in the extreme south and western edge of the Platte area as described in this book. The climbing consists of crack climbs on very nice granite on a crag 350 feet high situated in a remote setting. Of all the rocks covered in this book, McCurdy Park Tower offers the largest concentration of moderate routes in the Platte, especially crack climbs. Although the six-mile approach could act as a deterrent, it is well worth a weekend trip or two. All the routes can be done with a standard rack (up to 4").

Access and Approach:

From Colorado Springs drive west on U.S. Highway 24 to Lake George. Continue west 18 miles to the town of Twin Eagles. Park here and follow hiking trail #607 for 6 miles north to the Tower.

McCURDY PARK TOWER – West Face

A Numb Nuts 5.7
B Born Free 5.6
C Wings 5.7
D Notch Route 5.4
E Notch Chimneys 5.6
F Mountaineer's Route 5.5
G Recon Direct 5.5

H Sunshine Ridge 5.6
I West Bulge 5.7
J Tower Recon 5.6
K The Nose 5.7
L Blockbuster 5.7

McCURDY PARK TOWER – South Face

M Praying Nun 5.4
N Intimidation 5.8
O Layback 5.8
P Andersonville 5.5

McCURDY PARK TOWER – West Face

TWIN ROCKS

A Wild Raspberries   5.7 ★   pro: to 3½"
B Wild Raspberries (var.)   5.8+ ★
C Middle Crack   5.8 ★
D Main Dihedral   5.8 ★   pro: to 3½"; offwidth
E Flesh Grinder   5.10d ★   pro: wires, #1-4
     Friends; finger/hand
F Growing in Size   5.10b ★   pro: #1-4
     Friends; hand/offwidth
G Horizontal Bop   5.10b

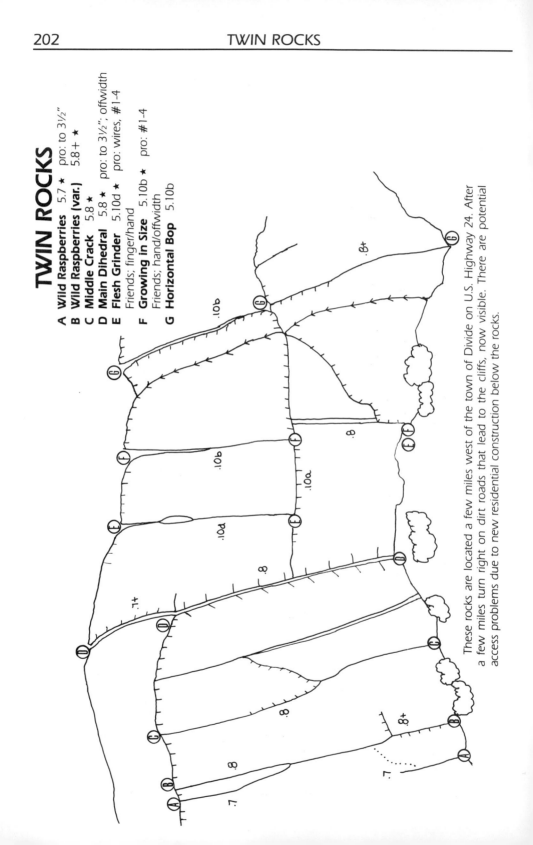

These rocks are located a few miles west of the town of Divide on U.S. Highway 24. After a few miles turn right on dirt roads that lead to the cliffs, now visible. There are potential access problems due to new residential construction below the rocks.

FIRST ASCENTS

LOVER'S LEAP
Original Route   U.S. Army or CMC climbers, circa 1930
Ye Olde Hysterical Route   FA unknown; FFA Maurice Reed and partner, circa 1975; 5.9 var FA
   unknown
Hubbel/Drier Route   Peter Hubbel and Mark Drier, 1979
Where Tunas Flop   Kevin Smythe and Terry Smith, 1987
Lover's Leap   FA U.S. Army or CMC climbers, circa 1930; FFA unknown
No Holds Barred   Claude Traufield and Peter Hubbel, 1987
Something for Nothing   Claude Traufield and Peter Hubbel, 1987
Procrastination   Peter Hubbel and Sara Brown, 1984
Winter Route   FFA unknown; var FFA unknown
Scare Tactics   Leon Henkelman and Andy Beal, 11/87
Shadow Dancer   Leon Henkelman and Andy Beal, 11/87
Love Me Do   Andy Beal and Leon Henkelman, 11/87
Where's the Beef   Leon Henkelman and Andy Beal, 10/87
The Cutting Board   Leon Henkelman and Andy Beal, 10/87
Mind Games   Leon Henkelman and Andy Beal, 10/87
Leon's Way   Leon Henkelman and Andy Beal, 11/87

NORTH TURKEY CREEK
Dotage   FFA unknown
Shadow Foxing   FFA unknown
A Bit of the Old One-Two   FFA unknown
Win One for the Zipper   FFA unknown
Captain's Corner   FFA unknown
Tonic   FFA unknown
Beginner's Route   FFA unknown
Pot Boiler   FFA unknown
Chalk Talk   FFA unknown
Young Lizards   FFA unknown
Warts 'n' All   FFA unknown
Bound for Glory   FFA unknown
Roof Route   FFA unknown
Queen of Hearts   FFA unknown
5.12 Crack   FFA unknown
5.10 Face   FFA unknown
5.9 Crack   FFA unknown
5.8 Crack   FFA unknown
Marginal Error   FFA unknown
Warhead   FFA unknown
King of the Jungle   FFA unknown
Young Lizards   FFA unknown
Chimney   FFA unknown
Valley Rescue   FFA unknown
Glory Hunters   FFA unknown
Aid Route   FFA unknown
Bell Route   FFA unknown
Bell Route Variation   FFA unknown
Sucker   FFA unknown

Green Slab FFA unknown
Green Slab Indirect FFA unknown
Wuthering Corner FFA unknown
5.8 Crack FFA unknown
Finger Crack FFA unknown
5.7 Corner FFA unknown
Left Crack FFA unknown
Right Crack FFA unknown

PINE AREA
ETIVE SLABS
Lost in a Blizzard Bob Kertzman, Rick Westbay and Dave Brower, 1986
Calm Before the Storm Bob Kertzman, Rick Westbay and Dave Brower, 1986
Storm Warning Bob Kertzman, Rick Westbay and Dave Brower, 1986
Weather Report Bob Kertzman, Rick Westbay and Dave Brower, 1986
Storm Watch Bob Kertzman, Rick Westbay and Dave Brower, 1986
Once upon a Thyme Dan McGee and Loren Trout, 1984
JAFC (Just Another Face Climb) Peter Hubbel and client, 1984
Paprika Plains Dan McGee and Loren Trout, 1984
Three's a Pair Peter Hubbel, Carlie Hubbel and Brett Bristol, 1985
Greenville Avenue Brett Bristol and John Durr, 3/87
Optical Illusion Brett Bristol and John Durr, 3/87
Hurdy Gurdy Man Peter Hubbel and Carlie Hubbel, 1984
Night Shift Peter Hubbel and Rob Donoho, 1980
Ah Youth Peter Hubbel and Rob Donoho, 1980
Parchment Farm Peter Hubbel and Carlie Hubbel, 1982
First Course Peter Hubbel and Rob Donoho, 1980
Tree Beard FFA unknown
Madness Strikes unknown
White Out unknown
Cash Sale unknown
Bonkers unknown
Red Clinic unknown
Loco-Motion unknown
Bloody Easy unknown
Not So Bloody Easy unknown
Diseased Mind unknown
Top Hat unknown
The Liturgy unknown
Fee-Ray Folly unknown

SPHINX ROCK
Talus Food Crack Dan Hare and Scott Woodruff, circa 1979
Black Crack Dan Hare and Scott Woodruff, mid 70s
Exit Stage Right Dave Bell (solo), 1979; (var) Peter Hubbel and Debbie Rothwell, 10/83
Plinth Robby Baker, solo, 1972. Bolts added by Peter Hubbel, Claude Traufield and Todd Lewis, 5/87
Lickety Split Dave Bell and Chris Bell, 3/79
Locksmith (Dihedral Route) FA unknown, circa late 1960's; FFA Dave Bell and Chris Bell, 4/79; (Dir. Var.) Dave Bell and Chris Bell, 9/79
Cheops Dave Dangle and Steve Jenkins, 9/85
Thinner Ken Trout and Miller, 1985
Crossing the River Styx Brett Bristol, John Durr, Marion Durr, Steve Brodhead and George Watson, 1986
Sphinx Crack (Fate Crack) FA Paul Sibley and Bill Roos, circa late 1960's; FFA Steve Hong and Leonard Coyne, 1982
The Crunch FFA unknown
Joint Venture Dave Bell and Mark Johnson, 3/79
Laundry Shoot Dave Bell and Mark Johnson, 3/79
The Turner Route FA Steve Turner and Kathy Turner, 1/69; FFA Howard Crow and Steve Turner, 6/72
Uh-Oh Dave Bell and Mark Johnson, 3/79
Return to Forever (Southeast Corner) FA Larry Arnold and Steve Turner, 12/68; FFA Eric Weinstein and Bruce Morris, 1977

Bottom Line Dave Bell (solo), 1979
The Slug Paul Sibley et al, late 1960s
Ptooeey Factor Dave Bell and Chris Bell, 7/84

SIDE SHOW SLAB
Mind Over Matter Dan Hutchins and Stu Ritchie, 4/86
Weekend Warrior Dan Hutchins and Stu Ritchie, 4/86

HONED ROCK
Mary's First Time Robert Blake and Wendy Winkler, 1986
So Honed yet so Stoned Robert Blake and Tripp Gordon, 1986
Snowbody's Business Claude Traufield and Peter Hubbel, 1/87

SQUAT ROCK
Miss Conception Dave Bell and Peter Hubbel, 4/83
Sex Favors Peter Hubbel and Sara Brown, 3/85
Jelly Omelet Peter Hubbel and Emily Busch, 6/86
Elusive Wapiti Peter Hubbel and Gregg Hinnen, 1/83
Elusive Wapiti Direct Richard Collins and Noel Childs, 1985
Higher Education Chip Wilson and Noel Childs, 5/85
Dead Gumbies Can't Dance Peter Hubbel and Brett Bristol, 5/85
Ghost Images Peter Hubbel, et al., 1985
Slimy Slit Tom Bohanon and Peter Hubbel, 4/83
Sticky Fingers Peter Hubbel and Tom Bohanon, 4/83
Peter's Out Peter Hubbel and Mike Smith, 5/83
Gob Knobbler Peter Hubbel and Tom Bohanon, 4/83
Hob Goblin Mike Smith and Peter Hubbel, 5/83
Casual Corner Peter Hubbel and Robin Hied, 5/83
Flamingo Road Peter Hubbel and Phil Ayers, 1984
Sad and Lonely Peter Hubbel and Claude Traufield, 1987
Dirty Pool Peter Hubbel and Claude Traufield, 1987
Lichen or Not Kirk Miller and Ken Trout, 1982
Lichen or Not Right Hand Nancy Dillingham and Carlie Hubbel, 1985
Di's Escape Diana Bailey and Peter Hubbel, 1985
Flamingo Toad Brett Bristol, John Durr and Marion Durr, 1987
Branded Gregg Hinnen and Peter Hubbel, 5/83
Urban Development Brett Bristol, Peter Hubbel and Chip Wilson, 5/85
Temporary Clemency Paul Heyliger and Brian Parsons, 1986
Kirk's Korner Ken Trout and Kirk Miller, 1982
Smut Puppy Noel Childs and Peter Hubbel, 1986
Urban Renewal Dave Gottenborg, Peter Hubbel and Emily Busch, 1/85
Misfit Kids Peter Hubbel, Dave Gottenborg and Emily Busch, 1/85
Lunge for Munge (tr) Jim Karn, 1986
Straitjacket Peter Hubbel, Emily Busch and Dave Gottenborg, 1/85
Powerlounger Peter Hubbel, Emily Busch and Dave Gottenborg, 1/85
Serenade Brett Bristol, John Durr and Marion Durr, 1987

DOODLE DOME
Crazy Corner FFA unknown
5.7 Face FFA unknown

DAFF DOME
Beeline John Bowman, et al., 1985
Bat Crack FFA unknown
Dr. Jekyl and Mr. Hyde John Bowman, et al., 1984
Rye Crisp Peter Hubbel and Rich Sutton, 6/83
Daffy Duck Peter Hubbel and Rick Sutton, 6/83

DING DOME
Fun Face Peter Hubbel and Rich Sutton, 6/83
Raindance Peter Hubbel, Gregg Hinnen and Mike Smith, 5/83

Easy Streak   Peter Hubbel and Mike Smith, 6/83
Ding Dang Doodle   Brett Bristol and Marion Durr, 1986
Captain Crunch   Mike Smith and Peter Hubbel, 6/83

BUCKSNORT SLABS
Left Out   Ken Trout and Rob Baker, 1984
Buck Fever   Peter Hubbel and Brett Bristol, 1986
Shake n' Bake   Ken Trout and Rob Baker, 1985
The Grand Slam   Peter Prandoni, Robby Baker and Ken Trout, 1987
Hurricane Gloria   Mark Rolofson and Mike Lowe, 1985
Good, Bad and the Ugly (Hooked on a Feeling)   FA Allan Pattie and Dave Bell, circa 1984; FFA
     Mark Rolofson and Scott Reynolds, 1985
Crack of Anticipation (Classic Dihedral)   Paul Sibley, Ron Cox and Carl Arndt, circa 1967
Slippery When Wet   Ken Trout, Tom Vanco and Rob Baker, 1984
Slippery When Dry   FA unknown FFA first lead by Dan Michael, circa 1987
Nuclear Burn/China Syndrome   Dave Dangle, Steve Jenkins and Dan Hutchins, 1986
Bushes of Beelzebub   Robert Sandefur and partner, 1968
Out and About   Dave Bell and Chris Bell, 5/79
Core Dump   Peter Hubbel and Brett Bristol, 1986
Crazy Face   Bruce Morris and Bill Feiges, 1977
Motor Mouth   Bill Feiges and Bruce Morris, 1977
Bats in the Belfry   Lee Marsh and Steve Brodhead, 1987
Gumbi Groove   Ken Trout and Rob Baker, 1986
The Boys are Back   Dave Bell and Allen Patttie, 8/86
Over and Out   Dave Bell and Chris Bell, 1979; (Eyeful var) Peter Hubbel and Sara Brown, 1985; (5.8
     var) Diana Bailey, Sara Brown and Lynn Fletcher, 1985
Easy Out   Chris Bell and Byron Nelson, 1982
One for the Road   Steve Manning and Tim Harrison, 11/87

MOTHERLODE DOME
No Glory for You   Steve Jenkins, Fred Kieth, Dan Schaeffer and Dave Dangle

THE EGGSHELL
The Terminator   Steve Jenkins, Dave Dangle and Fred Kieth

THE BEACH
Pirate's Cove   Marion Durr and Joslyn Hubbell, 1986
Sunburn   Brett Bristol and Joslyn Hubbell, 1986
Riptide   FFA unknown
Blonde Bomb   John Durr, Brett Bristol and Marion Durr, 1986
Cardiac Police   Brett Bristol, Joslyn Hubbell and Marion Durr, 1986
Clamdigger   Marion Durr and Joslyn Hubbell, 1986

THE WAVE
Unnamed   FFA unknown
Surf Bum   FFA unknown
Beach Bunny   FFA unknown

BANNER PEAK
Twinam/Bailey Route   Dave Twinam and Diana Bailey, 1986
Gambit Accepted   Peter Hubbel and Brett Bristol, 1985

THE DOME AREA
THE CRACK PRESERVE
Slot Trot   Noel Childs and Jerry Rock, 1985.

ANGLE IRON SLABS
Leftraction   Peter Hubbel (solo), 1980
Vacancy   FFA unknown
Purgatory   FFA unknown
Roadside Attraction   Peter Hubbel and George Fedoronko, 1980

Pure 'n' Simple   Peter Hubbel and Paul McLaughlin, 1984
Roadkill   Peter Hubbel and Tom Bohanon, 1981
Trifle Dicey   Dan McGee and Loren Trout, 1983
It Matters Not   Peter Hubbel and Paul McLaughlin, 1984
Schvondelagunst   Dan McGee and Loren Trout, 1983; var Peter Hubbel and Paul McLaughlin, 1984

THE BISHOP
Bishop Crack   Christian Griffith and Henry Lester, 1985
Lightning Crack   FFA unknown
Aid Crack   FFA unknown
Flounder   FFA unknown
Craftwork   Charlie Fowler and Chip Chase, 1981
Ellingwood Route   Albert Ellingwood, Agnes Vaille and Stephen Hart, July, 1924
10cc   Peter Hubbel and Mark Drier, 1981
Lichen Away   Peter Hubbel and Mark Drier, 1981

THE DOME
Prairie Dog Crematorium   Mike Dorsey and Dan Grandusky, 1985
Tube Terror   Jay Wilson, Mike Dorsey and Dan Grandusky, 1985
Sposi-Isaacs Route   Bruce Sposi and Gary Isaacs, 1981
A Day at the Beach   Dave McCanless and Mac McKeel, 1983
R.U. Redi   Jay Wilson, et al., 1986
Seamus   FA unknown, FFA unknown (possibly Noel Childs circa 1986)
YMCA (Left Side)   Peter Hubbel and Brian Brown, 1981
YMCA (Right Side)   Mark Drier and Peter Hubbel, 1981
South Side Johnny   Peter Hubbel and Brian Brown, 1981
Cruiser   Peter Hubbel and Brian Brown, 1981
Twist and Shout   Mike Dorsey and Dan Grandowsky, 1985
Day at the Beach   Dave McCanless and Ron Dawson, 1982
Sloe Gizz Fizz   Peter Hubbel and Mark Drier, 1981
Burke-Box-Ball Route   Joe Burke, Fred Box and Jenny Ball, 1983
Stars of Mars   Joe Burke and Marlene Griffith, 1985
Into the Abyss   Peter Hubbel, Dave Gottenborg and Claude Traufield, 8/87
Higbee/Reveley Route   Art Higbee and Chris Reveley, 1974
The Gig's Up   Peter Hubbel and Mark Drier, 1981
Dos Equis   Mike Smith and Ron Kirk, 1984
Dire Straits   Duncan Ferguson, early 1970s
Topographical Oceans   Peter Hubbel, Mike Smith and Gregg Hinnen, 1982
Bishop's Jaggers   Duncan Ferguson and Jim Walsh, 1972
Bishop's Move   FFA unknown
Sea of Holes   Ken Trout, Paul Franks and Brian Hanson, 1984
Pecker Wrecker   Peter Prandoni, Ken Trout and Rob Baker, 1985
Connections   Peter Hubbel and Mike Smith, circa 1983
Bolts to Somewhere   Mike Smith and Ron Kirk, 1984
Pornographic Motions   Steve Jenkins, Dave Dangle, 1986
The PTL Club   Peter Gallagher and Bob Robertson, 1986
Simpleton Crack   Jay Wilson, et al., 1986

LITTLE DOME
Ending Crack   Don Crawford, Eric Fagerstrom and Jack Britton, 1986
Beer Drinkers and Hell Raisers   Don Crawford, Eric Fagerstrom and Jack Britton, 1986
Arching Way   Peter Hubbel and Suzy Johnston, 1979
Flakey   Peter Hubbel and George Fedoronko, 1978; var Peter and Carlie Hubbel, 1983
Garden Party   Dave Gottenborg and Peter Hubbel, 8/87
Original Sin   Peter Hubbel and Dave Gottenborg, 8/87
Walking in the Rain   Dave Gottenborg and Peter Hubbel, 8/87

SUNSHINE WALL
Spot Light Kid   Chip Wilson and Noel Childs, 1982
Small Stuff   Kit Suddreth and Peter Hubbel, 8/83
Flakes of Wrath   Chip Wilson and Noel Childs, 1984
Grinder   Peter Hubbel and Kit Suddreth, 8/83

Fred the Crack   Bill Robert and Mac McKeel, 1985
We Scared o' de Goofa Man   Peter Hubbel and Rich Sutton, 1985
Witches Hex   Buck Norden and Chris Reveley, 1973
Squatters Rights   Chris Reveley and Dan Michaels, 1974; **variations**   Peter Hubbel and partners
Interceptor   Peter Hubbel and Claude Traufield, 1/87
Strip Teaser   Peter Hubbel and Claude Traufield, 1/87
Man on Fire   Peter Hubbel and Mike Smith, 1982
Arch Nemesis   Dan Hare, Noel Childs and John Durr, 11/87
Gunnin' for Buddha   Peter Hubbel and Claude Traufield, 1/87
Mister Skin   Peter Hubbel, Claude Traufield and Lee Marsh, 1/87
Forrest Route   Bill Forrest and partner, early 70's
Ward Cleaver   Dan Hare and Alan Bradley, 4/86
Meatcleaver   Maurice Reed and Bruce Sposi, 1983; var FFA unknown
Equinox   Chris Reveley and Dan Michaels, 1974
What Price Glory   Brian Parsons and Paul Heyliger, 8/86
The 26th Letter   Brian Parsons and Paul Heyliger, 8/86
Fallen Angel   Chris Reveley et al
Deception Past   unknown
Muddy Past   Mike Smith and Peter Hubbel, 1982
Wear Cattle   Ken Trout and Kirk Miller, 1/87
Standard Route   (first pitch) Chris Reveley and Jim Michael, 1970s. (final pitches) Chip Wilson and
    Noel Childs, 5/86
The Far Reaches   Bill Meyers, Ray Ringle and Mark Sonnenfeld, 10/85
Gonzo's Lament   Tom Bohanon and Peter Hubbel, 1982
Squish   Noel Childs and Dan Hare, 1987
Squash   Noel Childs and Dan Hare, 1988
Airborne Froth   Steve "Norman" Dieckoff, Noel Childs, Strappo Hughes and Jerry Rock, 6/88

SUNSHINE FACE
Fighting Gobblers   unknown
Turkey Foot Crack   FFA Larry Marquardt and Chris Reveley, 1974?
Astro Turkey   Kyle Copeland and Charlie Fowler, 1986
Unfinished   Olaf Mitchell, et al.
Rip Van Winkle   Greg Davis and Chris Reveley, circa 1975
Uncle Sam's Jam   Maurice Reed and Bruce Sposi, 1982
Opus   Maurice Reed and Bruce Sposi, 1982
Turkey Foot Tower/Shark's Fin FA unknown

THE CATHEDRAL SPIRES AREA
POE BUTTRESS
Jam   Peter Hubbel, Mike Smith and Greg Hinnen, 1982
The Maelstrom   Maurice Reed, Oliver Hill, George Saure, 1983
Brothers in Arms   Roger Briggs, Dan Stone and Chip Chase, 6/86
Uptown Toodaloo   Olaf Mitchell and Peter Prandoni, 6/87
Mississippi Half Step   Maurice Reed and Olaf Mitchell, 1985
Edgeofright   Noel Childs and Rufus Miller, 4/87
Tenacity of Purpose   Mike Smith and Malcolm McCormick, 10/83

BLOCK TOWER
Mr. Mantle   Olaf Mitchell with Maurice Reed (1st pitch) and Catherine Freer (2nd pitch), 1984
Hurt Dance   FA Chris Reveley and Dave Wright, 1974
Sex Dwarf   Peter Hubbel and Andy Archer, 8/84
Dance of Chance   Peter Hubbel, Mike Smith and Tom Bohanon, 2/83
Dance of Chance Direct   Paul McLaughlin and Rick Dulin, 1984
Bungi Man   Olaf Mitchell and Peter Hubbel, 4/83
Queer Bait   Mike Smith and Peter Hubbel, 6/82; var to start Phil Ayers and Emily Busch, 1984

CYNICAL PINNACLE
Round the Corner   Mike Smith and Peter Hubbel, 12/82
Who Cares?   (1st & 2nd pitches) Peter Hubbel and Brian Oliver, 1981; (1st pitch var & 3rd pitch)
    Bruce Sposi and Ed Garrity, 1981

Preparation H   Maurice Reed and Chip Ruckgraber, 1982
Potato Head   Peter Hubbel and Tom Bohanon, 3/82
Demolition Man   Mark Drier, Peter Hubbel and Gregg Hinnen, 1982; (var) Peter Hubbel and Gregg Hinnen, 1982
Buffalos in Space   Kyle Copeland, John McMullen and Greg Johnston, 1984
Busch Gardens   Tom Bohanon and Peter Hubbel, 3/82
Hand Job   FA Tom Fender and partner, FFA Ken Trout and Chris Hodge, 1973
Hand Job Direct   Chris Dodge and Ken Trout, 1973
Chip off the Old Buffalo   Ken Trout and Kirk Miller, 1987
Monkeys in the Forest   Noel Childs and Rufus Miller, 7/86
Breashears Crack   Dave Breashears, et al., 1975
Prayer Book (Wunsch's Dihedral)   FA Tom Fender and Bill Roos, circa 1964. FFA (2nd and 3rd) Steve Wunsch, 1972; (final bolt ladder) Jeff Lowe and Paul Sibley, 1977; (var to bolt ladder finish-Roger Briggs, 1976) (direct finish of original bolt ladder-Rolf Grange and Art Wiggins, 1983)
Center Route   FA Paul Sibley, Bill Roos, and Carl and Bernum Arndt, 1968?; FFA unknown
Rising Crescendo   Rob Wolfe and Oliver Hill, 2/85
Class Act   Olaf Mitchell, Ken Trout and Kirk Miller, 1986
Through Route   Paul Sibley and Bill Roos, circa 1974
Turf Spreader   FA Larry Dalke and Cliff Jennings, 1966. FFA Chris Reveley and Rich Lindall, 1975
Great Chimney   FA unknown (probably CMC climbers from the N side, circa early 60's)
Rubber Ducky   Dan Trygstad, et al., 1986
Rap Crack   Steve Hong, et al., 1981
Turf Spreader (Last Pitch)   Mike Smith and Tom Bohanon, circa 1982

ICEBOX WALL
Ice Age   Brian Oliver, Chris Allen and Peter Hubbel, 1981
Quaint Quack   Olaf Mitchell and Noel Childs, 1986
Prime Line   Olaf Mitchell and Jerry Rock, 5/86
Frigid Digit   Lindsay Broom and Mike Smith, 10/82

POWERHOUSE PINNACLE
Emotional Rescue   Mike Smith and Peter Hubbel, 11/82
Botany Bizarre   Mike Smith and Peter Hubbel, 11/82
Flight of the Rat   Peter Hubbel and Mike Smith, 11/82
The Bitch   Peter Hubbel and Brian Brown, 1983

THORNBIRD FACE
Quiet Desperation   Tom Bohanon and Peter Hubbel, 10/82
Mr. Clean   Tom Bohanon, Mike Smith and Peter Hubbel, 11/82
Mothergrunger   Peter Hubbel and Mike Smith, 11/82

BAD JU JU FORMATION
Bad Ju Ju   Olaf Mitchell and Noel Childs, 5/86

SNAKE BUTTRESS
Dr. Demento   Peter Hubbel, Gregg Hinnen and Mike Smith, 1982
Hodge Podge   Ken Trout and Rob Baker, 1974; (5.8 Var) Peter Hubbel, Bruce Sposi, Ed Garrity, 1982
Tronolane   Tom Bohanon and Peter Hubbel, 4/83
Rude Boy   Maurice Reed, et al., circa 1984
Jo' Bubba   (1st pitch) Peter Hubbel, Chip Wilson, Brett Bristol (2nd pitch) Noel Childs, Jerry Rock, and Chip Wilson, 5/86
Hubba-Bubba   Maurice Reed and Olaf Mitchell, circa 1983
The Rattler   Peter Hubbel, Gregg Hinnen and Dave Bell, 1982
The Rattler Direct   (1st pitch) Peter Hubbel and Brett Bristol, 1985, (2nd pitch) Peter Hubbel and Kit Suddreth, 7/84
The Viper   Gregg Hinnen and Peter Hubbel, 1982
Seven Sharp   Peter Hubbel and Mark Drier, 1982
Sidewinder   Peter Hubbel and Dave Gottenborg, 11/87
Mr. Pitiful   Peter Hubbel, Bruce Burnell and Andy Archer, 8/84
Hairless   Peter Hubbel, Bruce Burnell and Andy Archer, 8/84
Geek Crack   FFA unknown
Illusion Chain   Bruce Burnell, Andy Archer and Peter Hubbel, 8/84

POOP POINT
Uranus   Brett Bristol, Peter Hubbel and Jon Hall, 1/86
Hall's Balls   Jon Hall, Brett Bristol and Peter Hubbel, 1/86
Lies and Propaganda   Peter Hubbel, Brett Bristol and Jon Hall, 1/86

POOP SLAB
Rich's Route   Peter Hubbel and Rich Sutten, 1/83; (var) Peter Hubbel and Rich Sutten, 1/83
America's Little Dumplin'   Jerry Rock, Noel Childs and Dan Hare, 1986

TOP OF THE WORLD AREA
THE CHESSMEN
Three Stooges   Larry, Moe and Curly, 6/87
Parabolic Flight   Dave Bell and John Durr, 1987
Slit   Mark Drier and Peter Hubbel, 1981
First Aid   John Durr and Dave Bell, 1987
Short 'n' Sweet   Phil Ayers and Rick Dulin, 1983
The Anti Christ (Thin Ice)   FA Dave Bell and Chris Bell, 8/75, FFA Allen Hill, Scott Reynolds, Bryan Becker, John Catto, Miada Burkovensky, and Greg Liddy, 1987
Last Tango   Dave Bell and Mark Johnson(Jensen?), 7/79
Handcrack   FFA unknown
Trails of Tropical Lotions   Ron Olevesky, Dan McGee and Jim Karn, 1985. Lower portion done previously, FA unknown
Right Stuff   FFA unknown
Stuff 'n' Fuckit   FFA unknown
Toot Suite   Paul Sibley and Bill Roos, 1972
Low Pressure   FFA unknown
Destination Unknown   Peter Hubbel, Steve Jenkins, Fred Kieth and Rich Sutton, 1/83
Blues for Allah   FFA unknown
Secret Journey   Chris Gulepard and Greg Brazelton, 1984
Angel Eyes   Skip Hamilton and Paul Sibley, early '70s
Chamber Music (Fender Route)   Tom Fender and partner, 1969
Richart-Spaulding Route   Stan Richart and Don Spaulding, 8/56
Huston-Johnson Route (The Sandwich)   FA Cary Huston and Dale Johnson, 9/56; FFA Dan McGee, et al.

PARKING LOT ROCK
Latch Hand   Peter Hubbel and Rob Donoho, 1980
Buckbo   Peter Hubbel, et al., 1976
Handbo   Peter Hubbel, et al., circa 1978

SPOOF ROCK
Scab Labor   Dave Gottenborg, Peter Hubbel and Rich Dulin, 1987
Whiney the Pooh   Claude Traufield and Peter Hubbel, 1987
Punchline   FFA unknown
Newlywed   FFA unknown

GEMSTONE ROCKS
Just Say No   Noel Childs and Dan Grandusky, 1986
1986
Corporate Cowboy   Dave Gottenborg, Peter Hubbel and Claude Traufield, 7/87
5 Weird   Peter Hubbel, Gregg Hinnen and Mike Smith, 1982
Piece of Cake   Gregg Hinnen (solo), 1982; (5.10 Var) Peter Hubbel (tr), 1982
Agent Orange   Peter Hubbel and Gregg Hinnen, 1982
Group Therapy   (1st and 2nd pitches) Gregg Hinnen, Peter Hubbel and Dave Bell, 1982 (3d pitch) Ron Kirk and Lynn Thomas, 10/87
Sloppy Joe   Gregg Hinnen and Peter Hubbel, 1982
If 6 was 9   Peter Hubbel and Gregg Hinnen, 1982

CRACKED WALL
Benjamin   Tom Bohanon and Dale Lowry, 11/82
Sleight of Hands   Peter Hubbel and Kevin Smyth, 11/82

An Empty Bladder is a Happy Bladder Brett Bristol and John Durr, 1987
Whitman Sampler Brett Bristol and John Durr, 1986
You Won't Find This in Dallas John Durr, Marion Durr and Brett Bristol, 1986
Rodeo Brett Bristol and Ron Kirk, 1986
Leave it Blank Tom Bohanon and Dale Lowry, 11/82; (var) FA Peter Hubbel and Kevin Smyth, 11/82, FFA Peter Hubbel and Sara Brown, 1984
How the West was Won Peter Hubbel and Mark Drier, 1981
Odd Job Peter Hubbel and Brett Bristol, 8/85
Chicago Blues Peter Hubbel and Dick VanLandingham, 2/86

THE SLABBO
Whining Dog Peter Hubbel, Brett Bristol and Marion Durr, 10/86
Kentucky Long Rifle Brett Bristol, Marion Durr and Peter Hubbel, 10/86
Hand Jive II Brett Bristol, Marion Durr and Peter Hubbel, 10/86
The Pogue Peter Hubbel, Marion Durr and Brett Bristol, 10/86
Slime Mold Peter Hubbel and Andy Archer, 7/84
Fair Game Peter Hubbel and Marion Durr, 10/86
Crank Corner FFA unknown
Whiplash Smile Peter Hubbel, Claude Traufield and Jon Hall, 12/86
My Pet Monster Peter Hubbel and Claude Traufield, 12/86
5.10 Face FFA unknown, 5.8 var. FFA unknown
Boulderer's Delight Mark Drier and Peter Hubbel, 1981
Heinous Anus Peter Hubbel, Marion Durr and Joslyn Hubbell, 8/86
Hosemonster Peter Hubbel and Claude Traufield, 12/86

RAGNAROK
Where the Buffalo Cruise Steve Merritt and Brett Bristol, 1986
Twistin' the Night Away Olaf Mitchell and Jerry Rock, 5/85
Chasin' the Elements Chip Wilson, Peter Hubbel and Carlie Hubbel, 5/85
Fun Climb #101 Peter Hubbel and Chip Wilson, 4/85

THE BOULDER PILE
Dihedral Way Mark Drier, Peter Hubbel and Dave Bell, 1981
Warmer Crack Dave McCandliss, Peter Hubbel and Brett Bristol, 11/86
The Other Lee Marsh and George Watson, 11/86
Variations on a Theme in A Minor Brett Bristol, Dave McCandliss and Peter Hubbel, 11/86
Bushido Peter Hubbel, Brett Bristol and Dave McCandliss, 11/86
V-Slot Dave Bell, Mark Drier and Peter Hubbel, 1981
Sheer Lubacy Tom Bohanon and Peter Hubbel, 12/82; (var) Tom Bohanon and Peter Hubbel, 12/82
Springfest Peter Hubbel and Emily Busch, 9/87
The Combine Steve Manning and Deaun Schovajsa, 9/87
Commie Pinko Fag Peter Hubbel, Emily Busch and Claude Traufield, 9/87
Private Affair Brett Bristol and Diana Bailey, 1986
Illicit Affair Brett Bristol and Diana Bailey, 1986
Community Affair Tom Bohanon, Peter Hubbel and Deaun Schovajsa, 12/86
Tricky Dicky Peter Hubbel and Sara Brown, 10/85
Comedy Break Peter Hubbel, Jon Hall and Lee Marsh, 12/86
Steep Throat Unknown
Reveley's Crack Chris Reveley and partner, 1973
Comedy Club Jon Hall, Claude Traufield and Todd Lewis, 1/86
Pretty as a Pig Peter Hubbel, et al., 1/86
Pig Peter Hubbel and Jon Hall, 1/86
So Fine Peter Hubbel (solo), 11/86
Hesitation Blues Peter Hubbel and Marion Durr, 11/86
Stem to Stern Brett Bristol, Peter Hubbel and Dave McCandliss, 11/86
Pink Tights Marion Durr and Peter Hubbel, 12/86
Surprised Dick VanLandingham and Peter Hubbel, 1/86
Cheap Shot Peter Hubbel and Dick VanLandingham, 1/86
Mungeloid Peter Hubbel and Marion Durr, 1986
Pigmania John Durr and Marion Durr, 1986
Marion's Mirage John Durr, Marion Durr and Brett Bristol, 1986
Trial by Fire Rob Adair and Dan Hutchins, 1987

Piranha   Brett Bristol and John Durr, 1986
Conniption Fit   Peter Hubbel and Sara Brown, 1985
Conniption Direct   Peter Hubbel and Claude Traufield, 1986
Short as Shit, Hard as Hell   Brett Bristol, John Durr, Peter Hubbel, Deaun Schovajsa and Tom Bohanon, 1986
Blunt Object   Brett Bristol and Diana Bailey, 1987
Alterations   Peter Hubbel and Dick VanLandingham, 1986
Shadowline   Peter Hubbel and Sara Brown, 1985
Smoke em If Ya Got Em   Brett Bristol and Diana Bailey, 1986
The Surveyor   Peter Hubbel and Sara Brown, 1985
EB's Route   Emily Busch and Claude Traufield, 9/87
Arrowhead Arete   (tr) Claude Traufield, 9/87

GREEN SLAB
Omnique   Dave Gottenborg and Sam Green, 1986
Astral Pig   Noel Childs and Peter Hubbel, 1985
Rubble Ramble   Peter Hubbel and Noel Childs, 1985
Evening Light   Peter Hubbel and Sara Brown, 1985
Monkey See, Monkey Do   John Durr and Brett Bristol, 1/86

MYTOSUGIA FACE
Whisper to a Scream   Peter Hubbel, Jon Hall and Lee Marsh, 1986
Blood Pudding   Peter Hubbel and Sara Brown, 1985
Succubus   Lee Marsh, Peter Hubbel and Jon Hall, 1986

THE AERIE (Weasel Ranch)
Ides of March   John Durr and Lee Marsh, 3/87
Varicose Veins   Marion Durr and Joslyn Hubbell, 1986
Nuclear Waste   Dave Gottenborg and Tom Walker, 6/86
Small Loans, Easy Payments   John Durr and Brett Bristol, 1986
Belay Slave   John Durr and Diana Bailey, 1986
Spookshow   Noel Childs and Peter Hubbel, 1986
Horrorshow   Phil Ayers and Emily Busch, 1986
The Weasel   John Durr and Brett Bristol, 1986
Weasels in Lust   Brett Bristol and John Durr, 1986
Feeding Frenzy   Brett Bristol and John Durr, 1986
Shuwfalo   Brett Bristol and John Durr, 1986
The Naked Face   Brett Bristol and John Durr, 1987
Weasels Rip My Flesh   Phil Ayers and Emily Busch, 1986
Yabba Dabba Do   John Durr, Marion Durr and Brett Bristol, 1986
The Aerie   Noel Childs, John Durr, Lee Marsh, Ken Trout and Brett Bristol, 1986

END OF THE WORLD AREA
Cave of the Clan Bear   Rick Dulin and Phil Ayers, 1987
I'd Rather Stick Pins in My Eyes   Phil Ayers and Peter Hubbel, 1987
Chimney Sweep   Phil Ayers and Rick Dulin, 1987
Busy Bear   Claude Traufield, Karen Ann Young, Emily Busch and Peter Hubbel, 1987
Repo Man   Peter Hubbel, Karen Ann Young and Emily Busch, 1987
My Thang   Peter Hubbel and Dave Gottenborg, 1987

MALAY ARCHIPELAGO AREA
JAZZ DOME
Sweet Little Hollywood Flake   Ron Kirk and Mike Colasino, 1/86
Straight, No Chaser   Ron Kirk and Nicholas Kirk (at age 71!), 12/86
5.10 Head   Diana Bailey, Lynn Fletcher and Ron Kirk, 12/86
The Strat   Joe Burke and Ron Kirk, 1/86
Moonlight Cocktail   Ron Kirk and Lynn Fletcher, 12/86
Avalon   Lynn Fletcher and Diana Bailey, 1/86
Mystique   Diana Bailey and Lynn Fletcher, 1/86

DOME ROCK SLABS
Comfortably Numb Paul Heyliger and Brian Parsons, 1982

DOME ROCK
Central Slab John Ruger, Paul Sibley and Bill Roos, 1977
A3 Route FA Bill Roos and Carl Arndt, early '70s

ATLANTIS SLAB
Fluff Boys Peter Hubbel and Claude Traufield, 2/87
Soliloquy John McMullen, Tim Hudgel and Carl Rasmussen, 1986
Transformer Peter Hubbel and Claude Traufield
This Bolt's For You John McMullen, Tim Hudgel and Carl Rasmussen, 1986
Island Rhythm John McMullen, Tim Hudgel and Carl Rasmussen, 1986
The Leper (tr) John McMullen and Mark Rolofson, 1986
Snark Hunt Peter Hubbel and Claude Traufield, 1986
Dam the Water Board Ed Hackstaff, Marion Durr and Brett Bristol, 1987
No Bore A Bora John McMullen, Marc Hirt, Tim Hudgel and Carl Rasmussen, 1986
The Natives are Restless Charlie Fowler and partner, 1987
Seventh Wave Charlie Fowler and partner, 1987

GILLIGAN'S ISLAND
Mary Ann John McMullen (solo), 1986
Ginger John McMullen (solo), 1986

JAVA DOME
El Nino Tim Hudgel and Carl Rasmussen, 1986
Platte Magic John McMullen and Marc Hirt, 1986
Traditionalist at Work Bruce Hildebrand and Dale Haas, 11/87
Rock Lobster Tim Hudgel, Carl Rasmussen and John McMullen, 1986
Banzai Pipeline Lee Marsh and Ed Weidmann, 1971
Beach Blanket Bingo Tim Hudgel and Carl Rasmussen, 1986
Vertical Beach Party John McMullen, Tim Hudgel and Carl Rasmussen, 1986
The Unhead Lee Marsh and Ed Weidmann, 1971
Quit Your Beachin' Peter Hubbel and Claude Traufield, 1987

BALI DOME
Pee Wee's First Bolt Elaine Chandler and Dillon Williams, 11/87
Island Express Tim Hudgel, Carl Rasmussen and John McMullen, 1986
Good Left Hand John McMullen (solo), 1986

REDEMPTION ROCK
Sobriety Test Mark Rolofson and Elaine Chandler, 11/87

HALF DOME
Tin Can Alley Peter Hubbel, Dave Gottenborg, Sharon Murra and Deaun Schovajsa, 10/87
The Tube Robby Baker and Mike Surkalo, 1972
Party Time Lee Marsh and partner, circa 1976

NODDLE HEAD AREA
FIRST NODDLE HEAD
Sounds of a Desperate Man Maurice Reed and Doug Reed, 1982

SECOND NODDLE HEAD
Spinal Tap Peter Hubbel and Emily Busch, 10/87
Bullets for Bonzo Deaun Schovajsa and Claude Traufield, 10/87
Spinal Block Deaun Schovajsa and Claude Traufield, 10/87

THIRD NODDLE HEAD
Gone with the Wind Maurice Reed and Doug Reed, 1982
Intoxication Maurice Reed and Bruce Sposi, 1982
Once is Enough Maurice Reed and Doug Reed, 1982

New Creations Maurice Reed and Ed Garrity, 1982
Noodle Head Peter Hubbel and Emily Busch, 10/87

FOURTH NODDLE HEAD
Instant Exposure Maurice Reed and Doug Reed, 1982
Flights of Fantasy Ed Brown and Brian Perkins, 1984
Bed Lag Brian Perkins and Carl Perkins, 1984
Green Eggs and Ham Maurice Reed, Bruce Sposi and Ed Garrity, 1982
Die Too High FFA unknown
Too High to Die FFA unknown

DEEP CREEK DOME
On Butterfly Wings Rising Alan Mossiman and Tim Lane, 7/84

JACKSON CREEK AREA
JACKSON CREEK DOME
Creeper Peter Hubbel, Carlie Hubbel, Kit Suddreth and Brian Brown, 6/83
Living in Sin Alan Mosiman and Bill Coffin, 11/78 (South Face Chimney)
Missouri Breaks Chip Wilson and Kit Suddreth

SPIRE ROCK
Pontential FFA unknown
Nutbuster Peter Hubbel and Kit Suddreth, 1983

THE TAJ MAHAL
Standing in a Slide Zone Alan Mosiman, Jerry Harder, and Roger Overby
Pili Pili Steve Holonitch and Alan Mosiman
Chimneychanga Steve Holonitch and Alan Mosiman
Genetic Impressions Lee White and Mike White
West Face Route Dick Woodford and Cecil Ouellette, 1957
Inside Taj Mahal Larry Griffin, Lee Gillman and Sandy Kline

BUFFALO CREEK AREA
HUMPHREY'S DOME
Breaking Wind Peter Hubbel, Sara Brown and Dick VanLandingham, 6/85
Le Promenade Claude Traufield and Sharon Murra, 10/87
Brats in Bondage Dave Gottenborg and Claude Traufield, 10/87
Evening Light Kevin Cooney and Greg Davis, 5/84
Small Talk Kevin Cooney, Greg Davis and Neal Beidleman, 5/84
Small Talk Direct Greg Davis and Paul Meyers, 7/84
Central Chimney FFA unknown, circa 1960's
Sugar Magnolia Robby Baker and Chris Reveley, 1973
Wenches Dihedral Greg Davis and Kevin Cooney, 5/84
Frog Leg Michael Dorsey and Keith Brown, 1984
Squirrel Michael Dorsey and Keith Brown, 1984
Crack Attack Michael Dorsey and Keith Brown, 1984
Nacho Man Dave Gottenborg and Claude Traufield, 10/87
Elsewhere Peter Hubbel, Sara Brown and Dick VanLandingham, 6/85
Cashimoto Peter Hubbel, Sara Brown and Dick VanLandingham, 6/85
Cashimoto Direct Finish (1st pitch) Claude Traufield and Dave Gottenborg, 10/87; (2nd pitch)
    Deaun Schovajsa, Sharon Murra and Peter Hubbel, 10/87

HIDDEN VALLEY AREA
Guano Monster Peter Hubbel and Deaun Schovajsa, 11/87
Tit for Tat Dave Gottenborg and Sharon Murra, 11/87
The Arch Peter Hubbel and Brett Bristol, 9/84
The Cobra Chip Wilson and Jon Hall, 9/84
The Last Hurrah (tr) Rick Dulin, Peter Hubbel, Phil Ayers and Dave Gottenborg, 11/87
Easy Does It Brett Bristol and Peter Hubbel, 9/84
Face Route #425 Peter Hubbel and Brett Bristol, 9/84
Trojan Trauma Peter Hubbel and Brett Bristol, 9/85

GNOME DOME
Fat Head Peter Hubbel and Sharon Murra, 11/87
Leave My Monkey Alone Peter Hubbel and Sharon Murra, 11/87
Fat Freddy's Crack Sharon Murra and Peter Hubbel, 11/87

LITTLE SCRAGGY DOME
Second Thoughts FFA unknown; var. Paul Smith and Mike Leonard, 1974
Let Me Cry FFA unknown, circa 1974
Unnamed Ken Trout, Tom Vanco and Scott Fischer, 1983

ASSHOLE ROCKS
Share in Torn Feet Deaun Schovajsa, Sharon Murra and Peter Hubbel, 10/87
Slim Limbs Akimbo Peter Hubbel, Sharon Murra and Deaun Schovajsa, 10/87
Assholes and Elbows Deaun Schovajsa, Sharon Murra and Peter Hubbel, 10/87
Wild West Show Peter Hubbel, Sharon Murra and Jon Hall, 11/87
Psycho Killer Deaun Schovajsa, Peter Hubbel and Claude Traufield, 12/87
Mister Sol Peter Hubbel, Deaun Schovajsa and Claude Traufield, 11/87
Parallax FFA unknown
Anything Goes FFA unknown
Cardiac Crack Dave Bell and Chris Bell, 8/75
Southern Exposure Dave Bell and Byron Nelson, 10/75
Laughing Stock Mike Griffin and Ed Tobler, 1984
Worst Error Mike Griffin and Ed Tobler, 1984
Inflatulation Tom Bohanon and Dave Gottenborg, 12/87

DA BUTTS ROCKS
Buttkicker Dave Gottenborg and Deaun Schovajsa, 12/87
Roll Dem Bones Claude Traufield, Sharon Murra and Peter Hubbel, 11/87
Ho De Do Peter Hubbel, Deaun Schovajsa and Sharon Murra, 11/87
Dumb De Dumb Dumb 1st pitch Deaun Schovajsa, Peter Hubbel and Sharon Murra, 11/87; 2nd pitch Claude Traufield and Peter Hubbel, 12/87
Nazi's Demise Mark Drier and Gregg Hinnen, 1981
Smegma Burns (1st pitch) Gregg Hinnen and Mark Drier, 1981; (2nd pitch) Claude Traufield, Sharon Murra and Peter Hubbel, 11/87
Hymen Trouble Deaun Schovajsa and Dave Gottenborg, 12/87
Urine Trouble Dave Gottenborg and Deaun Schovajsa, 12/87
Showcase Dave Bell and Allan Pattie, 9/80
Cloudwalk Dave Bell and Byron Nelson, 7/77

REFUGEE ROCK
Kneeknocker Peter Hubbel, Mark Drier and Brian Oliver, 5/82

SKINNER MOUNTAIN
Attitude Adjustment Dave Bell and Chris Bell, 1982
Easy Out Dave Bell and Chris Bell, 1982
Central Corner 1st pitch Ken Trout and Kirk Miller, 1986; 2nd pitch Robby Baker and Peter Prandoni, 1986
Wally World Peter Hubbel, Dave Gottenborg and Claude Traufield, 8/87
Route to Baga 1st pitch Peter Hubbel and Claude Traufield; 2nd pitch Dave Gottenborg and Claude Traufield, 8/87
Eastern Front Lee Marsh and Peter Hubbel, 1986
Vegomatic 1st pitch Dave Gottenborg and Claude Traufield, 8/87; 2nd pitch Claude Traufield and Peter Hubbel, 8/87

GROVEL PIT
Dickin' the Dog Peter Hubbel and Lee Marsh, 11/86
Bonehead Lee Marsh and Peter Hubbel, 11/86
Compressor Peter Hubbel and Lee Marsh, 11/86
Matrix Lee Marsh and Peter Hubbel, 11/86

WIGWAM CREEK AREA
LITTLE WIGWAM DOME
Sloe Moe   Peter Hubbel and Sharon Murra, 11/87
Why Me?   Ken Trout and Brian Ferguson, 1982

ROCK ISLAND
Choulnard-Beckey Route   Phil Ayers, Peter Hubbel and Dan McGee, 1983

BEARTOOTH SPIRE
Rovin' Hoser   Joe Huggins and Kyle Copeland, 1985
Just Like a Virgin   George Watson and Steve Ilg, 1986

WIGWAM DOME
Wunsch Simulator   Ken Trout and Eric Winkelman, 1984
Turbo Betty   Charlie Fowler, Joe Huggins and Dan Mannix, 1985
Teepee Tower Cracks   Ken Trout and Eric Winkelman, 1984
T.B. Buttress   Ken Trout and Robby Baker, 1984; (direct finish) Noel Childs, Strappo Hughes, and
    Michelle Baur, 1987
Pow Wow Canal   Ken Trout, Robby Baker, Peter Prandoni and Kirk Miller, 1985
El Supremo   Ken Trout, Kirk Miller and Rob Baker; (4th pitch var) Rob Baker and Peter Prandoni, 1985
Violent Energy   Mark Rolofson and Tom Englebach, 4/86
Ramblin' Rose   Ken Trout, Brian Hansen and Kirk Miller, 1986
Lady Slipper   Ken Trout, Kirk Miller and Scott Vischer, 1986
Lord of the Flies   Steve Brodhead, George Watson and Gene Ellis, 1986
Trail of Tears   Kyle Copeland, John McMullen and Marc Hirt, 1985

THE SUN
Halogen Angels   John McMullen and Greg Johnston, 1985
Machination   John McMullen and Greg Johnston, 1985
Sketch Book   Charlie Fowler and Kyle Copeland, 1986
Better Lock Next Time   Kyle Copeland and Marc Hirt, 1985

THE MOON
One Small Step   Kyle Copeland and Marc Hirt, 1985
Lunar Kreep   John McMullen, Kyle Copeland and Marc Hirt, 1985
Luna-Sea   Kyle Copeland, Marc Hirt and John McMullen, 1985
Dark Side of the Moon   John McMullen and Kyle Copeland, 1985

WIGWAM TOWER
Ziegler/Doane/Kuglin Route
Pow Wow Prow   Doug Werme and V.J. Valente, 1985
Cap Rock Spire Gary Ziegler, Bob Doane, and Gary Boucher, 1962
Teeter Totter   Doug Werme and V.J. Valente, 1985
White Snake   Doug Werme and Cheryl Stomps, 1986
Lady Liberty   Doug Werme and Cheryl Stomps, 7/86

KEYSTONE BUTTRESS
Left Keystone Crack   Doug Werme and Cheryl Stomps, 1986
Right Keystone Crack   Bob Grundy, et al., 1985
A Snake on the Side   Doug Werme and V.J. Valente, 1985

BIG ROCK AREA
LITTLE CRAGS
The Crack of Life   Charlie Fowler, Joe Huggins, Dan Mannix and John Gills, circa 1986

HELEN'S DOME/SHEEP ROCK
Slightly Sloping   Greg DeWitt and Bill Anders, 1983
Howler   Greg DeWitt and Bill Anders, 1983

HELEN'S DOME
Moss Toss Dave Bell and Allan Pattie, 9/82
On the Bus Pete Williams and Keith Shoeptlin, 1982
Electric Koolaid Acid Test Keith Shoeptlin and Pete Williams, 1982
Borderline Boulevard Dave Bell and Mark Johnson, 8/81
Buffalo Tears Ken Trout and Dave Dunblazier, 1981
Buffalo Soldier Ken Trout and Dave Dunblazier, 1981
Beam Me Up Scotty Dave Dunblazier, Paul Braun, David Heinz, David Kozak and Ken Trout, 1983
Fools Gold Dave Bell, Chris Bell and Byron Nelson, 9/82; direct variation Egan and Hankins, 1985
Face Value Peter Hubbel and Dave Bell, 1981
Face Value Direct Dave Bell and Chris Bell, 1981
Solid Gold FFA unknown
Spree Dave Dunblazier and Cathy Bright, 1984
Pebble Beach Dave Dunblazier and partner, circa 1981

BABY HELEN
Leapin' Lizards David Kozak and Eric Boelke, 1984
Schizosphere Dave Dunblazier and Cathy Bright, 1985
Strange Attractor Dave Dunblazier and Cathy Bright, 1985
Twisted Laurel Dave Dublazier and Cathy Bright, 1985
Honk if You Love Climbing Dave Kozak and Eric Boelke, 1984

ACID ROCK
Scary Monsters David Kozak and Eric Boelke, 6/83
Four Eyes Ken Trout and Kirk Miller, 1978
Sandinista Dave Dunblazier and Paul Braun, 1985
Charlie Don't Surf Leonard Coyne and Ed Russell, 1977
The Divine Miss M David Kozak and Eric Boelke, 8/83
Erotic Plants Eric Boelke and David Kozak, 1983
Rap Route unknown

SHEEP ROCK
Smile for the Camel Mike Heartz, late 1970s
Route 1 Joe O'Laughlin and Steve Turner, 8/68
Acid Crack Ken Trout et al, 1973
Sheep Just Wanna Have Fun Dave Dunblazier and Cathy Bright, 1985
Velcro Strip Dan McGee, Ken Trout and Lynn Fletcher, 1984
Howler unknown
CMC Route John Sudar and Dick Yeatts, 1970
Tour de Platte Ken Trout and Kirk Miller, 1986

RAINY DAY ROCK
Crackola Peter Hubbel and Brian Oliver, 1980
Crackola Direct Diana Bailey and Marty Alfred, 1985
Natural Disaster Noel Childs, Chris Lange, Jerry Rock and Tim Johnson, 7/87
Toad Strangler Ken Trout and Kirk Miller, 12/86
Buffalo Bullion Kirk Miller and Ken Trout, 12/86
7-Up Peter Hubbel and Brian Oliver, 1980
8-Up Bruce Burnell and Marty Alfred, 1985
Never Had it Never Will Marty Alfred, Jim Karn, Dan McGee and Bruce Burnell, 1985
Shinola Bruce Burnell, Marty Alfred, and Jim Karn, 1985
Shits and Grins Marty Alfred, Bruce Burnell, and Jim Karn, 1985

THE COUCH POTATOES
Potato Peel Ken Trout and Mike Carr, 1987
Crash Diet Ken Trout, Kirk Miller and Rusty Kirkpatrick, 1987
Power Loungers Rusty Kirkpatrick, Ken Trout and Kirk Miller, 1987
Thunder Thigh Ken Trout and Marv Porter, 1986
Sweat Therapy Carr and Ken Trout
Potato Pancakes Ken Trout and Kirk Miller, 1986

No Mistake or Pancake Tripp Gordon and partner, 1987
Gong with the Wind Lee Marsh and Steve Brodhead, 9/87

THE FLAGSHIP
Bong for Glory Peter Hubbel, Claude Traufield and Lee Marsh, 8/87
Sorcerer's Apprentice Peter Hubbel, Deaun Schovajsa and Claude Traufield, 5/87

RENAISSANCE SLAB
Electrocutioner's Song Claude Traufield and Peter Hubbel, 1987
Hold On Lucy Deaun Schovajsa and Jon Hall, 5/87
Positron Peter Hubbel and Claude Traufield, 5/87
Harmonic Convergence Dave Gottenborg, Claude Traufield and Peter Hubbel, 8/87; var. (tr) Phil
   Ayers and Rich Dulin, 1986
Wood Nymph Peter Hubbel, Emily Busch and Claude Traufield, 1987
UMC Phil Ayers, Rick Dulin and Dave Gottenborg, 1987
Moribund Rick Dulin, Phil Ayers and Dave Gottenborg, 1987
Sideshow Dave Gottenborg, Claude Traufield and Peter Hubbel, 8/87

SUNSHINE DOME
French Curve Ken Trout and Kirk Miller, 1986
Heart of Darkness Noel Childs and Kirk Miller, 1987
Shining Path Ken Trout, Kirk Miller, David Kozak and Peter Prandoni, 1986
Tree Route (1st pitch) Maurice Reed and Mike Endicott, 1983
Sunshine Route Ken Trout and Kirk Miller, 1985
Original Earl Wiggins and Rob Fricke, fall 1974. **Narrow Escape** Steve Cheyney and Earl Wiggins,
   fall 74
Sunrise Ridge Steve Cheyney and Earl Wiggins, 1974
Easy Sun Mark Rolofson and Leonard Coyne, 7/75

LONGWATER DOME
Barracuda Roger and Bill Briggs, 6/86

BIG ROCK CANDY MOUNTAIN
Rotten Teeth Peter Gallagher and Peter Williams, circa 1984
The Original Route Don Doucette and Earl Wiggins, 1975
Hot Ice Cream unknown
The Original Route Don Doucette and Earl Wiggins, 1975?
Fields of Dreams Growing Wild Peter Gallagher and Peter Williams, 1979
Childhood's End Ken Trout, Eric Winkleman and Brian Hanson, with help from Robby Baker and
   Kirk Miller, 1984
Sweet Catastrophe (Bum Drop) Peter Williams and Peter Gallagher, 1980. FFA Chuck Grossman
   and Alan Hill, 1986
Petered Out Peter Williams and Peter Gallagher, 1980

TURKEY ROCK AREA
SHEEP'S NOSE
Ten Years After FFA Leonard Coyne, Dennis Jackson, and Mark Rolofson, 12/75
Seamis FFA unknown **Time to Space** Pete Croff and Mark Rolofson, 2/76
Chinook Peter Gallagher and Bob D'Antonio, 1982
Evening Stroll unknown
Hard Monkeys unknown
Harpoon the Mantaray unknown
Psycho Babble Bob D'Antonio and Mark Rolofson, 2/83
Jah Sport Harrison Dekker and Mark Rolofson, 2/83
Sheep with a Silver Tail unknown
Sheer Sheep Attack Bob D'Antonio and Bob Robertson, 1982
5.9 Dihedral unknown
An Apostle or Two Kevin Murray, Steve Cheyney, Bob Robertson and Peter Gallagher, 1982
The Arch unknown
Old Man Route unknown
Leaning Corner unknown

The Pimp unknown
Space Cadet Bob D'Antonio, 4/81
For Wimps Only Bob D'Antonio and Bob Robertson, 4/81
Lost in Space Direct Ed Lynch and John Pease, 1974
Friction unknown
Sparse unknown
Virgin Wool unknown
100% Wool unknown
Golden Fleece unknown
When Sheep are Nervous unknown
When Sheep are Safe unknown
Ozone Variation Brian Teale, Leonard Coyne and Ed Bailey, 1976
The Men from Wyoming unknown
Assassination Slab Bob Robertson and Peter Gallagher, 1984
Sheep and Wolves Clothing unknown
Lamb's Prey unknown
Direct Line unknown
Sheep's Dare Ed Russell and John Myers, 1978
Mr. Salty and the Crunch Crowd Ed Russell and Art Wiggens, 1978
Complications Bob D'Antonio and Bob Robertson, 8/81
Army Route the army?
Puppy Pee unknown

TURKEY ROCK – South Face
Direct Hit Pete Croff, John Hall and Steve Cheyney, 9/75
Southern Comfort Kurt Rasmussen and Steve Cheyney, 1972
Beginners Route unknown
Route 902 Doug Snively, Steve Cheyney and Steve Jones, 8/72
Northern Comfort Pete Croff, John Hall and Steve Cheyney, 9/75
Little Feat Kurt Rasmussen, 1972
Dash and Thrangle unknown
Messner's Delight Kurt Rasmussen and Steve Cheyney, 1973
Gobbler's Grunt Skip Hamilton and Steve Cheyney, early 70s
Second Coming Chuck Behrensmeyer and Jim White, early 70s
Safety Buffalo Leonard Coyne, Dennis Jackson and Ed Russell, 1978
Spring Turkey Richard Aschert and Bob Robertson, 1986
Turkey Shoot FA Don Doucette, Art Howells and Mike Dudley, early 1970s. FFA John Sherwood,
   Gary Garriet, 1975
Turkey's Dare Brian Teale and Dan Morrison, 1976
Glen's Pancake unknown
Nightime Madness unknown
Turkey's Forever unknown
Chopping Block Chuck Behrensmeyer and Molly Higgins, early 1970s
Pillar Variation unknown
Jump Start unknown
Vanishing Point Earl Wiggins and Steve Cheyney, 1975
Stewart's Crack unknown
Manimal One unknown
Great White Crime Bryan Becker, Brian Teale and Steve Cheyney, 1977
Satyr's Asshole Dean Tschappat and Don Doucette, early 1970s
Straw Turkey unknown
Brain Cramps unknown
The Eastern Front unknown
The Fiend John Sherwood and Don Doucette, 1970s
No Block Route unknown
Hallucinogenic Blues unknown
Uncle John unknown
Little Eddie Webster's Little Overhang Ed Webster and Kevin Murray, 4/78
Big Edward's Big Overhang Ed Webster et al
Casual Elegance unknown
Turkey Shit unknown

Mariposa unknown
Mad Max Mark Rolofson and John Allen, 6/81
Mad Max Direct John Allen, 6/81
Finger Crack unknown
Curving Crack Variation unknown
The Naked Edge Steve Hong and Steve Cheyney, late 1970s
The Roof unknown
Rastafarian Mark Rolofson and Mark Van Horn, 6/81
Finger Lickin' Good Earl Wiggins and Steve Cheyney, 1975
Wild Fire Mark Rolofson and Ed Russell, 6/77
Pullett Surprise unknown
Close to the Edge Steve Hong?
The Upside Down Jumping Whale unknown
Shear Shark Attack John Allen, 6/81
Wellflare Mark Rolofson and Greg Collins, 8/81
The Go Between Dale Goddard, 1986
Tofonareeker unknown
Dogs of Furniture Andy Parkin and Mark Rolofson, 4/82
Dogs of Furniture (var.) Jonny Woodward, 1986
Slab Center Pete Williams, 1983
History Lesson Dale Goddard, 1986
Mobius Trip Steve Cheyney, 1978
Look Ma, No Hands unknown
The Unic Horn unknown
The Golden Crack unknown

THE LEFTOVERS
Hang Ten unknown
Hang Twenty unknown
Chicken Legs unknown
Reptilian Wall unknown
Too Much Turkey Mark Milligan and Brent Kertzman, 1986
Captain Fist unknown
Too Much Crack Earl Wiggins and John Sherwood
The Throat unknown
Ding unknown
Dong unknown
Wild Cherry unknown
Flake Crack unknown
Alive n' Kickin' Leonard Coyne and Mark Rolofson, 1976
Temperature's Rising Pete Croff, Leonard Coyne and Mark Rolofson, 2/76

TURKEY PERCH
Bloody Englishmen unknown
Liquid Acrobat (tr) Leonard Coyne, 1978; (first lead) Steve Hong, 1980
5.6 Chimney unknown
Sangaphogos Dennis Jackson and Spanky, 1/76
Reefer Madness Dennis Jackson and Spanky, 1/76
Mark of Zorro unknown
Ragger Bagger Dennis Jackson and Spanky, 1/76
Gobble Up unknown
Stiff Little Fingers unknown
Steppenwolf unknown
Cold Turkey unknown
Moderate Cracks unknown
Honky Jam Ass Crack unknown
Left Handed Jew unknown
The Gobbler's Cobbler Steve Cheyney et al
Sandpiper Box Greg Collins and Mark Rolofson, 1982
Liberty Lady Greg Collins, 1982

TURKEY TAIL – South Face

Piece of Cake Jim Dunn and Ajax Greene, 1977
Vegetable unknown
Bald Turkey Peter Gallagher and Bob Robertson, 1982
Bitchin' Hot Mineral Neil Parker and Dave Finley, 6/81
The Flakes unknown
Dark Meat unknown
Turkey's Delight unknown
Rasmussen's Crack Kurt Rasmussen, early 1970s
Hummingbird Way (Snively's Crack) Doug Snively, 1973
Wild Turkey Jim Dunn and Chris Wood, 8/75
I Turkey Mark Sonnefield, Bill Myers, and John Steiger, 1986.
Whimsical Dreams Jim Dunn and Brian Teale, 5/75
Dekker Route Harrison Dekker, 1984
In Search of Unicorns Ed Webster, 1977
Wudamudafuka Jim Dunn and Chris Wood, 8/75
For Turkeys Only Jim Dunn and Bryan Becker, 10/75
Drumstick Direct unknown
Second Helpings Ed Webster and Steve Hong, 11/76
Turkey's Turd Jim Dunn and John Hall, 5/75
Squeeze Chimney unknown
Brush Turkey Bob Roberson and Harvey Miller, 1986. First top-roped by Harrison Dekker in 1984.
Jello Party Harrison Dekker, 1983
Spider Lady unknown
Sidewinder Jim Dunn and Steve Cheyney, 1/73
Wisecrack John Bachar et al, 1978
Snake Jim Dunn and Steve Cheyney, 1/73
Wishful Thinking Kurt Rasmussen and Jim Dunn, 6/75
Future Chic Charlie Fowler, 4/87
Hong Out Steve Hong et al
Journey to Ixtlan FFA Leonard Coyne, Peter Mayfield and Henry Lester, 1978
Rufus FFA Jim Dunn and Leonard Coyne, 1977
Beauty and the Beast John Allen, 6/81; 2nd pitch by Mark Rolofson and Allen
Double Trouble unknown
Turkey in the Straw unknown
Cheap Trick Mark Rolofson and Russ Clune, 7/80
5.6 Easy Offwidth unknown
5.9 Face unknown
Easy Crack unknown
East Side Story unknown
Camera Obscura Ed Webster, Ed Russel and Leonard Coyne, 1976
Inner Reaches Dennis Jackson, Mark Rolofson and Leonard Coyne, 10/75
The Flies Have Found Me Dennis Jackson and Kurt Gray, 6/78
Inner Sanctum Mark Rolofson and Leonard Coyne, 1975
Eclipse Dennis Jackson, Earl Wiggins, Steve Cheyney and Dave Schultz, 1975
Termination Dennis Jackson and Chris Wood, 1976
Live Fire unknown
Acoplopse unknown
Fuzzy Caterpillar unknown
Consternation unknown
The Chop unknown
Quivering Quill Jim Dunn and Earl Wiggins, 7/72

THE RIGHTOVERS

Sweet Turkey Brian Delaney and Jim Dunn, 4/77
Onassis' Crack Jim Dunn and Doug Snively, 10/75
Excellent Crack unknown
Easy Corner unknown
Flake Out Ed Russell and Leonard Coyne, late 1970s
Brown Sugar Leonard Coyne and Mark Rolofson, 1975
Scraggles unknown

Left Y Crack Bob D'Antonio, 1980
Back to the Zodiac Mark Rolofson and Eric Guerrein, 3/80
The Infraction Dale Goddard and Will Gadd, 1986
The Arsehole Kevin Murray and Jim Dunn, 7/75
Grunt n' Groan Mark Rolofson and Mark Van Horn, 6/81
Turkey Toot unknown

TARRYALL AREA
McCURDY PARK TOWER
Numb Nuts L. Gillman and Chris DePuy, 7/72
Born Free L. Bucholz and S. Robbins, 7/72
Wings Alan Mosiman and C. Winger, 9/81
Notch Route G. Parish and L. Griffin, 5/71
Notch Chimneys M. White and J. Todd, 5/71
Mountaineer's Route M. Lerner, G. Parish and L. Griffin, 5/71
Recon Direct R. Anderson and L. Griffin, 7/73
Sunshine Ridge R. Anderson and L. Griffin, 7/73
West Bulge J. Hajny and M. White, 7/71
Tower Recon S. Kline and L. Griffin, 5/70
The Nose J. Gingrich and B. Wehman, 7/73
Blockbuster L. Griffin, J. Berry and M. Berry, 7/72
Praying Nun J. Griffin and L. Griffin, 7/72
Intimidation S. Kline and A. Gordon, 5/71
Layback G. Baron and K. Lindquist, 5/71
Andersonville R. Anderson and L. Griffin, 7/73

TWIN ROCKS
Wild Raspberries unknown
Wild Raspberries (var.) unknown
Middle Crack unknown
Main Dihedral unknown
Flesh Grinder unknown
Growing in Size unknown
Horizontal Bop unknown

Mark Rolofson, Men at Work, North Gateway   Dan McQuade

GARDEN
OF THE GODS

Rising out of the foothills on the northwest side of Colorado Springs – between the city and Pike's Peak – are a group of soft sandstone monoliths known as the Garden of the Gods. This geologic wonder is one of Colorado's major tourist attractions. Owned and maintained by the city of Colorado Springs and located just minutes from downtown, the Garden offers convenient access for a fast climb after work or school. The approaches are usually only a few hundred feet from the car. Watching climbers is a popular part of the tourist attraction, and escaping the crowds present is in part the challenge of climbing here during the summer tourist season.

The Garden is a small climbing area, but highly developed, with over 220 routes and 68 years of climbing history. The protection is predominantly fixed and usually secure. A rack of quickdraws will oftentimes suffice. Several summits can only be attained via fifth class climbing routes though the larger monoliths have scrambling routes that lead to their summits.

The rock features are composed of two types of sandstone, Lyons Formation and Fountain Formation. North Gateway, South Gateway, and Keyhole Rock are composed of Lower Lyons Formation, a fine- grained, red sandstone. The middle section of the west face of South Gateway is composed of Fountain Formation, as are several of the free-standing spires. Fountain Formation is a coarse-grained sandstone with small pebbles embedded in it. Kindergarten Rock consists of Upper Lyons Formation and contains limestone ribs, making for sharp, incut holds.

The nature of the climbing varies dramatically in character, from the smooth friction climbs on the Drug Wall of South Gateway to slightly overhanging faces on sharp holds found on Kindergarten Rock. Most of the area's rock can be thought of as being slightly loose in comparison with almost any other established climbing area. Many handholds are reasonably solid but some loose holds are encountered and often used. Looseness in the Garden is usually not in the form of big, dangerous, loose blocks, but rather in the form of small, thin, fragile flakes that disintegrate to sand when pulled off. These flakes are usually not the size, shape, or weight to injure someone standing at the base of the rock. Naturally, some dangerous-sized loose blocks do exist and require extra care and delicate use. Much of the climbing in the Garden is found on steep faces with fragile, exfoliated flakes varying in their size and soundness. These flakes are generally small and the climber must learn to pull down and not out on such holds. These delicate routes are subject to change if they become popular. Many climbs are on vertical faces with small solution pockets and/or large potholes. The soft rock takes a little getting used to. Climbers who are capable of climbing 5.12 on solid rock may find some of the Garden's 5.8 and 5.9 routes to be horrifying. Not all routes suffer from a looseness, however; superb, nearly flawless rock is occasionally found.

The protection is another feature that is somewhat unique about this area. Most climbs are protected by drilled angle pitons and not regular construction bolts. Early pioneer Harvey T. Carter first developed this technique in the 1950s. He would drill a ⅝" hole about 3 or 4 inches deep. Into this he would hammer a sawed-off army angle. This was left as fixed protection, just as bolts are left fixed. The drilled angle has since become the standard form of fixed protection because of its reliability and safety. Chouinard hard steel angle pitons work, but soft iron pitons work better since they mold into the hole more securely. Occasionally a drilled angle will be found to stick out from the surface and should be tied off.

On some routes conventional ⅜" bolts will be found. These can be safe even though some loosen up in the hole. They are never as trustworthy as a drilled angle. In the aid climbing era of the 1960s ¼" bolts were often used, though their utility is, at best, limited to holding body weight.

Often potholes will form tunnels or bridges that can be threaded with slings to offer natural protection. If the bridge being threaded is more than a few inches in diameter it is generally reliable protection. Occasionally nuts or Friends can be cammed inside a pothole; Hexes and Tri-cams work well in most placements.

Routes that follow deep, continuous cracks take nuts and Friends easily. Small wired nuts can only be trusted, at best, for short falls. If the rock is sound, medium to large nuts or Friends can be reliable; some have held falls as long as 15 feet.

RULES AND REGULATIONS

The Garden of the Gods Park is administered by the Parks and Recreation Department of the city of Colorado Springs. Access to the climbing resource the park provides has, at various times, been challenged by those in city government. Fortunately, a compromise with those who would like to ban all climbing has been worked out, and the following guidelines, printed verbatim, should be respected by all visiting climbers.

RULES AND GUIDELINES FOR TECHNICAL ROCK CLIMBING
IN THE GARDEN OF THE GODS
Section 1 – Rules

1. For the purposes of these rules and regulations, rock climbing shall be defined as follows (18-5-105 of the Code of the City of Colorado Springs, 1980, as amended):

"Subsection B. Rock Climbing
1. Definitions:
   a. Rock scrambling is defined as climbing on a rock formation more than 10 feet above the valley floor, or base of the rock formation, without using proper equipment.
   b. Technical climbing is defined as climbing on a rock formation in parties of two or more, using proper equipment, which equipment shall, as a minimum, consist of:
      (1) A perlon or laid rope specifically designed and manufactured for use in climbing or mountaineering and which meet minimum Union International Alpinist Association Standards which standards as they presently exist or may hereafter by amended, are hereby incorporated by reference; and,
      (2) Carabiners to clip into the fixed protection (piton previously placed in the rock) or an assortment of artificial chock stones or pitons to adequately protect the leader's ascent, and allow the climb to be safely seconded.
2. Rock scrambling is prohibited in Garden of the Gods Park and North Cheyenne Canon Park.
3. Technical climbing is permitted in Garden of the Gods Park and North Cheyenne Canon Park except in areas posted by the Director (of Park and Recreation) as non-technical climbing areas."

2. All persons desiring to engage in technical rock climbing in the Garden of the Gods Park shall register with the Colorado Springs Park and Recreation Department. Registration shall be by mail or in person, at either the garden of the Gods' Visitor Center or Park and Recreation Headquarters. Climbers will be required to sign a "Rules and Guidelines" sheet, acknowledging they have read and understand the conditions governing climbing in the park.
3. The activity of bouldering (also called low traversing) shall be prohibited on the formations know as Sentinel Rock and Twin Spires.
4. The activity of sport rappelling shall be banned from all areas of the park. "Sport Rappelling" is defined as that activity of hiking or walking to the top or edge of any rock formation and rappelling downward. Rappelling in the park shall only be performed in conjunction with ascents by technical climbing.
5. The use of white chalk in conjunction with technical climbing shall be prohibited.
6. Only rust-colored slings (webbing) may be left on any rock surface.

Section 2 – Guidelines for Voluntary Compliance

1. The Park and Recreation Department will be undertaking a three-to-five-year scientific study on the effects, if any, of technical rock climbing in the Garden of the Gods. This study will address such issues as the geological, environmental, and aesthetic influences of various patron uses and activities on the ecology of the Garden, and appropriate long-term recommendations should any be necessary. As the Department prepares to enter into this study period, it would request specific voluntary compliance from technical climbers in the following two areas:
    A. Part of the proposed study will be an evaluation of the impact of technical climbing on the nesting habits of the White Throated Swift and Prairie Falcon. It is requested that climbers not disturb nests and known nesting areas of these two bird species, particularly on the formation called "Tower of Babel" and climbing route New Era.
    B. The study will also evaluate the fixed protection situation as it currently exists in the Garden. The Department requests that climbers refrain from placing additional protection items (pitons, expansion bolts, etc.) into the rock surface unless absolutely necessary for safety reasons.
2. It is requested that climbers schedule, plan, and conduct their climbs between the hours of dawn and dusk. Though it is recognized that some climbs may not end until after nightfall due to unexpected difficulties, the Park and Recreation Department strongly discourages any climbers from deliberately planning night or "moonlight" climbs in the Garden.
3. Climbers are advised that immediate climbing after rain, snow, or freezing temperatures may unnaturally hasten deterioration of rock surfaces. Participants are asked to refrain from climbing any formation that appears visibly wet or in a frosted condition.

Section 3 – Penalties

1. The failure of any climber to abide by the rules promulgated in Section 1 above shall be subject, upon conviction, to a maximum five hundred dollar ($500.00) fine, loss of climbing privileges for twelve (12) months, or both.

To reiterate, registration is required for all climbing in the Garden of the Gods, no bouldering is allowed, only chalk that matches the rock is permitted, and only rust-colored slings may be left at rappel sights.

The rock of the Garden is softer than just about any other established climbing area found in the United States. Most climbers will find this takes some getting used to. Some routes that harbor particularly loose and friable flakes, combined with runout protection may be noted as such with the route information. **The route descriptions may not state the exact rock conditions that you may find on the route. Once on the rock, you are on your own. Your judgement is your sole protection.**

THE CONDITIONS

Heavy rains and wet snow can leave the rock damp and fragile for up to a week afterwards. Climbers should let the condition of the rock decide whether to climb here. The soft rock actually absorbs and holds moisture (much like mud) after extended bad weather.

Noticeably damp rock should not be climbed on because the rock is more easily damaged in such conditions. It is also much less enjoyable climbing. If you respect the rock, stay off it when it is wet.

Wet conditions are most common in the spring, after weeks of wet snow or rain, though they can exist any time. Fall and winter are commonly noted for dry conditions. Cold winter snowstorms leave little moisture on the rock and pose no problem a couple of sunny days later.

ETHICS

This guide book is not designed to tell you what style you must climb in, but some ethics that affect climbers that come after you are particularly important since this area is already highly developed.

Don't add any drilled angles or bolts to climbs that have previously been climbed without them. On some climbs old manky bolts may need replacing. Remember to always remove the old bolt and redrill the old hole for reuse. This is a job best left to the experienced local climbers.

Don't chop bolts. Leave the fixed protection in place.

Don't take a hammer, chisel, et cetera to create a handhold. The whole idea is to climb the rock by means of its natural weaknesses such as face edges, potholes, solution pockets and cracks. On first ascents, some cleaning of very loose rock is common. Sometimes loose flakes are removed constructively to create a sharp edge for a handhold. Blatant chiseling into sound rock is never acceptable.

Don't litter. Remove all your trash and don't leave it on the route or on the ground. This includes cigarette butts and pieces of tape.

First ascents should be made only by those most experienced in the harder routes in the Garden. Placing bolts should only be done by those who are experts. Aid climbing and obnoxious bolt ladders are things of the past. New bolted free climbs should respect the lines of existing routes; squeezed-in lines are aesthetically offensive.

Spray painting on the rocks is ugly, unnecessary, and illegal.

Climb clean. There is no reason to carry pitons to place and remove on any free climb in the Garden. Nuts, Friends, runners, and fixed protection suffice on all existing routes. In fact, about 90 percent of the protection in the area is fixed.

Bothering wildlife or damaging foliage in any way is one of the most grievous offences.

ACKNOWLEDGEMENTS

The author would like to thank the following people who helped immeasurably in the compiling of the route information, not only for the Garden of the Gods, but for the Turkey Rock and Big Rock areas. Fred Aschert, Richard Aschert, Steve Cheyney, Leonard Coyne, Will Gadd, Peter Gallagher, Dale Goddard, Bob Robertson, Ken Trout, and Ed Webster.

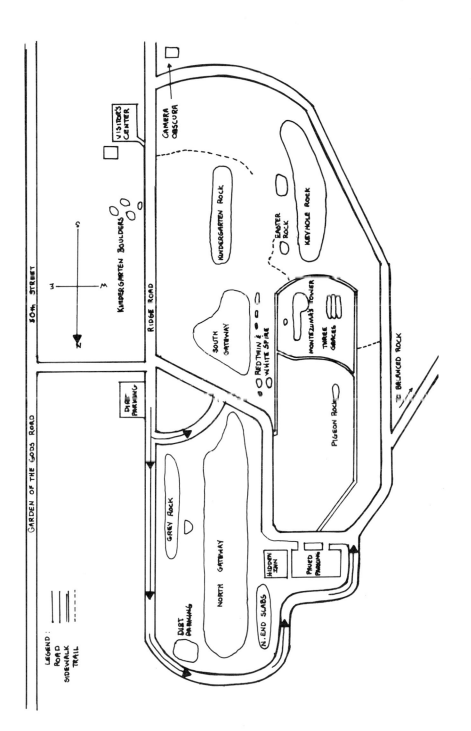

NORTH GATEWAY ROCK

This formation is composed of red, lower Lyons Formation sandstone. At 350 feet high, it is the largest butte in the Garden. The many routes lead to many different locations and summits on the rock. On the northwest end is the Tower of Babel. Just east of this tower are two other towers known as Middle and End Towers. A prominent summit window near the south end is the Kissing Camels, a popular tourist attraction.

DESCENT ROUTES: The two main descent routes off North Gateway Rock are the Tourist Gully and the East Ledges. The East Ledges start at the south end of the east face and work upward toward the north end, ending at Hidden Valley. This hidden terrace is on the back side of the Tower of Babel, Middle Tower, and End Tower. From Hidden Valley it is possible to rappel 150 feet down the east face from a large eye-bolt.

The Tourist Gully runs diagonally along the southwest face, the "Finger Face", to a large ledge on the upper east face. It is possible to follow this ledge north and find a way to the summit area. The Tourist Gully also connects up with the East Ledges near the summit of North Gateway. A series of chopped steps connect the 40 feet between the two ledges, making it possible to descend the Tourist Gully rather than taking the East Ledges. The East Ledges are a more dangerous descent; they are quite narrow in some places and can be icy in winter.

North Gateway Girdle Traverse   V 5.11 R   ★★★   The route starts by climbing all of **Anaconda.** Then downclimb the South Ridge of the Tower of Babel. Traverse south on Hollywood Ledge for several hundred feet to the top of the **Borgoff's Blunder** bolt ladder. downclimb this pitch! Back climb **Pete and Bob's — Borgoff's Blunder** link up. Then climb **Pete and Bob's** to North gateway's Summit. Now descend the Tourist Gully to the end of **Psychic Grandma.** Reverse **Psychic Grandma** to **Tidrick's** and ascend that route to its end. Descend **Boucher's Chimney** and scramble up along the East Ledges to Hidden Valley and the base of the South Ridge to the Tower of Babel. The **Girdle Traverse** ends here, unless you care to for for another lap.

Plus Four Crack   5.9 ★ At the top of the Tourist Gully a large ledge leads north. Above the ledge is a prominent offwidth crack. The crux is the overhanging start. At a roof 20 feet up, it is possible to either go left (5.5) or right (5.8) with hand jams. Some nuts are useful for the 5.8 finish.

NORTH GATEWAY ROCK – East Face

A Max's Mayhem   5.10– ★ loose   pro: #6 stopper to #11 hex

B-C Suggles-Fall Crack   5.8+ ★★

B Snuggles   5.8 ★   lieback/jam

C Fall Crack   5.8+ ★   offwidth

D Peterson's Crack   5.9 R ★   pro thin to #11 hex

E Boucher-Twombly Route   5.6 ★   It is illegal to climb over the Kissing Camels, at the top.

F Span Man   5.9

G Angle Tangle   5.7 A2   The second pitch goes free at loose 5.9.

Descent: An 80-foot free rappel leads from the top of Fall Crack to the east Ledges. If the slings through the tunnel thread should be missing, another descent is possible. Walk to the south end of the ledge and mantle on to a small pillar. Move onto the southwest face and follow a narrow ledge north. A few easy moves end on an exposed summit. Downclimb a short ridge to a large enclosed ledge. Walk north and rappel 60 feet down Boucher's Chimney to the East Ledges.

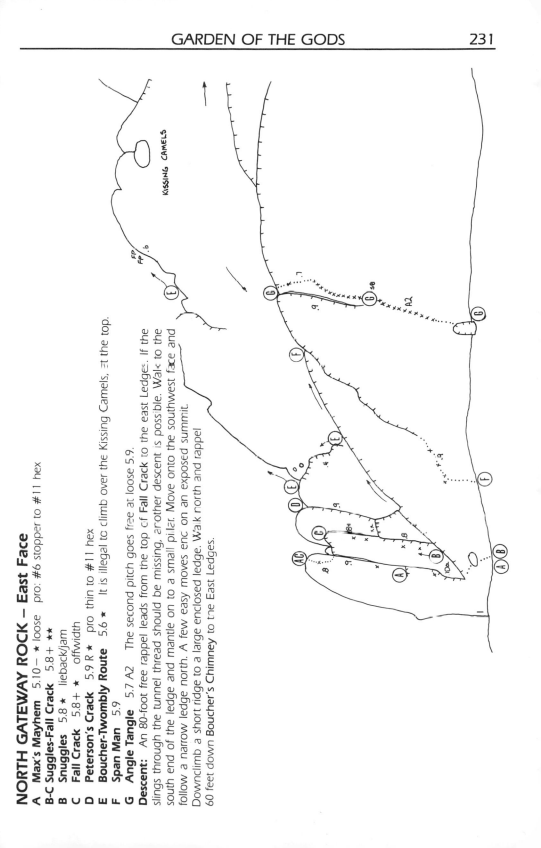

B

MIDDLE TOWER

C

TOWER OF BABEL

END TOWER

A

NORTH GATEWAY ROCK – North End

Mark Rolofson

A **North End Chimney**   5.6 or 5.7 R   ★   Both starts are shown.
B **Triple Exposure**   5.12c/d A0   ★★   pro: many QDs and #4 Friend for pitch 1. 2:
  #5 RPs and a #9 stopper. Pitch 3: #2-3½ Friends and #9-12 stoppers. Hanging belay.
C **Anaconda**   5.11   ★★★   pro: full rack of nuts, from a #5 RP to a set of Friends to a #4.

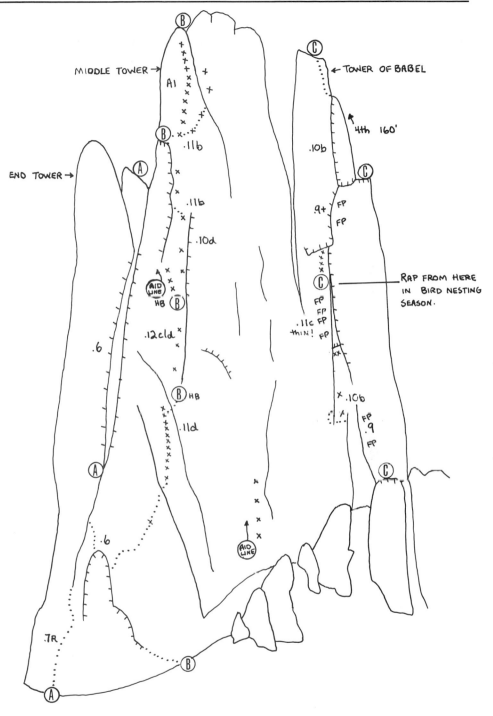

MIDDLE TOWER →

A1

.11b

END TOWER →

.11b

.10d

AID LINE

HB

.12cld

HB

.6

.11d

A

.6

.7R

B

A

B

TOWER OF BABEL

4th 160'

.10b

.9+ FP

FP

RAP FROM HERE
IN BIRD NESTING
SEASON.

FP
FP

.11c FP
thin! FP

xx

.10b

FP
.9
FP

AID LINE

NORTH GATEWAY ROCK – North End

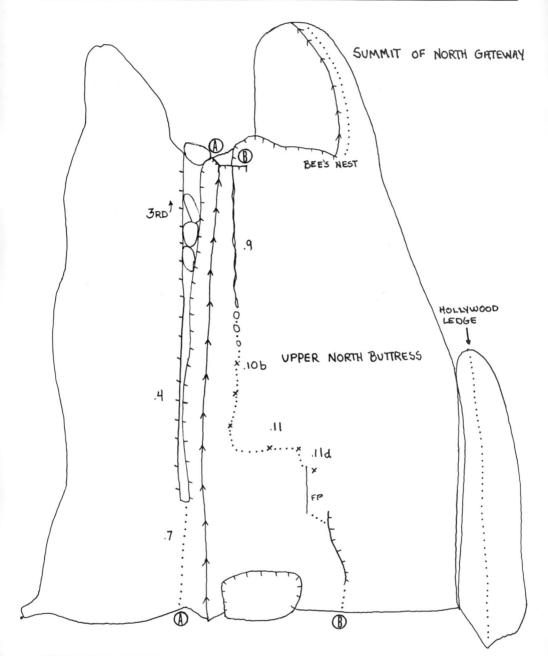

SUMMIT OF NORTH GATEWAY

BEE'S NEST

3RD

.9

HOLLYWOOD LEDGE

.4

X .10b

UPPER NORTH BUTTRESS

.11

X .11d

FP

.7

Ⓐ

Ⓑ

HIDDEN VALLEY

This hidden terrace is tucked between the Tower of Babel, Middle Tower, and End Tower.

A Tourist Trap Gully 5.7   Some nuts could be useful. Tourists who have tried to descend the gully from the summit of North Gateway are greeted by a smooth wall at the bottom and and soon discover that the chimney that they managed to slither down isn't so easy to scramble up.

B The Refugee 5.11+   ★★   In addition to quickdraws, bring a few medium stoppers and runners for tunnel threads.

NORTH GATEWAY ROCK – West Face

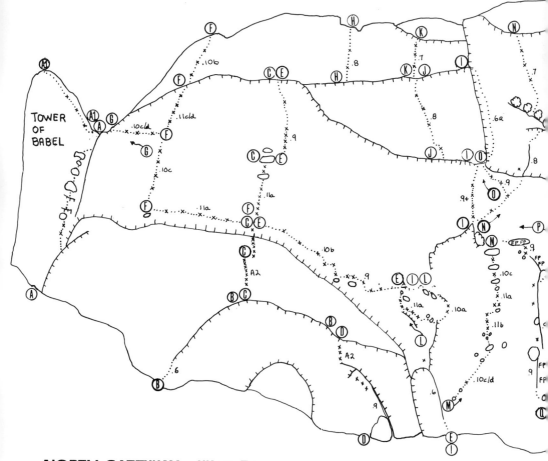

NORTH GATEWAY – West Face

A Water Crack 5.9+ R   pro: medium to #4 Friend

A1 S. Ridge of Tower of Babel 5.6-5.7

B Arching Crack 5.6   pro: to 3"

C Fuzzy's Farce 5.6 A2 (5.11−) ★   pro: wired nuts for bolt thread

D Murphy's Mistake 5.9 A2   pro: couple ¾" angles, to 4½" for start

E Over the Rainbow 5.11− ★★   pro: wired nut for bolt thread. Loose

F Touchy Situation 5.11+ ★★ loose

G Wimpish and Weak 5.10+   loose

H Pot of Gold 5.8

I Borghoff's Blunder 5.10− ★★   pro: some large nuts; runners for tunnel threads

J Henry the Pig 5.8 ★

K Vine Ledge Exit 5.7

L Rainbow Bridge 5.11− ★★

M Men at Work 5.11 ★★★

N Squids in Bondage 5.8   very loose

O Original line to Borghoff's Blunder 5.9 very loose

P Link up Traverse 5.9

Q Pete and Bob's 5.11 ★★ loose   pro: #7- 9 hexes useful

Q1 Low traverse var. to Pete and Bob's 5.10

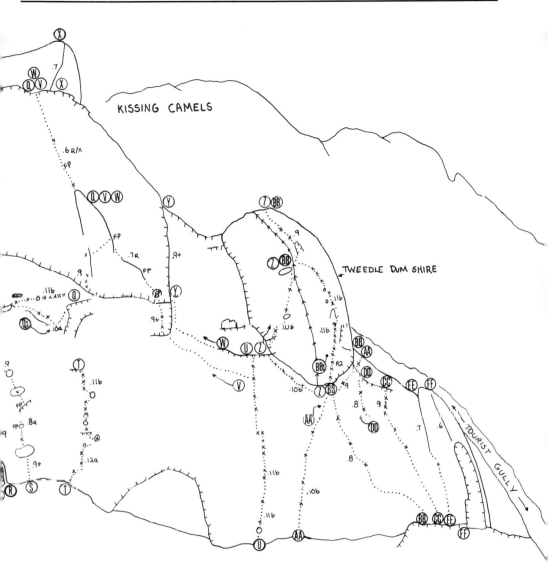

KISSING CAMELS

TWEEDLE DUM SHIRE

TOURIST GULLY

R Pete and Bob's Chimney 5.9 very loose

S Pete and Bob's Face

T Horribly Heinous 5.12− ★★

U Amazing Grace 5.11 R ★ loose

V Saving Grace 5.9+

W Indecent Exposure 5.7 R Approach is tricky. Ascend the Tourist Gully to near its end. Scramble up a short east-facing wall to a ledge. Downclimb a narrow exposed ridge. A rope may be desired. Rappel 60 feet to the ledge at the start of the climb.

X Punkin Crack 5.7

Y Escape Gully 5.9+ R

Z Fall from Grace 5.10 R ★ pro: medium to 3½"

AA The Warren Route 5.10b

BB The Zipper 5.11+ ★★★ pro: #3, #3½-4 Friend

BB1 Original Aid Line A2

CC Trigger Finger 5.9 ★

DD Fastest Drill 5.8

EE Cowboy Boot Crack 5.7 R ★ pro: small- medium nuts; #8 hex

FF Pillar Climb 5.6

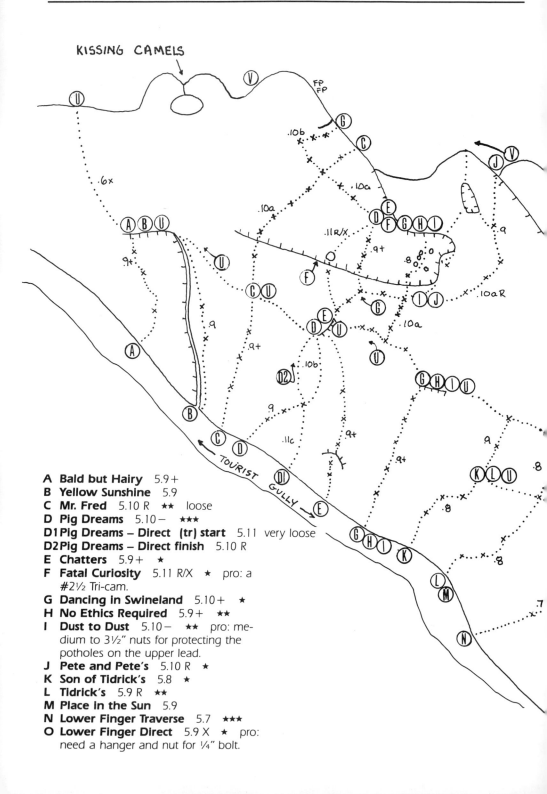

A **Bald but Hairy** 5.9+
B **Yellow Sunshine** 5.9
C **Mr. Fred** 5.10 R ★★ loose
D **Pig Dreams** 5.10− ★★★
D1 **Pig Dreams – Direct (tr) start** 5.11 very loose
D2 **Pig Dreams – Direct finish** 5.10 R
E **Chatters** 5.9+ ★
F **Fatal Curiosity** 5.11 R/X ★ pro: a #2½ Tri-cam.
G **Dancing in Swineland** 5.10+ ★
H **No Ethics Required** 5.9+ ★★
I **Dust to Dust** 5.10− ★★ pro: medium to 3½" nuts for protecting the potholes on the upper lead.
J **Pete and Pete's** 5.10 R ★
K **Son of Tidrick's** 5.8 ★
L **Tidrick's** 5.9 R ★★
M **Place in the Sun** 5.9
N **Lower Finger Traverse** 5.7 ★★★
O **Lower Finger Direct** 5.9 X ★ pro: need a hanger and nut for ¼" bolt.

NORTH GATEWAY ROCK – West Face (The Finger Face)

This wall provides a number of high angle face routes (70-90 degrees). The holds vary in their soundness. Many shaky flakes are found. Remember to pull down and not out! There are several safe routes on the face and the protection is entirely fixed with the exception of **Fatal Curiosity** and the upper lead of **Dust to Dust**.

The Finger is the giant flake on the south (right) end of the face. Until 1976, all the routes on the face started by climbing to the Finger. Since, many direct lines ascend the face, intersecting the older traverse lines of **Psychic Grandma** and **Tidrick's**.

P Finger Ramp 5.7 R ★
P1 Finger Ramp – variation 5.8 ★
Q Upper Finger Direct 5.9 X   pro: bring
a sling for a pothole thread. loose
R Upper Finger Traverse 5.9− ★
S Seam Wall 5.11 (tr) loose
T Short but Sweet 5.10b X or (tr) The pins
have been chopped.
U Psychic Grandma 5.9 R/X ★★ This is
a girdle traverse of the face.
**V Boucher-Twombly Route (upper
part)** 5.6

STAR POINT

THE FINGER

WHITE SPIRE AND RED TWIN

These two spires are the scene of much climbing activity and provide several fine routes. White Spire is the more popular of the two, even though **Potholes,** on Red Twin, is a frequently ascended climb. White Spire is 60 feet tall; Red Twin stands 70 feet.

RED TWIN

Red Twin is composed of Lower Lyons Formation sandstone. Three of the four routes on it are normally done as lead climbs. A belay and rappel anchor is located on the summit.

Potholes 5.6 ★★ pro: runners are useful.

This is the most frequently ascended route on Red Twin. The route, located on the north face, climbs up to a drilled angle on big holds, then up a series of long-shaped potholes. Inside these potholes a small pothole can be threaded. Where the potholes end, a drilled angle protects the face moves onto a small stance. Here, another pothole can be tied off. Move left and continue to the summit. To descend, rappel down the same face.

North Ridge 5.8 This seldom-done route ascends the north ridge, which is right of **Potholes.** There is no protection, so the climb must either be top roped or led 4th class.

Incline Ledge 5.8 The route is located about 25 feet left of **Potholes** on the east face. Ascend a sloping lege or ramp leading up and right. Near the end of the ledge is a drilled angle. From there, climb straight up over an overhang (5.8).

South Ridge 5.8 R The climb goes directly up the south ridge. Getting up to and just past the first pin is the (5.8) crux. From here, very moderate climbing leads up the ridge. One more pin is found for protection.

WHITE SPIRE

This rock is composed of very solid white Fountain Formation sandstone.

A North Ridge Eliminate 5.10 (tr) ★
B North Ridge 5.8 R ★★ pro: Hexes #5-8 are useful.
C Kor's Variation 5.10 ★ pro: bring a hanger for a ⅜" bolt.
D Mantle Route 5.11 − (tr) ★
E West Face 5.8+ ★
F South Ridge 5.6 ★ pro: medium to 3"

PIGEON ROCK

Pigeon Rock is a 40-foot spire to the north of the Three Graces. A rappel anchor consisting of fixed pins is located on the summit. None of the routes have any fixed protection and the South Ridge is the common route to the summit.

South Ridge 5.4 A (poor) runner placement can be found near the top of the ridge. The climbing is on big holds and is often downclimbed by experienced climbers.

West Ridge 5.6 or 5.9 (TR) Various top rope climbs can be found on the west face.

North Ridge 5.9 (TR) No protection is found.

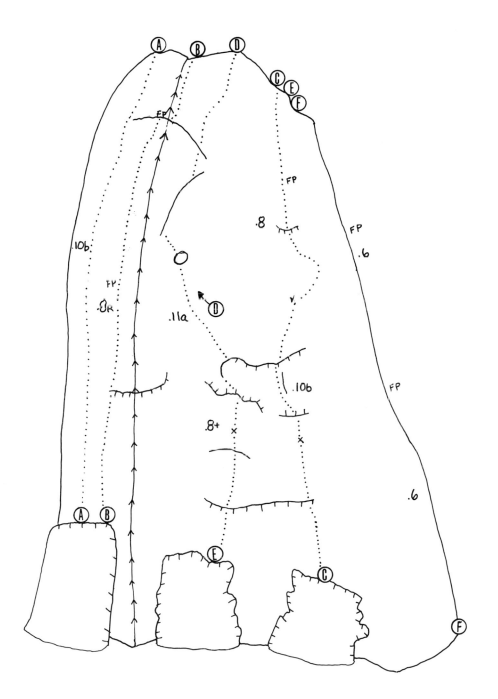

WHITE SPIRE

SOUTH GATEWAY ROCK – DRUG WALL (Northeast Face)

A Left Side 5.8   Direct start is 5.10.
B Rhineskeller 5.8   Nuts and perlon runners for thin pothole threads are needed for
   protection.
C Cocaine 5.10+   ★★★
D Cold Turkeys 5.11   ★★★   This is an 80- foot variation to **Cocaine.**
E Stalagmite 5.8   Nuts may be useful. very loose
F Ninety-Nine Percent Pure 5.11   ★★★   This is an excellent
   30-foot direct variation to **Cocaine.**
G Silver Spoon 5.6   ★★★
H There Goes a Neighborhood 5.10
I Tutor 5.8   ★
J Pure Friction 5.10 (TR)   ★
K Friction Solo 5.9 R/X
L Moderate Junk 5.5
M Chopped Steps
N The Fixer 5.10   ★★   The (grungy) second pitch is rarely
   done and requires a few small stopper and medium
   nuts to a #8 Hex.
O Rocket Fuel 5.11   ★★★
P Mighty Thor 5.10   ★★★
Q Crescent Corner 5.9+ R
R Notch Direct Bolt Ladder A3?   Poor bolts.
S Southeast Ridge of Block Tower 5.9–
T North Ridge of Block Tower A1?
   Bolt ladder.

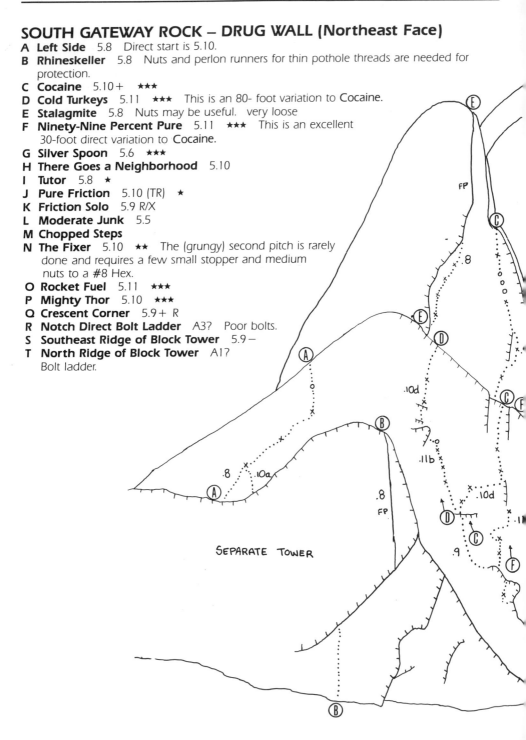

SEPARATE TOWER

SOUTH GATEWAY ROCK

This formation has several routes on its northeast and west faces. The south ridge provides an easy descent for most of the routes. South Gateway is composed largely of red, Lower Lyons Formation sandstone. The large whitish - colored area on the west face is Fountain Formation sandstone, a very coarse and granular rock quite unlike the softer Lyons sandstone.

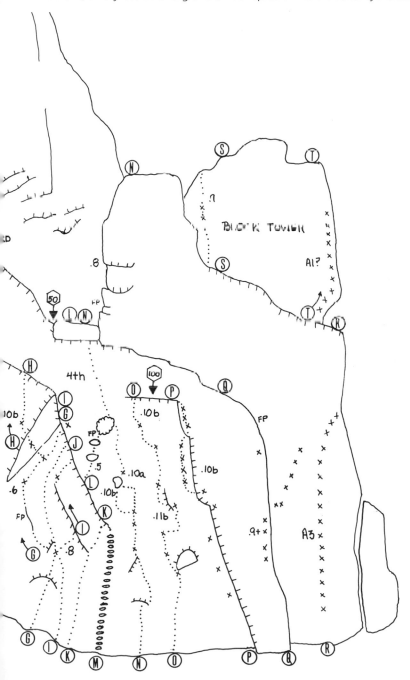

Mark Rolofson

SOUTH GATEWAY ROCK – DRUG WALL (Northeast Face)

SOUTH GATEWAY – West Face

Mark Rolofson

SOUTH GATEWAY ROCK – West Face

A Staircase 5.7 or 5.8 ★ pro: medium nuts.
 The first two pitches are shown on the topo. From the Notch, traverse left on a sloping, exposed ledge to a belay at the base of the **Southeast Ridge of Block Tower**. Ascend the north ridge to its highest summit. This part of the climb is almost never done.

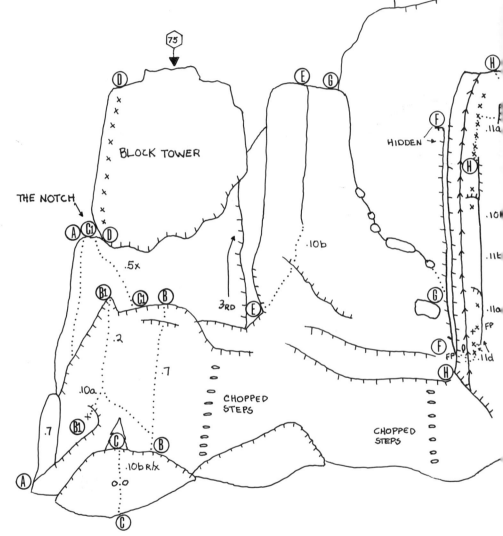

B Practice Slab 5.2 to 5.8 ★ There is no protection and the many possible routes are normally top roped.

B1 Insignificant, but There 5.10– This is a hard start to the left side of the **Practice Slab**.

C Dirty Sock 5.10 R/X ★ This is a high boulder problem that is often top roped.

C1 Notch Traverse 5.5 X The climb angles left from the top of the **Practice Slab** to the Notch. There is no protection.

D North Ridge of Block Tower A1?

E Tower Crack 5.10 (tr) This is an old aid line.

F Sandman 5.7 Very unpopular and gritty. Nuts useful. Loose

G Potholes Face 5.9 R

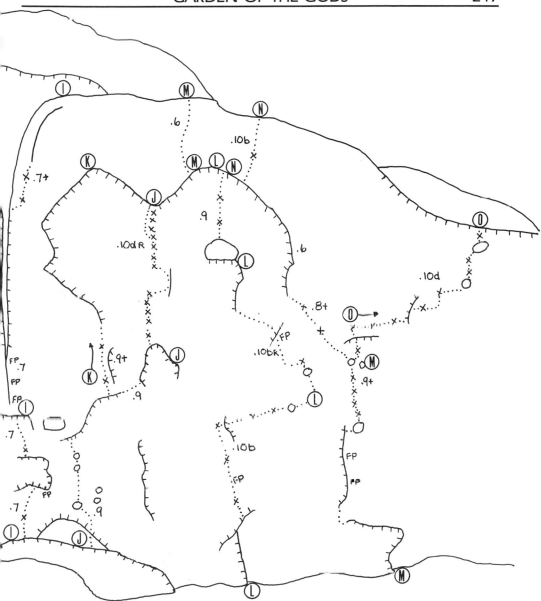

H Kor's Korner 5.12– ★★ pro: #5 RP to #10 stopper. Mulitple #5-7 stoppers may be useful. #1½ Friend.

I West Point Crack 5.7+ ★★ pro: medium to large nuts

J Pipe Route 5.10+ R ★ pro: (pitch 1) some nuts and plenty of slings for pothole threads. (pitch 2) A #7 or 8 Hex and 5-7 ¼" bolt hangers and nuts.

K Indian Head 5.9+ pro: many nuts small to large Loose

L Pipe Dreams 5.10 R ★★ pro: two #11 Hexes or similar needed on pitch 1; medium nuts on pitch 2.

M Credibility Gap 5.9+ ★★ pro: nuts not essential, but a #5 and 11 Hex useful.

N 5.10– Finish 5.10–

O Dog Day Afternoon 5.10+/5.11a Loose

SOUTH GATEWAY ROCK – West Face – South End

There are several good boulder problems and a few short climbs on the south end of the west face.

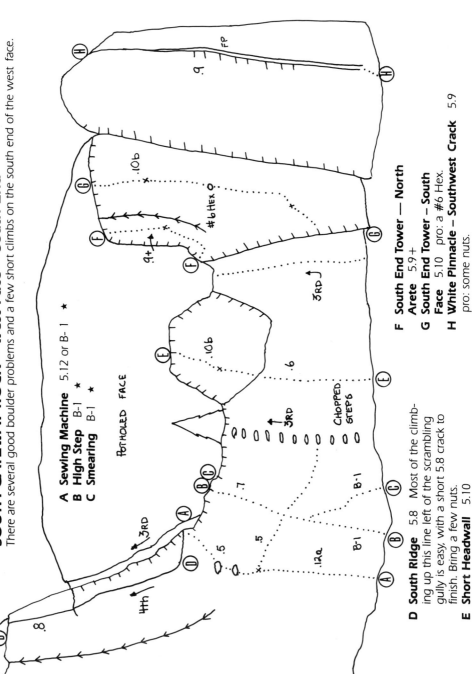

A Sewing Machine 5.12 or B-1 ★
B High Step B-1 ★
C Smearing B-1 ★

D South Ridge 5.8   Most of the climbing up this line left of the scrambling gully is easy, with a short 5.8 crack to finish. Bring a few nuts.

E Short Headwall 5.10

F South End Tower — North Arete 5.9+

G South End Tower – South Face 5.10   pro: a #6 Hex.

H White Pinnacle – Southwest Crack 5.9
pro: some nuts.

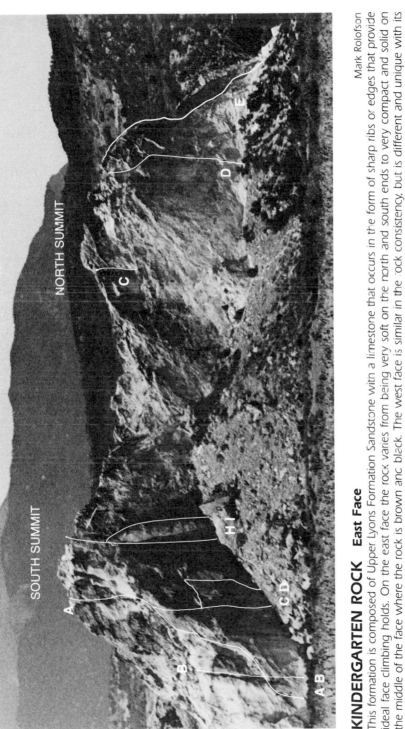

KINDERGARTEN ROCK East Face

Mark Rolofson

This formation is composed of Upper Lyons Formation Sandstone with a limestone that occurs in the form of sharp ribs or edges that provide ideal face climbing holds. On the east face the rock varies from being very soft on the north and south ends to very compact and solid on the middle of the face where the rock is brown and black. The west face is similar in the rock consistency, but is different and unique with its own character. The climbs are generally about two pitches in length. The crag is about 250 feet tall.

Descents For all climbs ending right of or near the south ridge it is easily possible to descend the south ridge (2nd to 3rd class). From the north summit, it is possible to traverse south to descend the south ridge. Another possibility is to descend the east face from the saddle on 3rd or 4th class (more dangerous and exposed). From the top of the 4th class above **Monster Walk** it is possible to walk north and descend a broken area on the west face. Because these descents are so easy, they are also popular for scrambles to ascend. Beware of people throwing rocks off the summit, especially during the summer.

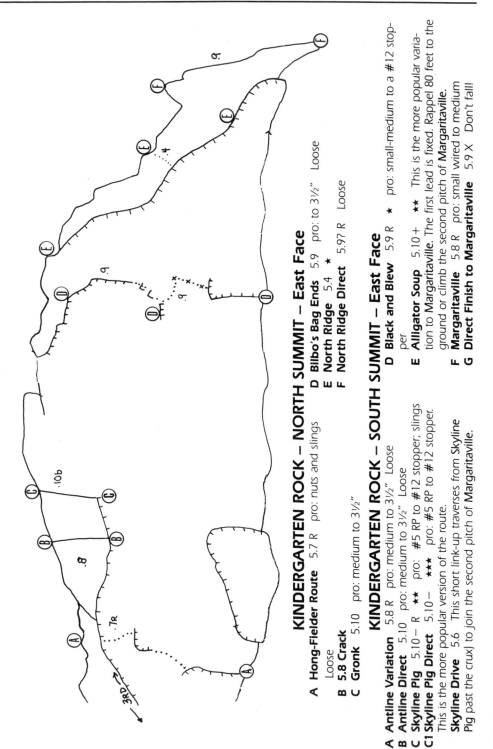

KINDERGARTEN ROCK – NORTH SUMMIT – East Face

A **Hong-Fielder Route** 5.7 R pro: nuts and slings
  Loose
B **5.8 Crack**
C **Gronk** 5.10 pro: medium to 3½"

D **Bilbo's Bag Ends** 5.9 pro: to 3½" Loose
E **North Ridge** 5.4 ★
F **North Ridge Direct** 5.97 R Loose

KINDERGARTEN ROCK – SOUTH SUMMIT – East Face

A **Antline Variation** 5.8 R pro: medium to 3½" Loose
B **Antline Direct** 5.10 pro: medium to 3½" Loose
C **Skyline Pig** 5.10 – R ★★ pro: #5 RP to #12 stopper; slings
C1 **Skyline Pig Direct** 5.10 – ★★★ pro: #5 RP to #12 stopper.
This is the more popular version of the route.
Skyline Drive 5.6 This short link-up traverses from Skyline
Pig past the crux) to join the second pitch of **Margaritaville**.

D **Black and Blew** 5.9 R ★ pro: small-medium to a #12 stopper
E **Alligator Soup** 5.10+ ★★ This is the more popular variation to **Margaritaville**. The first lead is fixed. Rappel 80 feet to the
ground or climb the second pitch of **Margaritaville**.
F **Margaritaville** 5.8 R pro: small wired to medium
G **Direct Finish to Margaritaville** 5.9 X Don't fall!

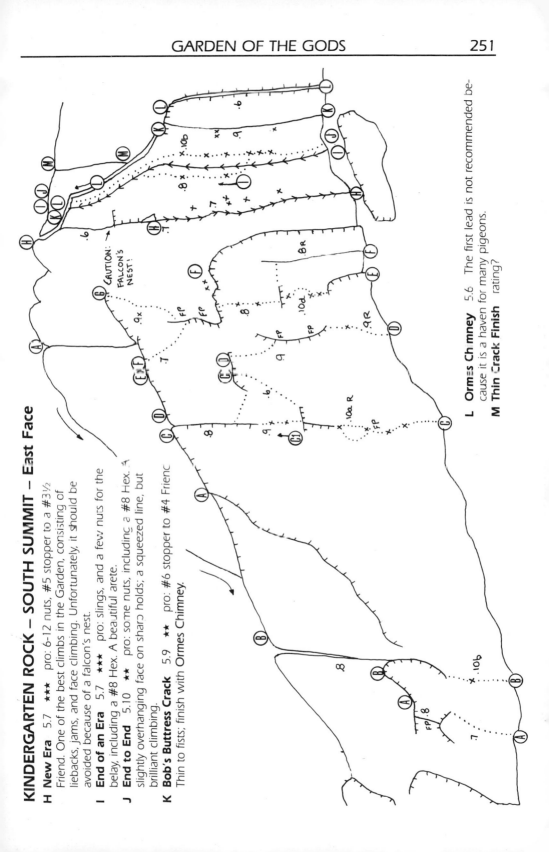

KINDERGARTEN ROCK – SOUTH SUMMIT – East Face

H New Era 5.7 ★★★ pro: 6-12 nuts, #5 stopper to a #3½ Friend. One of the best climbs in the Garden, consisting of liebacks, jams, and face climbing. Unfortunately, it should be avoided because of a falcon's nest.

I End of an Era 5.7 ★★★ pro: slings, and a few nuts for the belay, including a #8 Hex. A beautiful arete.

J End to End 5.10 ★★ pro: some nuts, including a #8 Hex. A slightly overhanging face on sharp holds; a squeezed line, but brilliant climbing.

K Bob's Buttress Crack 5.9 ★★ pro: #6 stopper to #4 Friend. Thin to fists; finish with Ormes Chimney.

L Ormes Chimney 5.6 The first lead is not recommended because it is a haven for many pigeons.

M Thin Crack Finish rating?

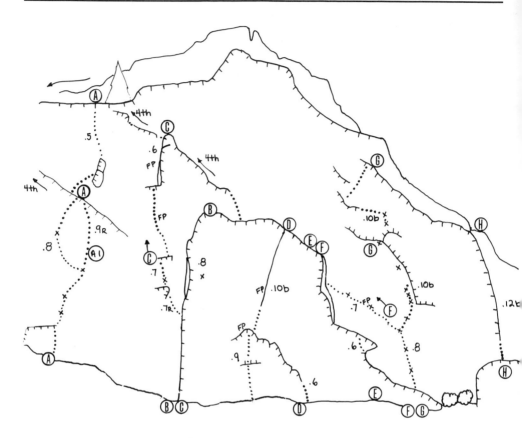

KINDERGARTEN ROCK – SOUTH SUMMIT – West Face

A Frankenstein   5.8 R/X   pro: tie-off slings for the chickenheads. Vertical face. Loose
A1 Frankenstein Direct   5.9 R/X   Vertical face. Loose
B Monster Crack   5.8   ★★   pro: medium to large nuts. Lieback/chimney.
C Son of Monster   5.7 R   pro: medium nuts.
D Scarecrow   5.10 R   ★   pro: #5 stopper to #3 Friend. Thin crack to hand jams. Loose
E Lance   5.6   pro: medium to 3"
F Sword in the Stone   5.8   pro: slings
G Footloose n' Fancy Free   5.10   ★★★   pro: ½ dozen nuts, mostly small/medium stoppers, but including a #3 Friend. Face/lieback.
H Fragile Dihedral   5.12 (TR)
   Right Side   5.4   On the south (right) end of the west face is a very moderate one pitch climb. Ascend a red ramp leading up and left. Reach a narrow ledge and traverse right to a short vertical crack, which is ascended to ledges on the south ridge.
   South End Slabs   5.4 to 5.7 X   To the right (south) of the previous route are several climbing possibilities up moderate slabs. No protection.

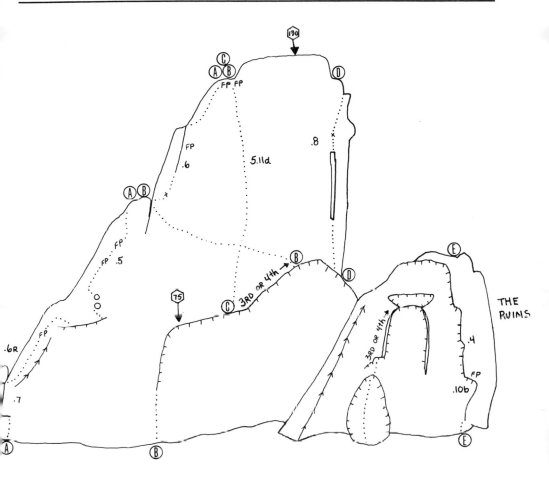

MONTEZUMA'S TOWER

A North Ridge 5.7 R ★★★ pro: medium nuts for belay.
B West Face 5.8?
C West Face Direct 5.11+ (TR)
D South Ridge 5.8 pro: some nuts.
E Ruins Crack 5.10 ★
 East Face 5.6 A2 (with A3-4 start) The upper ⅔ of the route ascends a (A2) bolt ladder. Either start with a 5.6 wide crack or nail up hairline cracks.

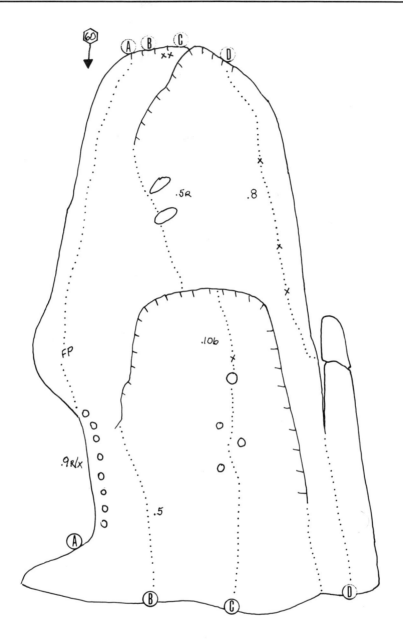

EASTER ROCK – West Face

This spire is located just east of the north end pinnacle on Keyhole Rock.

A North Ridge   5.9 R/X   ★
B West Face   5.5
C West Face – Right   5.10
D Silhouette   5.8   ★

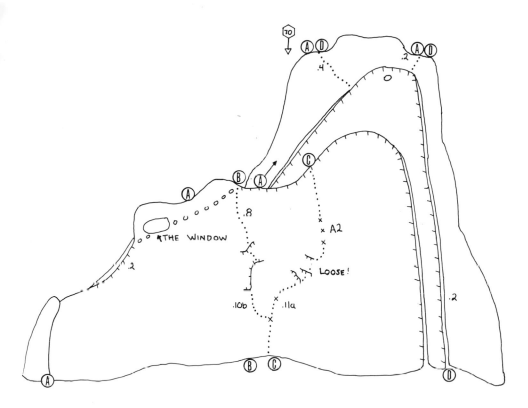

THREE GRACES – West Face

A Window Route   5.2 ★ 200 feet.   pro: A few nuts might be useful. Bring a runner for tunnel threads.

B Weenis Route   5.10 ★

C Original West Face   5.10 A2   80 feet

D Chimney Route   5.2 (tr) Directly below the summit a diagonal line ascends a shallow trough.

Wooly's B-Line   5.8   The route is located on the southeast side of the Garden, a few hundred feet past the Camera Obscura Shop.

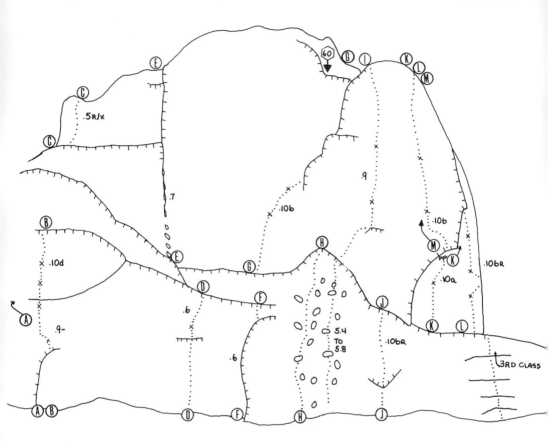

KEYHOLE ROCK – East Face
First Tier (Right) and North End Pinnacle

This short cliff is composed of Lower Lyons Formation Sandstone. Many short climbs from 30 to 100 feet long exist on both the east and west faces. Both sides of the rock are split by large ledges into tiers. These ledges offer easy approach and escape.

A Prodigal Son 5.8+
B Morning After 5.10+
C South Ridge of North End Pinnacle 5.5 R/X
D Short Face 5.6
E Hound Dog 5.7 ★ pro: nuts and Friends.
F Short Corner 5.6

G Fingerbanger 5.10
H Short Pothole Climbs 5.3 to 5.8?
I Status Quo 5.9
J Overhang 5.10 R
K Borderline Direct 5.10– ★ pro: #8 Hex
L Borderline 5.10 R ★ pro: #8 Hex
M Welcome to the Garden 5.10 ★

Montezuma's Tower Mark Rolofson

KEYHOLE ROCK – East Face

THIRD TIER

A **Cheap Thrills** 5.10
B **Potholes Line** 5.8
C **Ellingwood Chimney** 5.6 ★
D **Grovel Crack** 5.9 R
E **Upper Borderline** 5.11 ★★

T **South Ridge** 5.8
U **Macbeth** 5.10 ★

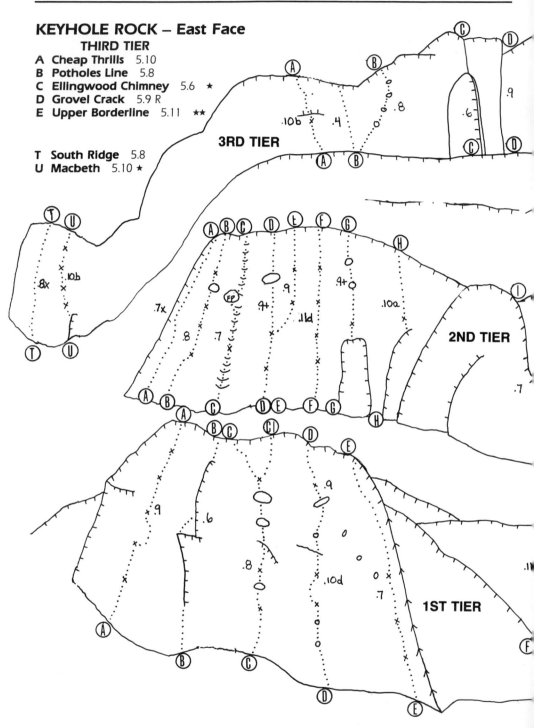

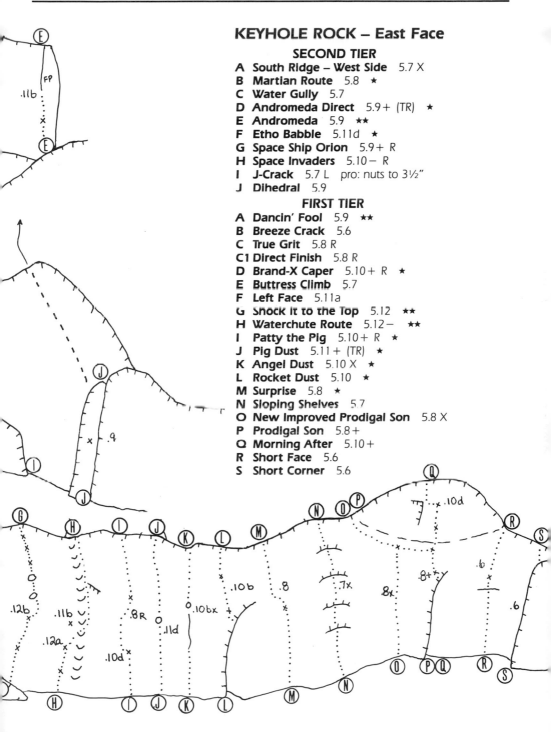

KEYHOLE ROCK – East Face

SECOND TIER
A **South Ridge – West Side** 5.7 X
B **Martian Route** 5.8 ★
C **Water Gully** 5.7
D **Andromeda Direct** 5.9+ (TR) ★
E **Andromeda** 5.9 ★★
F **Etho Babble** 5.11d ★
G **Space Ship Orion** 5.9+ R
H **Space Invaders** 5.10– R
I **J-Crack** 5.7 L   pro: nuts to 3½"
J **Dihedral** 5.9

FIRST TIER
A **Dancin' Fool** 5.9 ★★
B **Breeze Crack** 5.6
C **True Grit** 5.8 R
C1 **Direct Finish** 5.8 R
D **Brand-X Caper** 5.10+ R ★
E **Buttress Climb** 5.7
F **Left Face** 5.11a
G **Shock It to the Top** 5.12 ★★
H **Waterchute Route** 5.12– ★★
I **Patty the Pig** 5.10+ R ★
J **Pig Dust** 5.11+ (TR) ★
K **Angel Dust** 5.10 X ★
L **Rocket Dust** 5.10 ★
M **Surprise** 5.8 ★
N **Sloping Shelves** 5.7
O **New Improved Prodigal Son** 5.8 X
P **Prodigal Son** 5.8+
Q **Morning After** 5.10+
R **Short Face** 5.6
S **Short Corner** 5.6

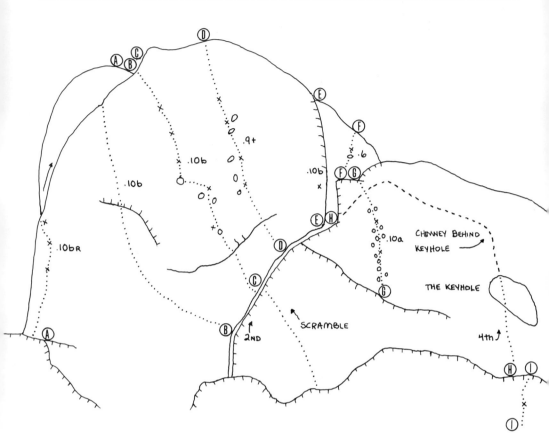

KEYHOLE ROCK – West Face
NORTHEND PINNACLE
A Borderline 5.10 R ★ pro: #8 Hex
B Small Overhang 5.10 (TR) ★
C BFD 5.10 ★★
D Ziggy Stardust 5.9+ ★★
E Punk Face 5.10
F Right Side 5.6?
G Punk Lives 5.10 − ★
H Keyhole Route 3rd or 4th
I Direct Start 5.6

BROKEN GLASS AMPHITHEATRE
Walk and scramble south up a gully above North End Pinnacle and the Keyhole. Gain the ridge on the west. A moderate scramble leads into the bottom of an amphitheatre or bowl-shaped pit on the west face. The climbs are located on the bulging west- facing wall. The floor of the amphitheatre is covered with broken glass from the reckless behavior of low-life tourists.

Broken Glass 5.9+ R ★   The route ascends the obvious line of potholes and shelves up the bulging wall. Move right and clip into a drilled angle. The crux moves finish the climb.

Solution Pocket Face 5.10 (TR) ★   Start about 10 feet right of **Broken Glass** and ascend the bulging wall with small solution pockets that lead to the peg on that route.

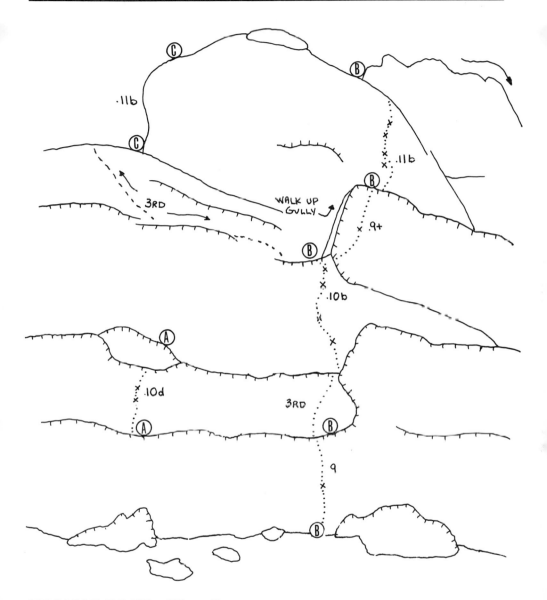

KEYHOLE ROCK – West Face
A Old Aid Bolts 5.10+ R
B Mission Impossible 5.11 R ★
C Upper Borderline 5.11 ★★

Tempest 5.10+ ★ A few hundred feet right of **Mission Impossible** are two thin bulging crack lines. On closer inspection only the right bears any semblance to a crack; this is **Tempest**. Ascend this line with two drilled angles. Bring a #4 Friend, a few small wired nuts, and slings for pothole threads.

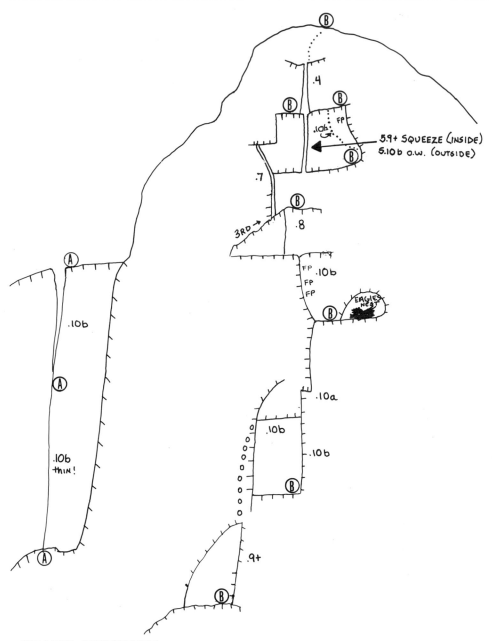

5.9+ SQUEEZE (INSIDE)
5.10b O.W. (OUTSIDE)

GRAND SPECIMEN

Grand Specimen is the left of two rock formations that can be seen from Colorado Springs above Cheyenne Canyon. Drive up the canyon, then head north on High Drive Road. Follow this down to a parking lot directly below the cliff. The hike up the hill takes at least an hour.

A Sweet n' Sour 5.10   pro: wired stoppers to tubes. Offwidth.

B Directissima 5.10 ★★★   pro: RPs, wired stoppers, Friends #1-4.

FIRST ASCENTS

NORTH GATEWAY ROCK
North Gateway Girdle Traverse Leonard Coyne and Ken Sims, 9/77
North End Chimney Stanley Boucher and Vernon Twombly, about 1946
Triple Exposure Doug Snively et al, 1972. FFA Will Gadd, Richard Aschert and Dave Dangle, 1986. The route still awaits a continuous free ascent.
Anaconda Layton Kor and Gary Ziegler, 1960s FFA Earl Wiggins, Jim Dunn and John Sherwood, 1975
The Refugee Mark Rolofson and Bob D'Antonio, 8/83

NORTH GATEWAY – West Face
Water Crack Michael Borgoff, late 1960s FFA Earl Wiggins and John Sherwood, 1975
Fuzzy's Farce FA Fuzzy Minch, 1960s? FFA Ed Webster and Bryan Becker, 4/78
Murphy's Mistake unknown
Over the Rainbow Ed Webster, Bryan Becker and Leonard Coyne, 4/78
Touchy Situation Richard Aschert and Scott Szcyzmak, 1/85
Wimpish and Weak unknown
Pot of Gold Ed Webster and Peter Mayfield, 6/79
Borgoff's Blunder FA Michael Borgoff et al, 1960s. FFA (pitch 1) Steve Cheyney and Pete Croft, 1960s
Henry the Pig Leonard Coyne, Ed Bailey and Mark Rolofson, 12/76
Vine Ledge Exit unknown
Rainbow Bridge Ed Webster and Peter Mayfield, 6/79
Men at Work Bob D'Antonio and Mark Rolofson, 4/83
Squids in Bondage Ed Webster, Leonard Coyne, Wendy White and Mike Heintz, 8/77
Original line to Borgoff's Blunder Peter Croft and Herby Hendricks, 1960s
Link up Traverse unknown
Pete and Bob's FA Pete Croft and Bob Stauch, 1960s. FFA (1st lead) Steve Cheyney (2nd) Bill Mummery and Mike Grey, 1968. (first continuous) Kurt Rasmussen, 1973
Low traverse var to Pete and Bob's Peter Gallagher and Mack Johnson, 12/79
Pete and Bob's Chimney unknown
Pete and Bob's Face unknown
Horribly Heinous FA Herby Hendricks, 1960s? FFA Bob D'Antonio and Mark Rolofson, 2/83
Amazing Grace Ed Webster, Earl Wiggins and Leonard Coyne, 1/77
Saving Grace Ed Webster and Leonard Coyne, 1977
Indecent Exposure Richard Cole et al, 1960s?
Punkin Crack Harvey Carter, 1960s
Escape Gully Harrison Dekker and Sue Patenade, 1982
Fall from Grace FA Leonard Coyne, Ed Webster and Ed Russell, 11/77. (first continuous) Ed Webster and Mike Mayers, 4/78
The Warren Route Robert Warren and Mike Johnson, 1983
The Zipper FA Harvey Carter and Cleve McCarty, around 1962. FFA Mark Rolofson and Jeff Britt, 2/84
Trigger Finger Dirk Tyler and Dave Hodges, 5/79
Fastest Drill Ed Webster, Mack Johnson and Dave Sweet, 4/78
Cowboy Boot Crack unknown
Pillar Climb unknown
Bald but Hairy Mark and Gary Hopkin, 3/78
Yellow Sunshine Scott Szcyzmak, 1985
Mr. Fred Richard Aschert and Fred Aschert, 2/84
Pig Dreams Peter Gallagher and Fred Aschert, 1981

Pig Dreams – Direct Maurice Reed, 1983
Pig Dreams – Direct finish Mark Rolofson, 1984
Chatters Bob Robertson, Bob D'Antonio and Larry Kledzik, 1982
Fatal Curiosity Richard Aschert, 1985
Dancing in Swineland Pete Williams and Pete Gallagher, 2/79
No Ethics Required Dave Bowman and Bob Robertson, 1980
Dust to Dust Kim Rogers and Gary Isaacs, 1973. Ed Webster and Pete Williams added a drilled pin
    to the upper pitch in 1976, unaware of the previous ascent.
Pete and Pete's Pete Williams and Pete Gallagher, 1/79
Son of Tidrick's Leonard Coyne and Gary Campbell, 1976
Tidrick's Rick Tidrick, 1960
Place in the Sun Ed Webster, Leonard Coyne, Kevin Murray, Bob Robertson, George Allen, Gary
    Hopkins and Pete Williams, 9/77
Upper and Lower Finger Traverse Paul Radigen, Art Howells, John Auld and Herby Hendricks,
    around 1960
Lower Finger Direct Max Hinkle, 1960s
Finger Ramp Richard Borgman and Steve Cheyney, 1960s
Upper Finger Direct unknown
Seam Wall Bob Robertson, 1982
Short but Sweet FA unknown. FFA Leonard Coyne and John Harrington, 1/77
Psychic Grandma Pete Croff and Bob Stauch, 1960s
Boucher-Twombly Route Stan Boucher and Vernon Twombly, 1945

RED TWIN
Potholes Mike Borgoff, 1950s
North Ridge unknown
Incline Ledge Harvey Carter, 1950s
South Ridge unknown

WHITE SPIRE
North Ridge Eliminate unknown
North Ridge Paul Radigen, 1950s?
Kor's Variation Layton Kor, 1960s?
Mantle Route Steve Cheyney
West Face Harvey Carter and Art Howells, 1960s
South Ridge Harvey Carter, 1950s

SOUTH GATEWAY ROCK
Left Side Harvey Carter, 1982
Rhineskeller Bob Stauch and Harvey Carter, 1960s
Cocaine Leonard Coyne, Ed Webster and Ken Sims, 7/77
Cold Turkeys Bob D'Antonio and Richard Aschert, 7/84
Stalagmite FA Richard Borgman FFA Dick Long
Ninety-Nine Percent Pure Mark Rolofson, 5/81
Silver Spoon Stewart Green, Steve Westbay and Kurt Rasmussen, 1970s
There Goes a Neighborhood Peter Gallagher and Bryan Beckerm, 1981
Tutor Larry Shurbarth and Greg Stevens, 1981
Pure Friction unknown
Friction Solo unknown
Moderate Junk unknown
Chopped Steps unknown
The Fixer Ed Webster and Leonard Coyne, 7/77
Rocket Fuel Mark Rolofson and Bob D'Antonio, 10/83
Mighty Thor Mark Rolofson, Bob Robertson, Murray Judge and Gugi Rylegis, 7/79
Crescent Corner Don Peterson and Helmut Husmen
Notch Direct Bolt Ladder unknown
Southeast Ridge of Block Tower Steve Cheyney, Bob Stauch and Pete Croff, 1960s
North Ridge of Block Tower unknown
Staircase Steve Cheyney, Bob Stauch and Pete Croff, 1960s
Practice Slab unknown
Insignificant, but There Mike Johnson and Bob D'Antonio, 1983
Dirty Sock unknown

Notch Traverse unknown
Tower Crack Bob Robertson, 1982
Sandman Harvey Carter, 1960s?
Potholes Face unknown
Kor's Korner FA Layton Kor and Gary Ziegler, 1965 FFA (pitch 1) Leonard Coyne, 1979 (2nd pitch and first continuous) Richard Aschert, 1985
West Point Crack FA U.S. Army, 1946 FFA Harvey Carter, 1950s
Pipe Route FA John Auld and Gary Ziegler, 1961 FFA Earl Wiggins and Jim Souder, 3/76
Indian Head Ed Webster, Steve Hong and Earl Wiggins, 11/76
Pipe Dreams Earl Wiggins, Steve Hong and Ed Webster, 2/77
Credibility Gap FA Gary Ziegler and John Auld, 1960s FFA Morgan Gadd and Skip Hamilton
Dog Day Afternoon Ed Webster and Mark Rolofson, 1/78
Sewing Machine unknown
High Step unknown
Smearing unknown
South Ridge Bob Robertson and Fred Aschert, 1982
Short Headwall unknown
South End Tower — North Arete Harvey Carter, 1982
South End Tower – West Face Harvey Carter, 1982
White Pinnacle – Southwest Crack Ed Webster and Harvey Carter, 1982

KINDERGARTEN ROCK
Hong-Fielder Route Steve Hong and Carol Fiedler, 1977
5.8 Crack unknown
Gronk Bryan Becker and Harvey Miller, 1977
Bilbo's Bag Ends Ed Webster and Bryan Becker, 5/77
North Ridge Bob Ormes, 1925
North Ridge Direct Stanley Boucher and Vernon Twombley, 1940s
Antline Variation Harvey Carter and Steve Cheyney, 1960s?
Antline Direct unknown
Skyline Pig Steve Hong and Steve Gropp, 1975
Skyline Pig Direct Mark Rolofson and Peter Phister, 10/78
Skyline Drive Bob D'Antonio and Harvey Arnold, 1982
Black and Blew Pete Croff and Steve Cheyney, 1960s?
Alligator Soup Leonard Coyne and Ed Russell, 9/77
Margaritaville Ed Webster and Mack Johnson, 6/77
Direct Finish to Margaritaville Earl Wiggins, Bob Robertson and Kurt Rasmussen, 1978
New Era Harvey Carter, 1950s
End of an Era George Allen and Ann Liebold, 9/79
End to End Mike Johnson and Ed Kalina, 1986
Bob's Buttress Crack FA Don Doucette and Mike Dudley FFA Don Doucette and Larry Hazlett, 1960s?
Ormes Chimney Bob Ormes, around 1925
Thin Crack Finish unknown
Frankenstein Ken Sims and Leonard Coyne, 1/77
Frankenstein Direct Earl Wiggins and Ed Webster, 2/77
Monster Crack Harvey Carter and Paul Radigen, 1950s
Son of Monster unknown
Scarecrow FA Harvey Carter and Gary Ziegler, 1950s FFA Jim Dunn and Stewart Green, 1973
Lance Albert Ellingwood, 1920s
Sword in the Stone Leonard Coyne and Ed Webster, 12/76
Footloose n' Fancy Free Leonard Coyne and Ed Webster, 6/77
Fragile Dihedral Bob D'Antonio, 1985
Right Side unknown
South End Slabs unknown

MONTEZUMA'S TOWER
North Ridge U.S. Army, 1945 FFA Harvey Carter, 1950
West Face John Auld
West Face Direct Jim Dunn, 1980
South Ridge Harvey Carter, 1950s
Ruins Crack unknown
East Face Harvey Carter, 1960s?

EASTER ROCK – West Face
North Ridge unknown
West Face unknown
West Face – Right unknown
Silhouette unknown

Wooly's B-Line unknown

THREE GRACES
Window Route unknown
Weenis Route Mark Rolofson and Bob D'Antonio, 1983
Original West Face Harvey Carter and Herby Hendricks, 1960s
Chimney Route unknown

KEYHOLE ROCK
Prodigal Son Peter Gallagher and Larry Shubarth, 10/80
Morning After Mark Rolofson and Bob Robertson, 12/80
South Ridge of North End Pinnacle unknown
Short Face unknown
Hound Dog unknown
Short Corner unknown
Fingerbanger FA Harvey Carter, 1960s? FFA Bob D'Antonio, 1982
Short Pothole Climbs unknown
Status Quo Bob D'Antonio and Harvey Carter, 1982
Overhang unknown
Borderline FA Harvey Carter, 1960s FFA Earl Wiggins, Leonard Coyne and Mark Rolofson, 2/77
Welcome to the Garden Bob D'Antonio and Ed Webster, 1982
Cheap Thrills Bob D'Antonio and Larry Kledzik, 1982
Potholes Line Harvey Carter, 1982
Ellingwood Chimney Albert Ellingwood, 1920
Grovel Crack unknown
South Ridge – West Side unknown
Upper Borderline Harvey Carter, 60s? FFA Bob D'Antonio and Ed Webster, 1982
Macbeth Larry Kledzik, 1981
Martian Route Harvey Carter, 1980
Water Gully unknown
Andromeda Direct unknown
Andromeda Dennis Harman, Bob D'Antonio and Larry Kledzik, 1982
Etho Babble Mark Milligan and Brent Kertzman, 1986
Space Ship Orion Bob D'Antonio, Dennis Harman and Larry Kledzik, 1982
Space Invaders Bob D'Antonio, Larry Kledzik and Dennis Harman, 1982
J-Crack unknown
Dihedral Harvey Carter and Bob D'Antonio, 1982
Dancin' Fool Peter Gallagher, Tom Eisenman and Larry Shubarth, 1980
Breeze Crack unknown
True Grit Pete Croff, Leonard Coyne and Mark Rolofson, 2/76
Brand-X Caper Ed Webster, Leonard Coyne, Steve Johnson and Mark Rolofson, 6/77
Buttress Climb Harvey Carter
Left Face unknown
Shock it to the Top Gene Smith and Bob D'Antonio, 1986
Waterchute Route FFA Leonard Coyne and Ken Sims, 9/77 (reconstructed by Mark Rolofson and freed by Bob D'Antonio after the route was mysteriously chopped.
Patty the Pig Bob D'Antonio and Ed Webster, 1982
Pig Dust Mark Rolofson and Bob D'Antonio, 1983
Angel Dust Mark Rolofson, solo, 1983
Rocket Dust Bob D'Antonio, solo, 1983
Surprise unknown
Sloping Shelves unknown
New Improved Prodigal Son unknown
Small Overhang Bob Robertson and Fred Aschert, 1981
BFD Bob D'Antonio, Peter Gallagher and Larry Kledzik, 1981

Ziggy Stardust   Bob D'Antonio, Peter Gallagher and Larry Kledzik, 1981
Punk Face   Bob D'Antonio and Larry Kledzik, 1981
Right Side   Harvey Carter, 1982
Punk Lives   Bob D'Antonio and Larry Kledzik, 1981
Old Aid Bolts   FFA Bob D'Antonio, 1982
Mission Impossible   FA Harvey Carter, 1960s FFA Bob D'Antonio and Peter Gallagher, 1982. (pitch 3)
   Peter Gallagher and Larry Shubarth, 1981
Tempest   Ed Webster and Mike Johnson, 1982
Broken Glass   Mark Rolofson and Bob D'Antonio, 1/83
Solution Hole Face   Mark Rolofson and Bob D'Antonio, 1/83

SAVE THE SOUTH PLATTE
AND STOP TWO FORKS DAM

A dam site for the confluence of the north and south forks of the South Platte River has been proposed by the Denver Water Board. Located 25 miles southwest of Denver, this region has been eyed as a premiere dam site for about 70 years. The Water Board submitted permit applications for Two Forks Dam on March 5, 1986.

The most recently proposed dam would be 615 feet high and innundate 8500 acres of land stretching along 30 miles of winding river. It would store 1.1 million acre feet of water. The reservoir would be filled to about 30% capacity by water from the South Platte River. The remaining 70% would be provided by the diversion of water over the Continental Divide from the western slope of the Colorado Rockies. Streams flowing east out of the Gore Range would be diverted into the Dillon Reservoir to provide water for the subsequent diversion into Two Forks Dam.

The dam site is located on some of the most heavily used National Forest lands in the state of Colorado. The increasingly popular South Platte area is enjoyed by climbers, hikers, fishermen, kayakers, campers and picnickers. The region features an elk and mule deer winter range, a bighorn sheep historic range, and a 20 mile stretch of Gold Medal trout fishery. It shelters eight species listed as threatened or endangered by the Federal Government, including the Montane Skipper Butterfly. As of June, 1988, these species were dropped from that list, in the height of the dam controversy.

Should the dam be built, several pristine climbing areas will be eradicated. The Malay Archipelago will be completely under water, and so will most of Dome Rock. Also affected will be access to Cynical Pinnacle and surrounding cliffs. Upstream waters will be flooded altering Big Rock Candy Mountain and Cheesman Canyon.

Construction is expected to take about seven years during which time the quiet dirt road will become very congested with loud machinery. The area will be completely shut off to climbers and recreation seekers at this time.

Naturally, there is much opposition to the dam proposal, with some of the strongest coming from residents of the South Platte valley. At recent public hearings, the majority of the speakers were vocal against the dam. Those opposing the dam include the U.S. Fish and Wildlife Service, the Enviornmental Protection Agency, and the National Audubon Society. Their efforts to date are not enough to stop the dam proposal. The water community, proponents for the dam, have called the enviornmentalists "outside interests."

Speakers in favor of the dam at public hearings have included the Denver Water Board, Denver Metropolitan water providers, Denver City Councilman Robert Crider, Charles Schinn Jr. (president) and other members of the Denver Home Builders Association, real estate groups, and Arvada city mayor, Bob Frie. These people possess powerful political and economic strength. Their goal was to start the dam project immediately, so that water could be stored for use by 1995. Without this water the Denver region would be unable to expand, according to their predictions.

Governor Roy Romer had the authority to approve or veto the dam proposal in June 1988. With immense pressure from both sides, he stated that "Colorado needs Two Forks as an insurance policy, not as a dam." He recommended that the U.S. Army Corps of Engineers issue a 25 year permit, and put so many provisons on the project that it is unlikely to see the dam built. If a dam is deemed essential, he suggested a better location would be at Eastabrook, near Bailey, and should be one-fourth the size. Other water alternatives will have to be examined first, he concluded. The final say on the dam goes to the U.S. Army Corps of Engineers, and they could possibly override the governor's decision to put Two Forks on hold. It is important to be aware of the following facts and arguments pertaining to Two Forks Dam:

• Costing $38 million so far, the enviornmental impact study is the most expensive one in U.S. history, according to Ed Reutz, proponent and spokesman for the Denver Water Board.

• The dam costs were estimated at $470 million, but this does not include post construction financing, transmission, and mitigation to offset enviornmental destruction. The actual cost will be closer to one billion dollars.

• The dam will dry up downstream water in Nebraska.

• The dam will divert water that presently goes to Gross Reservoir (near Boulder) via the Trans Continental Divide system, which is already in place. This will cause Gross Resrvoir to quickly dry up.

• Opponents say that if it is built it will be the "biggest ecological disaster in the state's history."

• It is "Colorado's biggest ecological controversy ever," say both sides.

• The Denver Region could cut its water use by 50% through xeriscaping (using native plants for landscaping). But this concept is unheard of in Denver, where green, freshly-cut lawns flourish.

I feel that if the project is approved it will demonstrate that big business has a free reign, and that Colorado government takes no pride in one of its most pristine natural wonders. Please join the fight to stop Two Forks Dam! Your letter of strong disapproval is most effective if sent to:

U.S. Army Corps of Engineers
Omaha District
215 N. 17th St.
Omaha, Nebraska 68102

Mark Rolofson, July 1988

INDEX